18. 10. '93.

Liam from Hazel
with love.

Walking through Ireland

Walking through Ireland

ROBIN NEILLANDS

LITTLE, BROWN AND COMPANY

A *Little, Brown* Book

First published in Great Britain in 1993
by Little, Brown and Company

Copyright © Robin Neillands 1993

Maps drawn by Terry Brown

The moral right of the author has been asserted.

A CIP catalogue record for this book is
available from the British Library.

ISBN 0 316 90427 9

Typeset by Solidus (Bristol) Ltd
Printed and bound in Great Britain by
BPCC Hazell Books Ltd
Member of BPCC Ltd

Little, Brown and Company (UK) Limited
165 Great Dover Street
London SE1 4YA

*This one is for Terry and Kay
with love and thanks, always.*

Contents

Acknowledgements

A great many people helped me on this journey, so my thanks to Philippa Reid of the Northern Ireland Tourist Board and John Lahiffe of Bord Failté (the Irish Tourist Board). Thanks also go to Daisy Roots for their excellent boots and Sprayway for some first-class raingear, together with thanks to Douglas Schatz of Stanfords Map Shop for help with the planning and route-finding, and to Terry Brown for the maps. Thanks also to Geoff Cowen and Major-General Julian Thompson, to Toby Oliver of Swansea Cork Ferries, and to the good people of British Midland and Aer Lingus. My thanks also to Matt Molloy of 'The Chieftains' for enduring my interviewing technique in Westport, and to Judith Greevan and Clovis Keath for some jolly company, and to a whole host of people who gave me a bed for the night or a helping hand along the way. Finally, as ever, to Estelle Huxley, for reading my notes and putting these pages together.

In so far as the collection of information is concerned, the advantages of travel may often be over-stated. So much has been written, so many facts are upon record about every country, even the most remote, that a judicious and persevering study of existing materials would no doubt enable a reader to fill himself with knowledge almost to repletion without leaving his chair. But for the formation of opinion, for the stirring and enlivenment of thought, and for the discernment of colour and proportion, the gifts of travel, especially of travel on foot, are priceless.

Winston Spencer Churchill
London, 1908

1

Preparations

> The great and recurrent question about
> ABROAD is, is it worth the trouble of getting
> there?
>
> Rose Macaulay,
> *Personal Pleasures*

Late one afternoon, halfway up the side of Carrantuohill,
with water pouring up my sleeves, I had a sudden thought:
Why am I doing this? People had been asking me that for
weeks but only now, with the end of my journey in sight, did
I ask the question myself. It would be nice to know the
answer but the only one I can offer, even now, months after
the walk ended, is the one the cowboy gave when they asked
him why he took off all his clothes and rolled in the cactus:
it seemed like a good idea at the time.

Sitting at home, with the map on the table and a mug of
tea at my elbow, the thought of walking across Ireland
seemed like a wonderful idea. Halfway up the cascading
waterfall that passes for the track up Ireland's highest
mountain, it simply seemed crazy. I can offer no reason for
deciding to do it, nor does there have to be one. I walked
across Ireland because I felt like it, because it was my fancy,
and given the time I might even do it again.

1

Now enter the walker, limping. In the case of the walker in Ireland, enter the walker wet and limping. Smiling though, because in spite of the roads and the weather and the blanket bog, Ireland is a happy country for a walker, a place that gives the heart a lift. I enjoyed walking across Ireland from North to South, and returned to my desk damp but cheerful and full of tales. All I have to do now is write this book, and I am at once faced with the same old problem: where to begin?

In theory, this ought to be easy, for surely the book should follow the walk. I begin at the beginning, go on to the end and then stop. If only it were that easy; but who can say when a journey really begins? It certainly does not begin at that moment when the boot first hits the footpath, but some time long before that, in the country of the mind. In the beginning is the idea, and even that takes some thinking about.

Working writers do not believe in the sudden flash of inspiration. Working writers do not have time for that sort of self-serving rubbish. Working writers believe that inspiration comes from applying the seat of the pants to the seat of a chair and staying there, scribbling or tapping away until something happens. I make this point because the idea of walking across Ireland did not come to me overnight, or even willingly. Quite the contrary. The idea of walking across Ireland came to me a bit at a time and overrode a far firmer resolve never to wear walking boots again.

I reached that decision one evening, some years ago, sitting on the beach at Tarifa on the southern tip of Spain. To get there I had made a 700-mile walk right across Spain, marching south from the coast of Biscay. It took weeks and during that time I had been blistered, thirsty and exhausted, been seared by the sun, put upon by Spaniards, set upon by muggers; enough was enough. I sat there on the sand looking out across the Straits of Gibraltar towards the winking lights on the coast of North Africa and considered taking my boots off and hurling them as far into the Atlantic as the remnants of my strength would allow. However, being a canny Scot, I kept them. They hung by their laces in the garage for a year or two, a gentle reminder of hard times now past. As the seasons passed they slowly turned green.

The snag is that hard times have a certain appeal. Note that 'snag is . . .' for it is a phrase that will appear constantly in this book. Walking is never without snags but without snags travelling would be very, very boring. Press anyone who likes to get out and hack it through the wild and they will eventually admit that the declared objective or reason for their journey is just an excuse. The real, deep-down reason is that for certain people hard times are a pleasant sort of pain in the neck. You may say, 'That's it, never again,' but after a while, say a year or so of soft living, you start to think about being on your own among the rocks. You fantasize about crawling ant-like across some wide savannah, you dream about the sharp sound of rain rattling against your waterproofs. Like Garbo, you want to be alone, goddammit!

Some little time-machine ticking away in your head then activates itself to put dangerous thoughts in your mind. Thoughts of wild places and windy days, of fords and footpaths and empty trails running off into the mist somewhere beneath the clouds. God! – you think – I was a *man* back then, and now look at me. When you start looking at maps and avoiding bathroom mirrors, the time has come to be off again. In my case this means going for a walk. I have walked across France and a couple of years after that I walked across Spain, and now here I was again, contemplating a walk across Ireland.

Travel – real travel – is becoming ever harder to find. Everything that can be discovered has been discovered and a lot of the wild has now been transformed into tourist resorts or theme parks. I do not resent this or deplore it; I simply state the facts. The traveller today has to think up new ways of getting in touch with the real world and so we have exotic travel. Stevenson began it in *Travels with a Donkey. Travels with my Microlight* is not the same thing somehow. The essence of real travel is simplicity, the art of drawing sufficient conclusions from insufficient premises, as Samuel Butler has it. For this reason, when I go travelling I prefer to do it on foot. Twenty-five miles under a 50 lb pack cuts everyone down to size.

I should make it clear now that this is not a book about walking. This is a book about Ireland. The walk is simply the theme, the storyline to hang the tales on, my way of getting from one place to another. It is also a way of linking up, in the story of a journey, the story of Ireland. Anyone looking for pages of lyrical prose on the joys of loop-stitched socks and cleated boots is in for a disappointment. That said, since these are matters worth considering by any traveller, they are also worth mentioning here, and there is a full kit list in the appendices.

First though, how was this decision to walk across Ireland arrived at? Slow and easy is the answer, by considering factors, by a process of elimination. Firstly, there is language. I don't think you can get to know a country well unless you speak the language at least adequately. Though British I can get along well enough in French or Spanish, but otherwise I am reduced to pointing out a line in the phrasebook. Even at that I am almost a linguist in Britain. I once met an Englishman in France who told me that he could get along everywhere on just two languages, 'English and Louder English'. He was bellowing at a Provençal waitress at the time and I have to say it seemed to work. He got the hot food and the cold wine and I got the opposite.

The British have a curious hang-up about languages and resist all efforts to learn them, but why is this? In the days of Empire the sons of the Raj exercised Dominion over palm and pine while nattering away to the natives in Urdu, Pushtu, Gurkhali, Swahili and all manner of arcane tongues, but the British of today come over shy if they have to speak to an Italian. I can't think why. Anyway, for the serious foot-powered traveller, a simple smattering of the language will not do. You have to be able to manage a few threats and insults as well, just in case you reach a spot where the men are vile or the natives hostile.

We found that out years ago when cycling across Arabia. We would shout a cheery '*Saa'ida*' to the wayside urchins of Jordan or Syria and they would reply with a volley of stones. The point is that a lack of the language is a limiting factor for the independent traveller, and I don't go where I can't speak the lingo. Some travellers may be able to learn colloquial Mandarin in a couple of weeks, but I am not one of them.

English is, of course, widely spoken in countries that don't interest me at all, such as Germany and Scandinavia. English, or a kind of English, is the common tongue in those countries like Canada or Australia, which are too big for a coast-to-coast tramp in the time available. I did not wish to walk one of the great American trails which are heavily infested with great American bores. I can still remember sharing a refuge in Colorado with a very 'green' American lady who was there to see the birds and the trees while they were, as she put it, 'neat in their Fall colours from Mother Nature's own boutique'. Her boyfriend entertained us by whistling birdcalls over dinner. It was a nightmare and three days of all that and no liquor soon had me looking for release in the clutches of the nearest grizzly.

So, you see the problem? Here I was, itching to be off, but having already walked across France and Spain I had run out of countries, and walking through Britain was out because John Hillaby had already done it. I needed a country where they spoke a tongue I could speak, and a country which I didn't know at all but which I could walk across in about six weeks. After that, arriving at Ireland was an accident. It simply swam slowly into my mind and stuck there, nagging. Before long I went out and bought a Michelin map and sat brooding over it, muttering to myself and scribbling on a notepad, and this is what I discovered.

Ireland is not very big. The distance North to South is only about 350 miles, and that allows for getting round some lakes and rivers, but people who have been in the middle of Ireland, and were Irish, told me that the middle of Ireland is boring. There is also the little matter of the River Shannon, which almost cuts Ireland in half and is difficult to cross except at certain places. Limitations once again dictated the route, and put the direct North to South route quite out of court to begin with.

If I walked across Ireland at all, I wanted to walk across the North. To walk across Ireland while skirting Northern Ireland, the embattled Six Counties of Ulster, struck me at once as a cop-out. I therefore studied the map of Northern Ireland for a suitable starting point and eventually came up with the Giant's Causeway, a World Heritage site on the North Coast of Antrim. Even I had heard of the Giant's Causeway. This was therefore selected as the starting point. Then comes the *diretissima* to the opposite coast, a straight line across country, like the one climbers follow to the summit of a mountain, the route taken by an imaginary drop of water trickling from the peak to the valley floor. I needed an objective because unless I knew where I was going I stood little chance of getting there.

A swift bit of work with a ruler gave me an axis of advance from the Giant's Causeway in Ulster to Valentia Island in the South-West, just off the Atlantic coast of Kerry. A rapid calculation on the scale showed that this was about 350 miles; nothing like the 700 or more miles I had walked across France or Spain, though hardly an afternoon stroll. All I had to do then was work out a way of getting there, and dividing my daily 15-mile stint into the total distance would give me my time scale. Well, part of it. Things never work out like that. I then emptied the shelves of the London Library and read everything I could find about Ireland. I ended up confused but it gave me a list of places I simply had to see. These I began to underline on the Michelin map and my direct route began to wobble a bit.

The Giant's Causeway, the North Antrim Cliff Path, Enniskillen, Drumcliff, Sligo, Westport, the Sperrins, the mountains of Croagh Patrick, Carrantuohill and the Twelve Pins of Connemara, Ballina and Castlebar, the Aran Islands, MacGillycuddy's Reeks ... all these and a score more were inked in on the Michelin map.

By now, a week or two into the thinking stage, I had covered the floor of my study with books and maps and pages of articles torn from magazines and newspapers. If anyone attempted to tidy this up I drove them off with wild cries. With all the various changes the distance I would have to walk soon got well above the 400-mile mark, and that was without the detailed route. When matters got really complicated I gathered up all the maps and guides and went round to see Geoff Cowen.

Geoff Cowen is a friend of mine. Today, Geoff closely resembles a barrel with a beard on top, but he used to hit the hills a lot in his youth, before he discovered rugby. Geoff is now seriously boring on the subject of rugby. However, he has many good qualities, like tolerance and a sense of humour, and very good Scotch. That apart, he is also a first-class planner.

Geoff actually likes planning. When I need a first-class plan I go round and order one from Geoff and he always comes up with the goods. Geoff has planned all my previous walks and he sometimes joins me for a few days on the trail to see if his plans really work. He was with me on the beach at Tarifa when the last walk ended and heard me vow never to go walking again. That might have been the reason why he was not too pleased to see me. He opened the front door, saw my armful of maps, and promptly slammed it shut again. I even heard the rattle of the chain.

'Go away,' he said through the letter-box. 'Whatever it is, I'm not interested. I don't want to get involved. You said you were never going walking again. You promised . . . so push off.' The flap snapped shut.

'Stop mucking about and open the door. I've changed my mind, that's all.'

'What mind? Do you remember what happened last time? You got set upon, and lost . . . you fell down a mountain and nearly died of thirst. And, anyway, you're getting too old . . .'

'I've thought of all that,' I said. 'This time it's going to be different. The walk will be much shorter and I certainly won't get thirsty. I'm going to walk across Ireland. Every other house is a pub and it pisses down with rain all the time.'

The door opened a fraction and the beard appeared. 'You're going to walk across *Ireland*? Have you never heard of the IRA? Come in and let me talk you out of it.'

During the planning phase, practically everyone I spoke to mentioned the IRA – the Irish Republican Army – and while I was walking across the North every conversation came round to the Troubles sooner or later. There seemed to be a general idea in England that the Provos were just waiting in the hedgerows for me to come ambling by and cause an international incident. I had already been to Ireland and I knew it simply isn't like that. Besides, I can't let a thing like that put me off or I would never go anywhere. The streets of my local town are not too safe after closing time . . . but let me talk of my first trip to Ireland.

I am a professional travel writer. From time to time Tourist Boards will invite me to visit their countries to see the sights and return with the wherewithal for some pages of glowing prose. Therefore, when I was offered a car and accommodation for a week-long tour of Ireland, I jumped at the chance. Then I thought of the distances and rang Carol, a fellow travel writer. She had just finished a long series of articles about car touring in the UK, so I suggested she join me in Ireland, sharing the driving and no hanky-panky. Honest.

All went well until we picked up the car at Belfast Airport.

'You drive,' I said, 'and I'll map-read our way out of town.'

'I can't drive,' said Carol.

I blinked. 'What do you mean, you can't drive? Everyone can drive.'

'I can't,' said Carol.

'What about all that "My Favourite Car Tours in East Anglia" stuff?'

'I wrote it,' said Carol, 'but Bill drove the car.' (Bill is Carol's husband.)

'Well, you'd better hop back on that plane and send Bill over. We've got a thousand miles to drive out here and I'm not going to do it all myself.'

After about two minutes I relented. This was a mistake. We got in the car and Carol guided me with unerring skill right down the Falls Road into an area where the Brits are, to say the least, unwelcome. Two days later she did exactly the same thing in the back streets of Londonderry.

'Carol,' I said, 'I don't want to be picky, but we have just passed a large sign saying, "You are now entering Free Derry". I had hoped we were going to Donegal.'

'Turn left,' said Carol. 'No ... right ... oh ... sorry!'

Turning right brought us to a dead-end in the middle of a housing estate. Facing us was a wall painted with the words, 'Brits out of Ireland' and a 20 ft outline of a man in a balaclava helmet carrying an AK47 Kalashnikov rifle. An interested group of teenagers, all carrying stones, appeared on the scrubby grass mound to my right. When I looked in the mirror I saw an armoured personnel carrier crawl across the intersection behind and block the road. Soldiers leapt from the rear doors and took cover in the gardens and behind the lamp-posts. One sighted his rifle on the back of my head. Then a stone skittered across the road and thumped into the fence. It was clearly going to be one of those mornings in Free Derry.

'I *really* don't want to be picky,' I said, 'but I think we are in the shit. So just get us out of here, fast.'

'I don't know where we are,' said Carol. 'Why don't you get out and ask someone?'

Was this woman mad?

Well, we got away. I drove over the pavement, over the grass mound, round the yobs, past the soldiers, round their APC, and away. I kept my foot down until we were over the Foyle and out in the country. Then I gave Carol a piece of my mind.

'Can't drive, eh?' I said to her, sourly. 'I'll tell you another thing. You can't read a bloody map either.'

The point is, though, that those were the only soldiers we saw all week. Even the North is not an armed camp, and everywhere we went the people were friendly. This time, however, I would be on foot, and that can make a difference. People who travel by car, or any form of transport, have both a protective carapace and a means of escape. People who travel on foot have to tread carefully.

Since I was planning not simply to walk but to walk on my own, a little on-the-spot advice might still be useful. Those of my friends who had soldiered in Ireland over the last twenty years were a little more specific and spoke with frowning brows of the provisional IRA – PIRA – the Provos, the ones who did most of the killing on the Republican side.

'I certainly think you should avoid South Armagh,' said an old Commando friend of mine. 'PIRA have a nasty habit of setting up their own roadblocks down there, and if you bump into one of those and they don't like the look of you, it might get . . . well, difficult. Otherwise you will be all right. There are some very nice people over there, as well as some real bastards. Just remember not to sing "The Wearing of the Green" in Union Jack areas, or "King Billy Slew the Papish Crew at the Battle of Boyne Water" in the Catholic ones, and you should be all right.'

'I'm known for my tact,' I assured him, 'but how do I know when I'm in a Protestant area or a Catholic one?'

'You'll know,' he said grimly.

My planned route across Northern Ireland took me well clear of the so-called 'bandit country' of South Armagh. From the Giant's Causeway it went first along the Antrim Coast to Coleraine and then south and west across the Sperrin Mountains to Omagh and Enniskillen, and so out of the North and into the Republic. This route took me through the only gap between the two arms of Lough Erne and out towards Sligo. Walking across Northern Ireland would take me about ten days. Northern Ireland is not very big, about 90 miles by 90 miles, with a darned great lake in the middle, but for such a little place it has seen a great deal of turmoil. Most of the places on the way there had seen their share of trouble in the last twenty-five years, but I have a simple way of avoiding trouble. If I think something is dangerous, I don't do it.

A glance at the map will reveal why my route led to Enniskillen. Not only was it more or less in line with my objective at Valentia Island, it also offered me the only direct way into the Republic, the Yeats Country and the beautiful

West Coast. Once across the frontier I would head like an arrow for the West Coast and try to pick up the long-distance footpath that ran south towards Castlebar and Westport. At Westport I would shin up Croagh Patrick – the Holy Mountain, a shrine to St Patrick.

From there I would wander south across the Twelve Pins to Connemara, heading for the ferry port at Rossaveal and hop on a ferry there for a peek at the Aran Islands out in Galway Bay; Inishmore, Inishmaan, Inisheer – the very names are like a song. This would take me to Galway and onto the Burren, that rocky moonscape of County Clare which everyone I talked to said I must see.

Once across the Burren which, it said on the map, has its own footpath, the Burren Way, I would be striding swiftly south towards the River Shannon, crossing at Killimer where the map promised a ferry towards the castle at Glin, another place I wanted to see. Once past Glin I would press on towards Tralee and across the Stacks Mountains and the Slieve Mish mountains towards Kerry and the MacGilly-cuddy's Reeks. These are Irish mountains and not very high, but the Irish call them mountains and that is good enough for me. Besides, one of the Reeks is Carrantuohill and at 3,414 ft this is a real mountain, the highest peak in Ireland. So I would have to climb that, come wind, come weather, but even that should not give me much to worry about. I had fallen down mountains much higher than Carrantuohill.

From the top of Carrantuohill I would see the fabled Ring of Kerry and the Dingle Peninsula, not to mention Kill-arney's lakes and fells, famous in song and story. After climbing Carrantuohill, a few more days should take me along the northern edge of the Ring of Kerry and so at last to my destination at Valentia Island. Geoff and I did our sums again and found that the distance had gone up to something nearer 500 miles.

Geoff and I spent several evenings on the whisky, working

all this out, and when we added it together the distance came to 451 miles without the inevitable diversions, so we added 50 miles for those. This walk would be much shorter than my previous expeditions across France and Spain but we both knew that good as Geoff's plans are, things never go as intended. Nor do I wish that they should. In spite of all that poring over maps, or perhaps because of the whisky, we had failed to notice the big snag with Irish walking: no footpaths.

I didn't actually notice the absence of footpaths in Ireland until I was about three days into the walk, and when it finally dawned on me the discovery came as something of a shock. The thought itself simply didn't occur to us at the planning stage. Damn it, every country has footpaths! How else do farmers get to their fields and the villagers to church? I was so sure that Ireland had footpaths that I didn't bother to check any more than someone buying a city guide checks that London has streets. On mainland Britain there are 140,000 miles of rights-of-way, in England and Wales alone, but in Ireland . . . none. Well, very few. The Irish don't worry about this, but then the Irish don't worry much about anything. The Irish walkers I met actually got quite lyrical about walking on mountains 'in their natural state'. Let me tell you that a mountain in its natural state is a place best avoided.

I must not go too far on this point. Ireland does have *some* long-distance footpaths and bridleways, but there are not many of them. Those footpaths that do exist tend to run around the coast or along the banks of rivers. That web-like maze of footpaths that enable the walker to hack his way right across England or France, or even Spain, simply does not exist across the Irish Sea. Had I wanted to go on a long walk, like the 500-mile circuit of the Ulster Way, no problem – though much of that is on lanes and tracks – but I didn't.

I wanted to walk directly across Ireland as I had across France and Spain, marching from one place to another, avoiding roads wherever possible. But here was a country without footpaths, so that idea went out of the window.

We might have noticed this sooner had we found large-scale maps, but the bulk of Irish topographic mapping is still on half-inch-to-the-mile maps, which is too small a scale to use accurately for walking. Northern Ireland does have newly-revised 1:50,000 ($1\frac{1}{4}$" mile) maps, and certain popular holiday areas of the Republic are currently being re-mapped to this scale or larger, but for an independent wandering, north-east to south-west walk, the long-distance walker is very much on his or her own.

Once I had made this Ghastly Discovery I went into the causes in some depth and found, inevitably, that it was all the fault of the English. Well, the Anglo–Normans. At a time when the Saxon peasantry were establishing footpaths across the lords' lands – 'Got to get to church/market/your demesne, m'lord' – back there in the 11th and 12th centuries, the Anglo–Norman invaders were taking steps to see that few rights-of-way were ever established in Ireland, and so it remains. British farmers, who by and large hate walkers, must wish the Normans had been equally intransigent here. The Ordnance Survey were duly apologetic when I rang to complain, but since no one else had complained and the Irish farmers don't really mind if people tramp across their fields, setting up rights-of-way at this late stage seemed a mite superfluous.

Well, up to a point, but the point is this: there are very few footpaths in Spain and I managed well enough there, but Spain is a dry country. Walking directly across Ireland on a compass bearing didn't work out too well. I used a compass bearing when walking directly across the high, hot *meseta* of Castile, but you can't do that in Ireland. Ireland is wet. Ireland has rivers. Three days into the walk, just after the

Ghastly Discovery, I tried a compass walk across the Sperrin Mountains, but it was not a success. Let me explain why.

First, you have to scramble over a wall or through a hedge or across a chain-link fence. There are several of these as you move down the valley. At the bottom of the valley is a river, too deep to cross, and since there is no footpath there is no footbridge or ford. Let us suppose you find a way across the river. Nicely wet, you then proceed uphill over yet more fences, hedges and walls – knackering stuff this at my age, with a 50lb rucksack on my back – and then you get to the bracken-cloaked uplands. This is certainly open and fence-free but covered in clumps of heather and bracken and well supplied with bogs. The bogs will be oozing with water and cut about with deep trenches, or peat hags. Put your weight on your stick to steady yourself for a leap across a boggy bit and it slides like a sword into the soft body of the hill, taking you with it. It took me hours to get across the tops of the Sperrins and when I arrived at the far side I was covered in mud and smelling like a polecat.

The local people don't seem to mind all this. They talk about the pleasures of walking on mountains 'in their natural state' and even wonder aloud how they would manage on rights-of-way or waymarked trails. Wouldn't that be boring? It would be better, is the answer – much better. My on-the-spot decision after the Ghastly Discovery was to head at speed on lanes or farm tracks out to the West Coast, where there must surely be a coastal footpath. To get there I could use roads, lanes, farm tracks, railway lines, whatever I could find heading in the right direction. Bog-trotting was not a serious option.

Apart from the fact that many people, and I mean Irish people, told me that the centre of their country was boring, this is the main reason why, after leaving the North at Enniskillen, I headed through Sligo for Westport and Connemara. Out in the Wild West there must be fewer fields and more established footpaths. Out there I could surely find a route that would take me south. Out there in the West, or so I was told, the country is empty of people and very beautiful, and this at least turned out to be true. In my dreams today I can still see Connemara in September. There was all that beauty in abundance, but very few footpaths.

Making this discovery about the maps and the paths was a reminder of how little I really knew about Ireland. The North has been in the news every day for 20 years, and I know and like a lot of Irish people, but Ireland itself I hardly knew at all. Getting to know Ireland was the object of this journey, but a few statistics always help at the start, if only to get the basics right and get the scale of the place firmly in the mind.

The island of Ireland covers an area of about 33,000 square miles. That is tiny compared with the 220,000 square miles of France, and makes Ireland about one-third the size of mainland Britain. Into this area fits a small population of about 5 million people, of which $1\frac{1}{2}$ million live in Northern Ireland. The majority of the people in the North are Protestant, while nearly 95 per cent of the people in the South – the Republic – are Catholic and from that fact stems many a tale and much of the problem.

Historically, the island of Ireland can be divided into four provinces, each a former kingdom: Ulster, Munster, Connacht (or Connaught), and Leinster. These date back to the Ireland of pre-history when this island was occupied by the semi-legendary Fir-bolg people, and the kingdoms were still in place when St Patrick arrived in the 5th century, and for hundreds of years after that, until Strongbow arrived at the end of the 12th century. It had been borne upon me when reading the books about Ireland, that this would be a journey through time as well as space, for Ireland has never given up on its history. What happened in the past has relevance today, as I was to discover later.

My most urgent concern, as the day of departure drew near, was the weather. In Ireland it rains. On the West Coast they get over 80 inches of rain a year, which keeps the ground wet but supplies the country with those 'forty shades of green' and creates that Emerald Isle the poets sing about. Small, underpopulated, wet, green, divided; these were the basics of the Ireland I hoped to discover. I soon realized that Ireland is much more complicated than that.

The complication of Irish history was just one of the things I hoped to unravel on this journey. No one goes on a long walk, right through a country, simply to go for a walk. There have to be more reasons for it than that; some of these you know at the start, some you discover on the way. Little of this was known to me as I tried to get the basics right and turned my mind to kit.

With kit comes more thoughts of weather and terrain, because if you can be sure of the weather and terrain you can cut down on the kit, and this is important because kit means weight. Some long-distance walkers are kit-freaks, always adding some knick-knack because 'it weighs nothing'. In this they fool themselves; everything weighs something. Some of the kit I already had, like my wonderfully comfortable Daisy Roots boots. These were still in a good state after walking right across Spain and on a lot of other trails. I had my great big green Karrimor rucksack and a lot of ancillary gear, but given the Irish weather I needed some state-of-the-art raingear because it tends to rain a bit in Ireland. A 'soft' day in Ireland actually means that the rain is coming down like stair-rods. One friend I consulted told me that if I was lucky on my journey it would only be pissing down with rain for 90 per cent of the time.

I therefore consulted my good friend, Clive Tully, who is gear adviser to the hard-hitting gentry of the Royal Geographical Society. Clive advised me to get a set of Gore-Tex Sprayway raingear, the complete set of cagoule and

overtrousers which, he said, would be proof against everything but a tidal wave. A set of Sprayway Gore-Tex raingear
was duly acquired together with a set of gaiters to keep the
boots dry. It was perhaps inevitable, therefore, that the sun
shone down all day for the first ten days of my trip.

Then there were maps, which I have touched on before. I
like maps. I will happily spend an evening with a map spread
on the table, picking out the Roman roads and the churches
'with spire or steeple', working out routes from here to
there, humming happily to myself the while. For maps I
went to see Douglas Schatz at Stanfords Map Shop in
London's Long Acre, and we spent more hours there,
spreading maps of Ireland over his wide, glass-topped
tables, and here again I met that snag. The Northern Ireland
maps are fine. Elsewhere you must still cope with maps that
should have 'Here be leprechauns' written on them; they are
also set to a very small scale. There is also the snag that
many Irish maps are out of date.

As a rule I don't mind old maps. I work on the theory
that there will usually be more landmarks on the ground
now than there were back then when the map was made,
and provided I can proceed in the right direction I am
happy enough. This is another theory that does not work
in Ireland, because of the mists, the bogs, the rivers and
the lakes. Just wandering along in Ireland will soon have
you waist-deep in a bog or deliriously lost. It pays to walk
in very short stages, from one clear landmark to the next,
or go on lanes and roads, and in the end I had to go on
lanes and tracks because the long-distance trails either did
not go in my direction or were lanes and tracks anyway.
I don't like walking on roads. Roads are for cars or cycles,
not for walkers, not least because tarmac plays havoc with
the feet.

Time was pressing as winter gave way to spring, but I had
my kit in the rucksack and if it weighed far too much at least

that was ready. I still had to furnish my mind. To do this I had to do the background reading. There is a saying, old but true, that if you want to learn anything about a country you have to take a lot of learning with you. This is true of any journey, for the more you put into it the more you get out of it, but it is particularly true of Ireland. I read all I could about Ireland and ended up confused, but I have been confused before. Experience helps, for I knew I could sort it all out piece by piece as I trudged across the country. That indeed was now the object of my journey. If I had simply wanted to go for a walk I only had to step outside my own front door. Walking across Ireland is more complicated because Ireland is a complicated country.

See me then, in the early days of summer, getting ready for my walk across Ireland, my rucksack full of equipment and my brain full of confusion. I had found a theme, to explore the history of Ireland as I walked along, and to discover and identify all those people who rose from the pages of the history books and went parading through my mind. Who were Yeats, O'Connell, Patrick Pearse, Wolfe Tone and the rest? What really happened during the Great Hunger, and above all, why did the English push into Ireland with such tenacity when all the Irish wanted them to leave? I didn't know, but I would find out as I wandered along through the Irish summer, over the hills and down the coast. I would drink in the pubs and sleep in the Bed & Breakfasts, and hear the old tales and make some sense of it. I might even enjoy myself.

All this reading and planning took months. I am a freelance writer and I have to work for a living every day. When I stop working, I stop earning, so devoting five or six weeks of my time to a walk is a real investment. It usually takes about two years to squirrel away the days until I have enough in hand for a five-week trip. I decided to go in June, but even that fell back a bit, and losing that time put me under pressure. There was also the little problem that I never had the time to get fit.

Meanwhile the mountain of kit grew. Before long my rucksack was so heavy I could hardly lift it off the floor. When I was helped into it I tottered about the kitchen, crashing into the furniture. I had decided to take everything I could possibly need to cope with the Irish weather and whatever difficulties might fling themselves across my path. I finally found time to go out for evening walks and some long weekend tramps, so when I eventually got to the airport I was as ready as I could be and a lot more prepared than I had been on other occasions. I still felt quite intrepid standing there at Heathrow in my weather-beaten Rohan clothing among all the suits: but before we begin this journey, a final word of warning.

There is a lot of conversation in this book. The Irish are a talkative people and I spent a lot of time in their pubs, resting my feet and drying my clothing. When you do that you soon get into the 'crack', so it may help if the reader can imagine at least 50 per cent of the speech with an Irish accent. It will also help if the reader can accept that at least 50 per cent of the speakers were usually drunk.

2

Setting Out

They say it is the fatal destiny of that lande, that
no purposes, whatsoever meant for her good, will
ever prosper or have good effect.

Edmund Spenser,
A View of the Present State of Ireland, 1596

Living as I do in the South of England, I had always nursed
the idea that Ireland lies directly to the West, roughly level
with our Southern parts. In fact, the coast of Antrim, where
my journey would begin, actually lies a long way north, level
with the Mull of Kintyre in the Western Highlands of
Scotland. So we flew north and west, across the middle of
England and the March of Wales, over the Irish Sea, and in
very little time were crossing the coast of Northern Ireland
and beginning our descent.

Watching twenty years of trouble on my TV screen must
have an effect, but I am old enough to know that violence
anywhere in the world is usually confined to a few parts of
the country and on an episodic basis, so I am happy to say
I was not in the least apprehensive about the first part of this
journey. In fact, I was looking forward to setting out across
the North and being on my own. The last few days before
setting out on any expedition are always the worst. All the

21

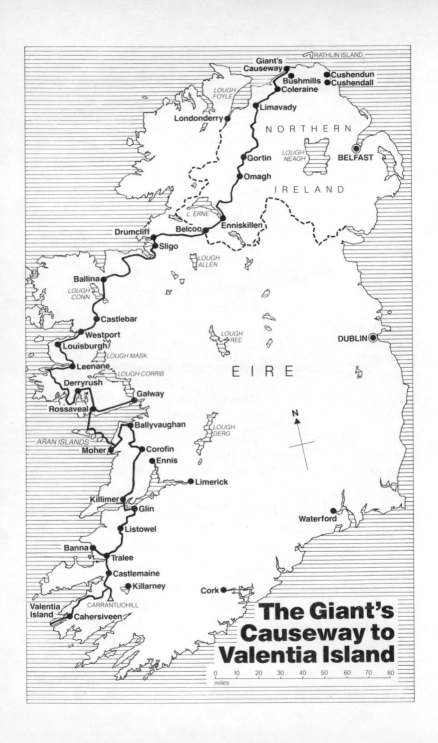

The Giant's Causeway to Valentia Island

preparations are made, the gear packed, the farewells said. There is nothing left to do but go, and here you are with two or three days in hand and nothing to do but wait. The waiting is always the worst part. Once the journey has begun everything slips into place.

One of the many things people do not know about Ulster is that it is very beautiful. Like the rest of Ireland it endures a fairly relentless rainfall and is therefore noticeably lush and green. It is also very well cared for, a tidy land, patchworked with little farms. The farms really are small, with an average size of about 70 acres, and some of them are still worked in the traditional '*conacre*' system, where some of the fields, or grazing, is let out on a seasonal basis to a smallholder, to graze his stock or produce one crop.

Northern Ireland is quite a small province, covering an area of roughly 180 square miles, a green and fertile farmland which cradles Lough Neagh, the largest lake in the British Isles. The River Bann flows out of Lough Neagh in two directions, to the North and the South, and the destination on my first day's walk was the town of Coleraine, which lies on the River Bann as it flows into the Atlantic on the Antrim Coast. I could hardly wait to get going.

As the aircraft began to circle over Belfast, a voice in my ear said, 'There's the Maze,' and there indeed it was. Below the wing-tip lay the roofs of Ulster's most secure and notorious prison, standing out clearly in the afternoon light. I had never seen it before, but those H-Block roofs were unmistakable. The Troubles had given my mind a little nudge and we were not even on the ground yet.

'There's a lot of hard men penned up in there,' said my companion, but his tone was non-committal. This was a second lesson learned. In Northern Ireland you don't commit yourself too much until you know who you are talking to. That apart, this was an ice-breaker, my first contact with a local, and he was friendly. He was also very pleased that I had come to Northern Ireland and wished me all the best on my journey. He even gave me his phone number in case I should get stuck. If there is any truth in the saying that you only get one chance to make a first impression, then my first impression of the Ulster folk was favourable and it remained so.

The people of Northern Ireland are very friendly and I'll make that point here so that I don't have to go on and on about it. They are friendly because that is the way Ulster people are, but also because they feel themselves traduced by the media and neglected by their fellow countrymen on the Mainland. As a result, anyone from the Mainland who comes wandering among them, especially on foot, is sure of a good welcome.

As on my first visit, there seemed to be no particular security at Belfast Airport. Some Army helicopters were egg-whisking away on the far side of the airfield, but otherwise there was no sign of military activity at all. There was not even a policeman on the airport concourse, so I collected my rucksack from the carousel, staggered around while pulling it on, and made my way out to where Philippa Reid was waiting for me. Philippa was with the Tourist Board and had volunteered to drive me up to the start of my journey on the Antrim Coast.

'Where do you want to go first?' she asked. 'A quick tour of Belfast or straight up to the Glens of Antrim?'

I decided to pass on the city. Belfast is a rather splendid town which became rich in the last century from the flax and linen trade and then from shipbuilding and engineering. As a result it has some fine public buildings and parks and nothing could less resemble the Irish Beirut of popular imagination. However, like many Northern Irish towns, the centre of the city is a Control Zone, where it is forbidden to leave cars unattended, and this, though very sensible, restricts the opportunities for a quick stroll about. Besides, cities are all much the same and having finally arrived I wanted to get started, so we set out at once for the Glens of Antrim. On the way there I had my first lesson on the origins of Northern Ireland. You have to begin somewhere, and this seemed as good a place as any.

The story of Ireland is so long and so complicated that it is hard to know where to begin, but since relevance is all, it might be as well to begin by looking at the root causes of the present Troubles, which began in Ireland in the early decades of the present century. This is looking at Ireland through the wrong end of the telescope, but at least it provides a starting point for a long series of 'whys'.

The best way to tell any story is from the beginning, but I was starting my journey not simply in the North, but in the place where the long and turbulent history of Ireland has come to its latest, but by no means its first, fruition. History is like that. A situation does not simply occur. It arises from what happened before, and contributes to what happens afterwards. To begin in the present does at least mean that the story starts with a situation which is widely known if not generally understood.

The Irish date the troubles of their country all the way back to 1170, to the Norman invasion of Leinster by the mighty Strongbow, Earl of Pembroke. He was brought into Ireland by Dermott MacMurrough, King of Leinster, and offered the hand of the King's daughter if he would help MacMurrough in his local wars. Strongbow came over with a strong force of bowmen and mailed and mounted knights, and having married Dermott's daughter he became King of Leinster when MacMurrough died in 1171. Thus the English gained their entry into Ireland.

To be quite accurate, Strongbow was neither all Norman

nor all English. His King, Henry II, was an Angevin and
Strongbow was of French descent, as were all the knight-
hood of England at that time. This only confirms the deep-
seated English belief that if you look at the troubles of
Europe you will generally find a Frenchman at the bottom
of them.

We shall come back to Strongbow, but for the moment I
was more concerned with how Ireland came to be parti-
tioned into Northern Ireland and the Republic. Partition
arose from the desire for Independence and, at least in my
opinion, Partition lies at the bottom of all the troubles
Ireland has seen since 1919. The basic fact that underpins
the story of Ireland and runs like a steel hawser through her
history is that the Irish always wanted to be free of that
foreign domination introduced by Strongbow, and clung to
that need with a most intense tenacity. The Scots and Welsh
may have settled for the Union, but the Irish only wanted to
be free. By the turn of the present century they had that
freedom almost in their grasp.

For over a hundred years, Ireland had been struggling to
free itself from the Act of Union of 1800, which abolished
the Irish Parliament in Dublin and effectively made England
and Ireland one country. Many of the leading advocates for
Irish Independence during the 19th century were Protestant,
but when it came to the point of emancipation, there was a
problem, and on that problem the country split. The
Protestant majority of the North would simply not consent
to live in an independent, Catholic Ireland. They still won't,
and that is the root and branch of it.

A Home Rule Bill had been introduced in the English
Parliament of 1886 by Charles Stewart Parnell, a famous
man in Irish history, but the House of Lords, who had a veto
at that time, swiftly rejected it. In 1893 the Irish members
tried again with similar results, and yet again in 1912. By
now the tide of opinion had turned and after two years of

debate the Home Rule Bill finally went through in the summer of 1914.

Then came the Great War and implementation of the Home Rule Bill was suspended until the end of hostilities. There was no conscription in Ireland, but when the war began Irishmen flocked to the Colours in their tens of thousands, assured of their own country after the war; but some did not believe this promise, or could not wait, and in 1916 they rebelled. The Easter Rising of 1916 was vastly unpopular with the Irish people, at least until the British foolishly executed sixteen of the leaders. After that, the Independence movement began to press for immediate Home Rule. A Declaration of Independence was read out, without the agreement of Westminster, in the newly-formed Irish Parliament – the Dail – in January 1919, and matters were clearly coming to a head.

Then came the brief but bloody Anglo–Irish war, between the British irregulars, the notorious 'Black and Tans', and the Irish Republican Army which was then just what it claimed to be, the Army of the Irish Republic. During this time there was violent anti-Catholic and anti-Independence rioting in the North and the IRA gained a great deal of credibility by defending the Catholic population against attacks from the Protestants and, indeed, from the Police. However, the leaders of the Irish Government came to accept that they could not hope to gather in the intransigent Protestant community of the North and they therefore agreed to Partition, and the six counties of Ulster with Protestant majorities among the population became the UK Province of Northern Ireland.

In 1920 the Government of Ireland Act established the 'Six Counties' of Northern Ireland and the Irish Free State of Twenty-Six Counties. The Free State then had Dominion status, rather like Canada and Australia, and remained closely lined to the British Crown. This fact infuriated the men of the IRA, who felt that the Anglo–Irish Treaty, which set up the Free State, was a sell-out to both the Protestant majority and the British Government.

So far, so straightforward, and I now had an outline of the facts behind the Troubles. The cost of founding the Free State was Partition, and the consequences of that fact we live with to this day. The reasons for Partition are simple. The Protestant people of the North flatly refused to submit to the rule of a Catholic Irish Government. As the Loyalists put it bluntly at the time, 'Home Rule means Rome Rule'. There was nothing new about this, even at the turn of the century, and having set out the causes of partition it might be as well to look at the actions which led to its acceptance, at least in the North.

The Protestants of Ulster had decided to fight Home Rule long before the First Home Rule Bill was promulgated in 1886. By 1913 they were importing arms, ready to fight if Home Rule was forced upon them. The leader of the Protestants at this time was Sir Edward Carson and he made it clear that if the Home Rule Bill went through the Protestants of Ulster would fight. That aroused the Government of the day and warships were sent to the port of Belfast hoping to coerce the Protestant population. Such gunboat diplomacy had no effect whatsoever on Protestant opinion, which soon received another boost to its intransigence.

In 1914, on the very eve of the Great War, came the 'Curragh Mutiny', when certain officers of the British Army stationed at the Curragh near Dublin, made it clear that they would resist any attempt to use them in coercing the North. Though hardly a mutiny at all, it was evident to all concerned that the Army could not be relied upon to suppress a Protestant rising in the North, and the British Government – not for the first or last time in Ireland – found itself on the horns of a dilemma. If they did not grant Home Rule there would certainly be a rebellion in Ireland. If they did grant Home Rule there would certainly be civil war between Protestants and Catholics. Their solution to the problem was Partition.

Partition lies at the root of the present Troubles in Ireland because large sections of the Republic's Government and people have always refused to accept it. They rejected the Treaty that produced it, even in the early days of the Free State. In their Constitution the Government and People of Ireland still lay claim to the North and declare that the territory of the Republic of Ireland shall be 'the whole island of Ireland', a phrase that makes many of Northern Ireland's politicans hyperventilate.

If upsetting certain Neanderthal politicians was the worst of it, the effects of Partition might be quite bearable. In spite of this *de jure* opposition, the politicians of the Republic rub along happily enough with their Northern counterparts. The wild card is the IRA, for as soon as the Free State was established, they started a civil war against those who had agreed to the Treaty.

This is a swift, hand-gallop through Irish history and all I knew about it when I arrived. Most of the events and people were just names to me, and since I am interested in history I suspect they are not even that to most people. However, my interest lies not so much in what happened, but why, and that is far more complicated. The story of Ireland has to be absorbed in small amounts or it becomes indigestible.

Enough of this for now then, except for one final point. There is a problem with 'Ulster', with the word as well as the place. As with many other things in Ireland, when you speak of 'Ulster' you speak in codes. The present province of 'Ulster', usually referred to in the Republic as 'The Six Counties', is both a code and inaccurate because the original province of Ulster had nine counties, not six. The current Six Counties are Antrim, Armagh, Down, Fermanagh, Tyrone and Londonderry, or at least Londonderry to the Unionists – the Republicans or Catholics call it simply Derry, and that name applies to the city as well as the county. In former times, before Partition, the Province of Ulster also included the counties of Monaghan, Cavan and Donegal, which now lie in the Republic. It is therefore more correct to refer to what the English call 'Ulster' as 'Northern Ireland' in the North and 'The Six Counties' in the South.

I had my first lesson on all this from Philippa as we drove north out of Belfast, and very useful it proved. The distraction was the scenery, which was green and beautiful and very, very peaceful. Northern Ireland has its problems but compared with many other places, Northern Ireland is a prosperous place, and it shows. The fields are well tilled, the hedges trim, the farms neat, the villages tidy. Northern Ireland is easy on the eye.

I did soon notice that, as my Commando friend had told me, there was no difficulty in telling which were the Catholic villages and which were the Protestant ones. The former flew the Irish tricolour and had green, orange and white stripes painted on the pavements. The Protestant ones flew the Union flag and had red, white and blue stripes on the pavement. It was not very subtle but I was already beginning to grasp that there were two Irelands, even here in the North.

The advantage with being the passenger in a car is that you have time to look around and take in the scenery. This part of Ulst ... the North, the glens of Antrim, is very beautiful, a rippling mixture of rounded moor-topped hills and lush river valleys, bathed now in a soft early evening light that threw cloud shadows over the hilltops.

There are nine glens in Antrim, each with its own descriptive name; there is Glenarm, the Glen of the Army, and Glenariff, the Glen of the Plouhmen, Glencorp, the Glen of the Slaughter, and so on. Two of these glens, Glentaisie and Glenshesk, run out at Ballycastle, a seaside resort on the North Coast of Antrim. The countryside here has a well-tended look that comes from centuries of pastoral care and is a restful, gentle place. Were it not for the Troubles I would not mind living here myself. It took an effort to drag my mind away from the view and back to the situation.

The present Republic of Ireland was the Irish Free State from 1920 until 1937, when it became Eire. Eire became the Republic of Ireland in 1949. Now it gets tricky again and more codes come to the surface. If someone refers to the Republic as 'The Free State', in the North this probably indicates someone of a Republican persuasion, since this implies that Northern Ireland is not free. Safer then to refer to it as 'The South', or more correctly, 'The Republic'. The person who calls the Republic the 'Free State' will probably also refer to the North as 'The Six Counties'.

I trust this is confusing because it confused me. In practical terms none of this matters. Whatever titles you use, the Irish people, North or South, will understand what you mean and in the case of a visitor from the Mainland they will make allowances for your ignorance. For a local person these names are codewords, a way of identifying where the speaker stands, confirming his political opinions, even his religion. We may live in an ever more secular world, but in Ireland religion is a force to be reckoned with, a fact to consider.

On that first visit to Northern Ireland, I remember propping up a bar, deep in one of those long rambling conversations with the barman. He told me he could always tell a Catholic from a Protestant. He didn't know exactly how he could, but he could.

'Well, it beats me,' I said, 'but then I've never understood religious differences anyway . . . maybe that's because I'm an agnostic.'

The barman shook his head. 'Well, you couldn't be one of

those up here, so you couldn't. Up here you'd either have to
be a Catholic agnostic or a Protestant agnostic.'

The great thing with a walk is to get on with it. Before I set
off I am always mildly apprehensive, wondering if this time
I have bitten off more than I can chew. That feeling departs
the minute I get going. Once I have started on my journey
I want to get my boots on a footpath as soon as possible, for
that is the only way I know of to get into a daily routine. It
is the routine, and nothing else, that gets 20 miles or more
a day out from under your boots. It was now a warm and
glorious evening and both Philippa and I fancied a little walk
before dinner.

The main road to the seaside resort of Ballycastle skirts to
the west of the glens of Antrim and passes through the
village of Armoy. Then it flows round the smooth bulk of
Knocklayd Mountain, which isn't quite a mountain, being
less than 2,000 ft high, and so down to the coast and
Ballycastle. Just to disprove my statement that Ireland has
no footpaths, three long-distance footpaths converge hereabouts: the Moyle Way which comes over Knocklayd and so
north, the province-circling Ulster Way which follows the
spectacular East Coast of Antrim past Cushendall and
Cushendun and, to the west of Ballycastle, the North
Antrim Cliff Path which I would follow on the morrow
towards the Bann estuary. Meanwhile there were places to
see hereabouts.

Ballycastle is a very pretty fishing port and a resort town,
one of those places with pubs and teashops and lots of
whitewashed houses with B & B signs outside. There was a
noticeable lack of neon, thank God! Just out to sea lies the
boomerang shape of Rathlin Island and away to the east the
soaring cliffs of Benmore, or Fair Head, which drop for
600 ft sheer into the sea. This is a spectacular and very
beautiful coastline, and the path runs right along it. Beyond

Fairhead and well out to sea lay another coast, a loom of blue and purple hills, mysterious in the heat haze.

'What's that over there?' I asked Philippa, pointing.

'That's Scotland,' she replied. 'The Mull of Kintyre.'

'My God ... it's very close.'

'Only 13 miles,' she said. 'They say that in the old days the Puritan people used to row across to church ... it's no distance but the North Channel is very wild when the wind gets up, so I rather doubt it.'

Here was a little point of understanding. With Scotland that close, it is no wonder that the Irish – who were then called Scots – found it so easy to invade Kintyre back in the Dark Ages. No wonder either that centuries later the stern Calvinist Presbyterians found it so easy and so beguiling to leave their heather-clad hills and damp glens to cross the narrow sea and take up residence in the rich farmlands of Ulster, where they proceeded to multiply. In fact, the Scots were coming here long before that, and one of them has provided another of those popular local legends, which like so many of these Irish stories, may not be a legend at all.

In the early part of the 14th century, the would-be King of Scots, Robert the Bruce, fled across the sea to Rathlin Island, just off the Antrim Coast, where he hoped to avoid the English and have a good think. It was while he was sheltering in a cave on Rathlin he saw the spider trying to climb to its web and was thus encouraged to return to Scotland and try, try again, until he expelled the English, defeated them at Bannockburn in 1314 and gained the throne of Scotland. So legend has it – and legend is a potent force hereabouts; but how many people today remember the story of Robert Bruce and the spider? True or not, there is a Bruce's Cave under the lighthouse on the north-eastern tip of Rathlin Island, so if it ever happened, it probably happened out there.

Rathlin Island lies in plain sight from Ballycastle and there is a daily ferry in the summer which takes visitors out to see the gulls and the seals or spend an hour or two ashore. The population of Rathlin is less than 100, most of them fishermen, and there is a notorious whirlpool off the southern tip of the island known as the Swallow of the Sea, which is pointed out by the boatmen and must have been there for centuries since it nearly swallowed St Colomba back in the 6th century.

Ballycastle has other claims to fame. The big event of the year hereabouts is the annual Lammastide Fair which began in 1606 and used to last a week or until the pubs ran dry, whichever was the sooner. Now it lasts just two days and is mainly devoted to selling sheep and ponies, for the Ulster folk are great horse-lovers. The Lammastide fair is so famous there is even a song about it:

> Did you treat your Mary-Ann
> To dulse and Yellow Man
> At the Old Lammas Fair in Ballycastle . . .

It probably sounds better set to music, but what is dulse and Yellow Man?

'My husband loves dulse,' said Philippa, 'but I can't stand it. It's a sort of seaweed and you chew it . . . ugh! Yellow Man is toffee, hard as a rock. They have to smash it to bits with a hammer before they weigh it out . . . it's terrible for the teeth but people love it.'

In Elizabethan times Ballycastle used to be the fief of an Ulster warlord, Sorley Boy Macdonnell, a great rogue who lived hereabouts in Elizabethan times and is buried in the chapel at Bonamargy, just outside the town. This is all Macdonnell country, and I would be bumping into Macdonnell monuments for the next few days. Right now I still felt like a walk and I especially wanted to walk across the rope bridge to Carrick-a-Rede Island. This is the sight that appears on all the local postcards and although it formed no part of my route across Ireland, I hadn't come this far to miss it. Walking across it was another matter, mainly because I hate heights.

To get to the Carrick-a-Rede bridge you have to walk a bit from the National Trust car park along a short section of the North Antrim Cliff Path. There are marvellous views from here, east to the sheer drop of Fair Head and west into the sun towards the Giant's Causeway. Carrick-a-Rede actually means the 'Rock in the Road', which is very Irish and makes no sense, though it is said to refer to the route taken by the salmon on their way home from the Atlantic.

The island is a hump of rock set in the shallow blue waters just offshore and the salmon fishermen store their nets out on the island during the annual salmon run along this coast. They put up the rope bridge in the spring and take it down in the autumn, and the visitors just love crossing it. I would not let any children of mine out on this walkway.

To get to the island means a very jittery walk along a swaying two-plank-wide rope bridge, 80 ft above the sea. Neither Philippa nor I have much of a head for heights, let alone for standing about on this creaking, swaying contraption while the other one took photos. Even so, we did it and then we had a little climb about the rocks before setting off again east for the little town of Bushmills.

Bushmills sprawls. Most Irish towns, north or south, large or small, support or have supported a weekly market, with the result that the main streets always seem unnaturally wide, though not so wide that the locals find it unnecessary to double park their cars. These wide streets give the towns a helpfully spacious air, helpful because by and large, Irish towns are not pretty. The shop-fronts tend to be narrow, though the interiors, especially the pub interiors, are frequently vast. The attraction comes from the colours of the paint, those blues and pinks, purples and bright vermilion with which the Irish love to paint their shops and houses. It strikes the visitor as garish for a while, but you soon get used to it and the colours stand out well in that clear rain-washed Irish light.

Bushmills is a famous town in Ireland and famous for the best of reasons. This is the home of the Bushmills Whiskey distillery – and please note here that Irish whiskey is the one with the 'e'. This distillery at Bushmills opened for business as long ago as 1608 and claims to be the oldest legal whiskey distillery in the world. Philippa had a bottle of it to cheer me on my way and a glass of Bushmills marked the end of every day in this tramp across Ireland after that; the pages of my notebook are dotted with it. I can even still smell it if I sniff hard.

My destination that evening was the Auberge de Seneri, a curious name for a hotel in this part of the world. The Auberge is owned by a Frenchman, Jacques Defres, who is waging a lifelong campaign to put some spark into Irish cooking. Jacques offered to drive me up to the start of my walk next morning, and helped me into my room with the rucksack, grunting under the weight in a most gratifying fashion, and Troubles or No Troubles, the dining room was crowded, loud with cheery Ulster voices.

One gets the impression that Ulster folk lurk indoors of an evening, but nothing could be further from the truth. Ulster folk love company and almost every bar I ever went into was jammed to the doors.

There may be time for another spot of history before dinner. Further confusion reigns among visitors over the difference between the Unionists and the Republicans. A Unionist is someone – probably but not necessarily Protestant – who believes in maintaining the unity of the United Kingdom which, it will be recalled, consists of Great Britain and Northern Ireland. A Republican – who is usually but not necessarily a Catholic – backs the Republic of Ireland's constitutional claim to 'the whole island of Ireland'. On the other hand, a Unionist can also be a Loyalist – loyal to the Queen and the Union, but sometimes of a more violent kind. Thus you will hear of 'Loyalist para-militaries' but never of Unionist para-militaries.

Similarly, the more extreme Republican factor will be described as Nationalists, and beyond that we move into the dark areas occupied by the Irish Republican Army, which like most other institutions hereabouts has split into two parts. The official IRA, the original IRA, has currently abandoned violence and it is the Provisional IRA – PIRA or the 'Provos' – which does most of the killing hereabouts and has become one of the most efficient terrorist organizations in the world. The IRA, Official or Provisional, has its origins in the last century, but takes what justification it can for its current barbarities from what is seen as the error of Partition.

The setting up of the Irish Free State and the Province of Ulster led to civil war, not between North and South or Protestant and Catholic, but between the citizens of this new Free State. The cause of this was the Anglo–Irish Treaty of 1921. The Treaty was passed in Ireland by only a very narrow majority, and many of the population were dead set against it, preferring to hang on for full Independence and a United Ireland. The Free State was then torn by civil war between the pro- and anti-Treaty-ites, which effectively meant between the Free State Government and the IRA. Michael Collins, one of the heroes of the struggle for Independence, and one of the signatories to the Treaty, said at the time, 'I have signed my death warrant'. This turned out to be true. The Irish Civil War was fought to a very bloody conclusion, and the Irish Government had few qualms about executing members of the IRA.

Thirty-four Republicans were shot by firing squad on the orders of the Irish Government in January 1923 alone. More than 13,000 Republicans were gaoled and many of them endured weeks on hunger strike.

This civil war was brief but bloody and when the Government won the IRA went underground. The Republican Party's political arm, Sinn Fein, then refused to take up their seats in the Dail, which they regarded as an unworthy Assembly, representing as it did only part of the country, and because it meant swearing an oath to the titular sovereign, King George V.

Sinn Fein was the main Republican party of the day, and although they won a majority of seats in the post-war elections of 1919, they refused to take their seats in Westminster. The Republicans then set up their own Parliament – the Dail – in Dublin. The leader of this party was a survivor of the 1916 Easter Rising, Eamon de Valera, who was actually in gaol when the Dail first sat.

Eamon de Valera eventually came to accept the Anglo–Irish Treaty that set up the Free State, broke away from Sinn Fein and founded a new party – Fianna Fail – in 1926. The problem in Ireland was then, and to an extent still is, between those who accept the partition of Ireland until such time as the majority of the Northern Ireland people reject it, and those who feel that Partition should end forthwith and the British should be driven out of Ireland, by force if necessary. Seventy years after the signing of the Anglo–Irish Treaty that issue is kept alive by the IRA.

I would rather let the local people explain this dilemma. They are the ones who have to live with it or die because of it. I suppose, in retrospect, it might have been simpler and maybe wiser, to withdraw completely from Ireland in 1921 and let the Irish fight the matter out among themselves. The Irish are good fighters but also very sensible folk. Perhaps, when it came to the sort of massive killing that everyone feared, and still fear, they would have drawn back from the brink. Who knows? Partition came about from the best of intentions as the only available solution to an intractable problem. Only now can we see that the problem was not solved but deferred.

I tried to get all this straight as we drove across Antrim, and over drinks before dinner, sad stuff to hear in this beautiful mellow countryside, where everything seemed so peaceful, but it is something I wanted to get straight while there was still someone to ask. To the casual observer passing through the Province, Northern Ireland is a peaceful place, not a bit like the TV image. We had not seen one roadblock on our journey up to Bushmills.

'It depends on the day,' said Philippa, calmly. 'On some days you run into vehicle checkpoints – VCPs – every few miles. The soldiers stop you, look at your driving licence, look in the boot . . . and goodbye. It's really no bother. Don't go thinking that it's dangerous over here.'

I won't. Unless you are unlucky and in the wrong place at the wrong time, Northern Ireland is perfectly safe. Unless you are a soldier or a policeman or have made yourself a target in some way. The thought is always there though. As I was to discover on my walk, the people I met are almost eager to talk about the Troubles, especially to an outsider. It seems to ease them in some way, but you cannot take too much of it. There is no solution in sight and all the talk dries out on the rock of intransigence. Enough I say for now, and so to dinner.

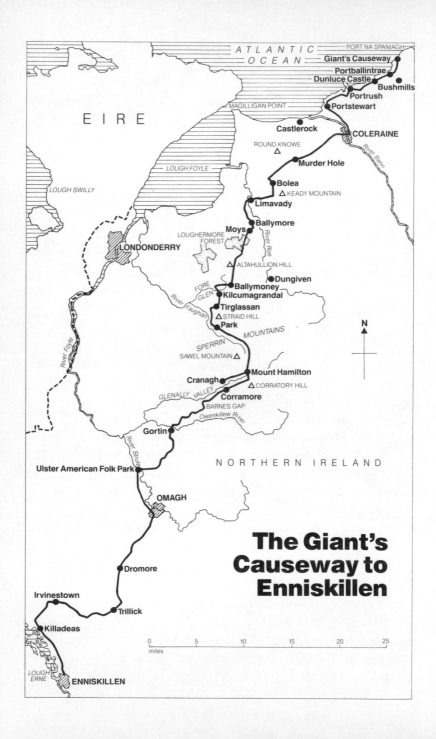

ATLANTIC
OCEAN

PORT NA SPANIAGH

Giant's Causeway
Portballintrae
Dunluce Castle
Bushmills
Portrush
Portstewart

MAGILLIGAN POINT

EIRE

Castlerock

COLERAINE

River Bann

ROUND KNOWE
△

LOUGH FOYLE

Murder Hole

Bolea
△ KEADY MOUNTAIN

LOUGH SWILLY

Limavady

Moys
Ballymore

River Roe

LOUGHERMORE
FOREST

LONDONDERRY

△ ALTAHULLION HILL

Dungiven

FORE
GLEN

Ballymoney
Kilcumagrandal

River Faughan

Tirglassan
△ STRAID HILL

Park

MOUNTAINS

SPERRIN

SAWEL MOUNTAIN △

N

River Foyle

Mount Hamilton

Cranagh
△ CORRATORY HILL

GLENALLY VALLEY

Corramore

BARNES GAP

Owenkillew River

Gortin

River Strule

Ulster American Folk Park

NORTHERN IRELAND

OMAGH

The Giant's
Causeway to
Enniskillen

Dromore

Irvinestown

Trillick

Killadeas

0   5   10   15   20   25
miles

LOUGH
ERNE

ENNISKILLEN

3

The Coast of Antrim

This lande of Irelande is uneven, mountainous,
soft and watery. It has bogges even on the tops of
mountains, not bearing man or beast, and such
bogges are found all over Ireland.

Fyles Morrison,
Secretary to Lord Mountjoy,
Deputy in Ireland for Queen Elizabeth I.

In spite of all the warnings I had received about rain and
mist and sudden storm, I began my journey on a beautiful
day. Ireland makes up for a somewhat indifferent climate by
looking outstandingly lovely when the sun deigns to shine,
and on this morning, on the North Coast of Antrim, it
looked glorious. The day promised to be hot and, truth to
tell, I was not too happy about this, weight-wise. Lugging a
heavy pack is best done in cool temperatures but it was
already warm at 9.30 in the morning and with the sun
shredding the sea-mist down below the cliffs it promised to
be a good deal hotter by the end of the day.

The Giant's Causeway and the coast round about it is
owned by the National Trust, who maintain the only road
down to the Causeway from the cliffs to the sea. The
Causeway is Ireland's only World Heritage site, a fact I

learned in the Visitors' Centre at the top, and since the Causeway lay to the east and my path to the west, I saw no reason to lug my rucksack all the way down the hill and back up again. The man in the National Trust shop agreed to keep an eye on it so, stick in hand, I swung off down the road. After a mile or so I came upon the Causeway and the starting point of my journey.

This part of the Antrim Coast would be remarkable enough even without the Causeway, for the cliffs are high, running up to 600ft in places, very dramatic and topped with jutting pinnacles or stacks. The road down to the Causeway leads past a headland called the Great Stookan, while ahead and to the east lies the headland called Port na Spaniagh, where the *Girona* galleon came to grief in 1588. This was one of the many losses sustained by the Spanish Armada down the West Coast of Scotland, and it has endowed Ireland with a fine collection of 16th-century treasure.

The Spaniards knew that Ireland was a Catholic country and came into this coast hoping for shelter and fresh water. The captain of the *Girona*, Don Martinez de la Casa de Rioja, may have been hoping to make a landfall by Dunluce Castle, which was held by the notorious rebel Sorley Boy Macdonnell, but he ran his ship onshore further east and she broke up in the storm. Over a thousand men were drowned. Instead of a warm welcome those who got ashore were knocked on the head for their possessions and only nine men survived. The wreck of the *Girona* lay offshore until it was discovered in quite shallow water and recovered from the sea in 1967. The treasure of the *Girona*, a wealth of gold and silver plate, weapons and cannon, is now in the Ulster Museum in Belfast and well worth seeing.

The Giant's Causeway is an equally remarkable natural sight. It consists of three reefs, the Grand, Middle and Little Causeways, composed of about 40,000 dull-red hexagonal blocks and looks rather like a giant's Lego set, clumsily fitted together. When he came past here in the 18th century, Dr Johnson remained unimpressed. 'Worth seeing, but not worth going to see,' he said grumpily, but his verdict on this curious collection of blocks and columns hardly seems valid. On this brisk spring morning, with the oyster catchers '*peet-peeting*' about among the rocks, the blue sea crashing in and the blocks standing up in fluted columns, the Causeway looked very well worth visiting. Besides, there are at least three theories as to how the Giant's Causeway got there, so I sat down on a convenient pillar, warming myself in the sun and read all about it in the handbook.

There are two scientific explanations. The 'Vulcanists' believe, probably correctly, that the Causeway is the result of volcanic action about 60 million years ago, when a volcano spread lava out to form these basalt formations and cut out the deep channel to Scotland, which is now filled by the Irish Sea. That seems simple enough, though other volcanoes have wrought similar havoc without creating such strange formations.

The second scientific explanation comes from the 'Neptunists', who hold that the columns are the result of chemical reaction on the sedimentary rocks. This seems a bit far-fetched even to a layman, but since my ignorance of science is, to say the least, profound, I will settle for the fact that this is one of the wonders of the world, the 'eighth wonder' according to the Tourist Board. It is certainly quite remarkable.

I actually prefer the third, or Irish version of how the Causeway was created, which I picked up from Philippa the night before. Long long ago, back in the time of Irish legend, the giant Finn MacCool, or Fionn MacCumhaill, lived hereabouts. Finn was a feisty fellow who greatly enjoyed his daily slanging match with the giant Fingal who lived across the water in a cave on the island of Staffa, just off the coast of Scotland. MacCool bellowed insults at Fingal, and Fingal bellowed insults back, and then matters escalated, as matters will, and events took a nasty turn. The two giants stopped hurling abuse and started hurling stones.

One day, Finn MacCool picked up a handful of land – quite a large handful evidently, for the cavity thus created became Lough Neagh – and hurled it at Fingal. He missed by quite a margin for the handful fell in the sea to the south and became the Isle of Man, which gives you some idea of the scale of things. Incidentally, I don't necessarily believe all this ; I'm just passing on what I was told.

MacCool then decided to build a Causeway across to Staffa and settle Fingal's hash once and for all. So work began and the Causeway gradually crept out across the sea, but as he got closer to Staffa, MacCool realized that Fingal was a lot bigger close-to than he had appeared to be from a distance. He therefore fled back to Ireland with Fingal in hot pursuit and took shelter in his mother's cottage.

Now this Finn MacCool was not just a mass of brawn. He had a brain or two about him somewhere and so, putting on baby clothes, he leapt into a handy cot. He had just stuck the dummy in his mouth when Fingal came hammering on the door. There was a lot of hammering and bellowing before Fingal thought to peer through the window . . . and there was MacCool lying in his cot.

'Dear me,' thought Fingal – or thoughts to that effect – 'If the babies hereabouts are as big as THAT, I can't imagine how big that bugger MacCool will be . . . so I'm off back to Scotland.'

Well, it's a good tale. The Causeway may well have extended right across to the Western Isles at some time, because there are vestiges of it on the Scots' side, but whatever the truth of it, Volcanic, Neptunic or legendary, it remains a most remarkable sight.

There are many thousands of these basalt columns, and

having climbed over them and pondered about them and sat on them for over half-an-hour thinking philosophical thoughts like, 'Why don't I do this more often,' I persuaded a gentleman to take my Start-of-the-Walk picture and made my way back up to the Visitors' Centre. There I spent another half-hour examining the displays and drinking tea and otherwise messing about. I had no particular desire to heave on the rucksack and set out for Valentia Island. Apart from anything else, the damned thing was heavy.

However, needs must. The man in the shop gave me a heave on with the rucksack and off I went over the wind-tugged grass out onto the North Antrim Cliff Path, heading west for Portrush. There is a 5-mile local walk here for those with less serious intentions, while the North Antrim Cliff Path runs for a total of 42 miles along the cliffs and beaches from Fair Head to Magilligan Point. This bit of the path between the Causeway and the mouth of the River Bann is very easy-going and, in the event, turned out to be one of the most scenic parts of my entire journey.

This was in the late spring, but I had flown north from my home in England and gone back a little in the season. The primroses were still out here, along the Antrim Coast, and were lying in great yellow patches in every sheltered corner. Great drifts of sea-pinks cascaded down the cliffs and the grass under my feet was soft and springy. It all made for delightful walking. Gulls, terns and kittiwakes zoomed about my head or sat nesting in the crevasses of the rocks below, so what with one thing and another I had plenty to entertain me as I made my way along the Cliff Path to the beach at Bushfoot Strand and on to Portballintrae, a little port set in a rocky loop along the coast, and so to Dunluce Castle.

I like castles. I will walk miles out of my way to see a good castle, and Dunluce Castle is well worth seeing, a most romantic-looking place seen from across the headland. This is the castle that appears on all the local postcards, and like all such places, Dunluce has picked up some good stories down the centuries.

Dunluce began as a 13th-century medieval keep which belonged to the de Burghs – or Burkes – but it really came to prominence in the 16th century when this castle was the home of Sorley Boy Macdonnell, Chief of the Macdonnell Clan who ruled most of Northern Ulster. Like many other local warlords, Sorley Boy eeked out his rents with cattle raids on his neighbours and piracy off the coast. He paid little or no heed to the laws or wishes of his leige-lady, Elizabeth I of England, and ignored all her edicts. Therefore, in 1584 Elizabeth's Deputy in these parts, Sir John Perrot, marched against Dunluce with a siege-train, pounded the castle with artillery and forced the Macdonnells out. Sir John then installed an English garrison, dusted his hands and departed.

Sorley Boy brooded over this for a year or so and then attacked the castle in his turn. He gained access by first getting half-a-dozen men onto the seaward ramparts, from where more Macdonnells were hauled up the cliff in baskets. The garrison was slaughtered and the English commander hanged from the walls in a cage. However, all this fighting had left Dunluce in a very dilapidated state, and it remained that way until the *Girona* galleon came to grief on the rocks to the east. Those of the crew who staggered ashore were killed by Sorley Boy and his men and the loot from the ship helped to repair the castle.

This slaughter of their Spanish enemies enabled Sorley Boy to make his peace with the English, though to keep in with the Spaniards he also smuggled the few survivors of the *Girona* back across to France. The Macdonnells lived on in Dunluce for another fifty years until 1639, when one night, and quite without warning, a portion of the cliff fell into the sea, taking with it the outer walls, the kitchens, the dinner in the oven and most of the cooks. Sorley's descendants, the Earls of Antrim, hung on to what was left until the mid-1600s, since when Dunluce has stood empty. It has now been partially restored and is a fine sight to see, standing high on the wild green cliffs of Antrim.

Looking at Dunluce took my thoughts back to the 16th century, when the reasons for the English attitude to Ireland and the Irish came into sharp focus. While always wishing to be independent, the Irish had always been seen as a source of rebellion and disaffection by the English Crown. They had supported the House of York during the Wars of the Roses, which did not endear them to the Tudors, but matters took a more serious turn after the Protestant Reformation. The Irish people remained stoutly Catholic and the Protestant tide never swept far up their beaches. The Irish were therefore seen as a base for the Counter-Reformation, the western arm of the Franco-Spanish pincer that could crush the English like a nut.

The English remit in Ireland did not extend very far. In practical terms it existed only within a few hundred square miles around Dublin, generally known as 'The Pale'. This name arose from the word 'paling' for the planks of a fence, and gives us the expression about people living 'beyond the Pale'. Life 'beyond the Pale' in the mid-16th century was nasty and brutish but free. The Irish lords ruled the Irish land and paid only nominal allegiance to the English king. The Irish had their own laws, the Brehon Law, which dated back to Celtic times, and they had no need of foreign statutes or advice. Fearing a Catholic rebellion, Henry VIII decided to change all that.

In 1534, Henry decided that *all* Irish land was to be surrendered to the Crown, which would then redistribute it to loyal adherents, who would be left in no doubt as to where their true allegiance lay. This shocked the Irish lords, for it put an end to their independence and the well-tested laws that had ruled their lives for a thousand years. Naturally they resisted. Henry had too many problems at home to apply his will in Ireland but his daughter, Elizabeth I, was a different person and not one to tolerate defiance.

Elizabeth's problems with Spain and her support for the Dutch fighting the Spaniards in the Low Countries made her very sensitive indeed to unrest or rebellion in Ireland. A succession of her best captains and favourites was dispatched to keep the Irish in order, and when they returned one after the other, with only failure to report, she decided on a drastic solution. If she could not change the Irish lords, then she would change the Irish people. Thus began the 'plantations', the 'planting' of Irish land with English and Scots settlers.

Next to Strongbow, the Plantation of Ulster – and many other parts of Ireland as well but particularly Ulster – is often cited as the worst offence in the long list of Irish grievances against the English Crown. The 'planting' of Scots and English settlers in Ireland took place in the 16th and 17th centuries, but the effects endure to this day. In a sense this is surprising because Elizabeth I was, within reason, fairly tolerant on religious matters. 'I seek no windows into men's souls,' she often declared, and in general she meant it. This tolerance did not, however, extend to Jesuit priests who, if caught, were hanged and gutted, or to any Irish Catholics who showed significant signs of independence.

Elizabeth was determined to enforce her will and the English law in Ireland. She did not trust the great Anglo–Irish lords, the O'Neills and the Macdonnells and the rest, who had become 'more Irish than the Irish,' and her 'Deputies' were English peers who went to Ireland to do her bidding and make their fortunes. The result was rebellion. There were six major risings in Ireland during Elizabeth's reign, all put down at great cost and with growing ferocity.

Sir Henry Sidney, writing to the Queen's Council in 1576, declared, 'I cannot tell the name of every varlet that hath died since I came here, by law and martial law and in the fighting, but the number is great, and the rest tremble. Down they go in every corner, and down they shall go.'

The end result of this conflict was to establish a permanent division between the Protestant English and the Catholic Irish, which came to a head in the person of Hugh O'Neill, the Earl of Tyrone, who then ruled most of Ulster. O'Neill had been brought up at the English Court and was believed to be loyal to the Tudor Queen. He was, however, more loyal to Ireland. After forging an alliance with another Ulster earl, Hugh O'Donnell, the Earl of Tyrconnell, he rose against English domination in 1598 and defeated Elizabeth's forces at the Battle of the Yellow Ford, near Armagh.

Three years later, the war still continuing, Elizabeth's worst fears were realized. A Spanish fleet arrived at Kinsale, landing Spanish soldiers to aid the rebel Earls, but this disparate collection of soldiers proved no match for the English army of the new Deputy in Ireland, Lord Mountjoy. Mountjoy smashed the Spanish–Irish army outside Kinsale and the Earls were forced to submit. They were pardoned by the Queen, and Hugh O'Donnell died soon afterwards, but O'Neill found it impossible to live, or at least live happily, under English domination. In September 1607, O'Neill and the new Earl of Tyrconnell, Rory O'Donnell, took ship for France and never returned. This 'Flight of the Earls' marked the end of Gaelic Ireland and the start of a struggle we have yet to resolve.

O'Neill had been given his lands back after submitting at Kinsale, but after his flight they were given away or sold to English settlers. Most of his lands were in the old province of Ulster, in the countries of Donegal, Tyrone, Derry, Armagh, Fermanagh or Cavan. The 'planting' idea was not new but this time those invited to start 'Plantations' saw a profit in it. Chief of the planters was the Corporation of the City of London. They were granted land in County Derry, which then became Londonderry, and distributed that land among their Livery Companies – the Goldsmiths, the Innkeepers, the Drapers, the Fishmongers, who were directed to find and settle Englishmen on Irish lands.

They succeeded all too well, and traces of the 'Plantation' survive to this day – there is still a Draperstown in Londonderry. But they also failed. The English came but the native Irish did not leave. They stayed on as workers or tenants on the land they had previously owned. By the 1630s about 14,000 settlers had arrived, half-English, half-Scots, all Protestant, and the seeds of the present conflict had been sown.

For a time it seemed likely that what had happened before would happen again. The Irish are a personable people and it was thought that the incomers would inter-marry with the local people and again become 'more Irish than the Irish', but then two events occurred which drove a Protestant stake into the Irish heart; the coming of the Puritans, who won the English Civil War under Cromwell, and the arrival of William of Orange in 1688.

The process of 'planting' continued throughout the first half of the 17th century and reached its peak in the bloody years after 1649, when Oliver Cromwell came to Ireland and drove the Irish west into Connaught. The idea was that of Elizabeth I, to drive the native people off their lands and replace them with loyal Protestant settlers. Ulster was now largely 'planted' with Scottish Presbyterians, whose descendants live in Ulster to this day and still maintain strong links with their distant connections in Scotland, which lies just a few miles off the Antrim Coast. The Catholic supporters of 'Celtic' and the Protestant supporters of 'Rangers' give weekly proof of this during the football season in Scotland.

* * *

It was now mid-day and time for a rest so, having dumped my pack in the café just across the road from Dunluce, I toured the castle with a group of visiting Irish–Americans. They were openly surprised that a 'Brit' should dare walk around Ulster without an armed guard. 'Do you find the people, well, friendly?' they asked, curiously. 'In spite of everything?' added one gentleman, quoting a few examples, like the Plantings and the Famine of the 1840s. He looked very sceptical when I explained that the Potato Famine was not actually my fault and the local people knew it. When an American lady asked when the British would leave Ireland, I said when the Americans give Dakota back to the Sioux, or when the majority of the local people wanted us to, whichever was the sooner. One tries to be amiable but there are limits.

After Dunluce the path went down to the seashore, while I followed a rough track along to the river that curves round between the links of the Royal Portrush Golf Club. This is just one of a dozen golf courses along this coast, all doing good business on this pin-bright morning. I was still new to Northern Ireland, and still surprised at the normality of it all. I went over the dunes, which was hard work on the soft sand, pulling myself up the slopes with handfuls of marram grass, and then down onto Portrush beach, which was fairly crowded on this sunny Saturday afternoon – normality again.

Portrush is set on a stiff finger of land sticking out to Ramone Head and the flat outline of the Skerrie Islands a mile or two offshore. Then on, along the coast, towards the rushing estuary of the River Bann by Portstewart. A raft race was being held on the Bann, but I had been trudging along for five hours now, though with fairly frequent stops for rest and a cup of tea. I now decided it was time for a decent drink, so I looked around for a typical Irish pub and decided to go into the first one I found. To be honest, Irish pubs don't change much and one is as good as another.

Portstewart is a fairly large resort and my first Irish town. The streets of Portstewart are lined with pastel-painted houses and the shop fronts are painted in more vivid colours. The Irish like bright colours and sales of purple or vermilion paint must be considerable. Half the commercial premises in Portstewart seemed to be pubs and most of the pubs were crowded.

I was to become well acquainted with Irish pubs over the next few weeks, so there is no need to labour the description except to say that Irish pubs are places for talking and drinking. There is no space in Irish pubs for horse brasses, jovial 'mine hosts' or poker-work signs saying, 'If you don't see what you want behind the bar she has probably left'. Irish pubs – bars is a better description – are not like that at all. The outsides tend to be covered with bright-coloured plastic and the door can be difficult to find. Most of them are named after the owner, so that 'The Red Lion' and 'The Wheelwright's Arms' are replaced by 'O'Malley's' or simply 'Paddy's'.

Once inside, the bar will either be jammed or empty, depending on the time of day. The first one I entered had no one in it but a man behind the bar, reading a newspaper. He continued to read as I staggered in, found a table in the gloom and proceeded to divest myself of two cameras, a rucksack, my notebook, my glasses, my sunglasses, a map and my walking stick. All this took some time. Only when I was standing at the bar, pulling my sweat-soaked shirt away from my back, did he take any interest at all. When I asked for a glass of dry white wine, he became positively alarmed. If I had asked for a glass of hemlock it could not have caused more consternation.

'Gentleman wants a glass of wine, so he does,' he bellowed up the stairs at the back.

More sounds of astonishment drifted down from the

upper reaches. After a while a bottle of wine – sweet and white – was unearthed from somewhere out the back. I *hate* sweet white wine, but after causing all that fuss what could I do? Fortunately, I was saved by a shortage of equipment – no corkscrew. This was the first bar I have ever been in that hadn't got a corkscrew. On the other hand that meant I needn't drink sweet white wine, and I never again asked for a glass of wine in an Irish pub. I settled instead for a glass of Smithwicks and a chat. We discussed the weather, which was unseasonably hot, and the prospects for the salmon fishing, which were noticeably bad, and then, inevitably, we got round to the Troubles. When it comes to discussing the 'Troubles' with total strangers it pays to be non-committal.

'I don't understand the cause of it at all,' I ventured. 'Seems a terrible pity in such a beautiful country.'

'It's because of the bastards,' declared the barman.

'The IRA?'

'Those . . . and the others. The Protestant bastards . . .'

'Oh . . . but. . . .'

'. . . and the Army. They are *all* bastards. They don't come in here, y'know, so they don't. I won't have soldiers in here, so I won't. Bastards, all of them!'

I like a man who hedges his bets. It may make no sense to hate everyone but it certainly makes life simpler.

4

Coleraine to Limavady

I would define Ireland as a region of good eating
and tolerable company, where a man from
England may sojurn some years with pleasure,
make his fortune and return home, having gathered the spoils by doing us all the mischief he can
and by that gain credit at Court.

Jonathan Swift, 1729

I left the Antrim Coast at Portstewart and could have wished
to stay on it a lot longer. The full distance along the coast
from Fair Head to Magilligan Point would make a good
three-day tramp, but there was no time for that now. The
day was getting on and I was tiring but I was not done yet.
There were still a few miles to Coleraine.

Portstewart is a Victorian resort, and rather snobby. In the
last century the townspeople even rejected the offer of a
railway station in case it let the vulgar people in. It still
looked reserved but rather charming, a place to linger in on
this warm afternoon. The heat was now quite shattering and
the sea was therefore pulling the crowds down onto the long
beach of Portstewart Strand, where the surfing is said to be
the best in Ireland.

No surfing today though. On a day like this the sea lay like a mill pond, the waves lazily lapping on the beach as I took off my long socks and went for a paddle. Resting the feet and keeping them cool is one of the great ways to stave off the blisters, so I had half-an-hour here before setting off along the edge of the River Bann for Coleraine. I had walked a good deal further than I intended for the first day and I was already very tired. The place I had arranged to stay in lay just across the river from Portstewart but the only bridge across is at Coleraine.

Coleraine is not a pretty town. The pretty parts lie by the river, and it has seen more than its share of Troubles in the last few years. Six months after my visit a huge IRA bomb devastated the heart of the town and this was just one incident among many. There was no sign of any trouble now. When I came limping in about teatime there was not a soldier or a policeman in sight, even around the large crowd enjoying the local regatta by the bridge. In the early days of my walk it seemed strange to find people in Northern Ireland doing normal things like working and enjoying themselves on a golf course or a river, but I was already starting to get used to it.

They have held an annual regatta on the River Bann at Coleraine for about 150 years and rowing eights and cox'd fours were zipping about the surface of the river like so many aquatic insects. I did think of tottering into one of the riverside pubs for another chat with the locals, but I had really had enough for one day. Maybe I am getting too old for this. Now I only wanted to get free of the pack and out of the boots. This was when I discovered that my night-stop at Norrie and Billy's 'Bed & Breakfast' was another two miles out of town. Discoveries like that can really break your heart.

There is no cure for it but to press on, so on I went, ever slower now, out of town a bit and then up a side road, back towards the Bann estuary, stopping every so often to check my map for the location of the guest house. While I was doing this a very ramshackle Land Rover came bouncing down the road towards me and pulled up alongside.

'You must be Rob,' said the lady driver. 'No one else would carry a great pack like that on a day like this.'

'I am,' I replied, 'and you must be Norrie.'

'I am,' she said. 'So hop in and we'll away to the regatta.'

Norrie was a smiling, busy lady of a certain age and she drove the Land Rover with the ease of Boadicea handling her chariot. In other words, rather fast. Within minutes I had been co-opted into helping Norrie tow away the Finishing Line Box from the lawn on the far side of the river. This box also served as the Finishing Line Box at the local horse races and moving it involved recruiting a certain amount of help from the locals and some tricky driving round the town. It was well after six o'clock before we were back at Norrie's house and I was able to settle down in my socks for a pot of tea and some scones.

Maybe it isn't too early to say more about the hospitality of the Ulster people. It isn't reserved for the visitor, it's simply there. Anyone can say, 'Make yourself at home,' but they don't often mean it. In any Northern Ireland home, on the other hand, I always had my boots off and a cup of tea in my hand ten minutes after arriving. I was settling down for a good 'crack' with Norrie when her husband Billy came in, a big, fit, jovial man, a sports-lover, a put-a-right of local problems. Billy was just looking in for dinner before rushing out again to a local Sports Council meeting, and although he invited me to go along for the evening and have a bit of singing with the regatta crowd, I had done enough for one day after 25 miles on road and footpath.

Instead I stayed in and had a good chat – or 'crack' as they call it hereabouts, with Norrie. The 'crack' is an Irish institution, but it is one of those local words it is hard to put your finger on. The implication is that a good 'crack' means a good time, but it means also that there will be witty or amusing, or at least worthwhile conversation. I love listening to good conversation, and nowhere is it better than in Ireland.

'Billy was in the police,' said Norrie suddenly. 'During all the Troubles. I'm glad he's out of it now, I can tell you. I was worried all the time.'

There is not a lot you can say. I am not a politician or a pundit. I don't have any answers. I'm just trying to understand. I don't live in Northern Ireland so I just asked the usual questions, especially the one the local people will have to answer sooner or later. How or when will it end? The present Troubles have been going on for twenty-five years; over 3,000 people have been killed, thousands more injured, property destroyed, lives wrecked. Still it continues, so where will it end?

'I don't know when or where it's going to end,' said Norrie. 'I can see no end to it. There's so much hate here, you see, so little understanding. Billy is a Protestant and I'm a Catholic, you know. When we got married the families were, well . . . upset. My folks soon got to like Billy, but you feel the hate, the distrust, everywhere. My sister-in-law swore she would never buy a car from a Catholic . . . now isn't that daft? The car doesn't have a religion. She said the car was fine and the man was honest, but she just wouldn't feel happy about it. How can it end when even good people feel like that?'

God knows – as they say in Ireland – but He's not telling.

It is also curious that while the distrust between the communities is certainly there and the extremists thrive on it, outsiders like myself are hardly aware of it. On that day, and all other days, everyone I met was charming. It took some time and a great deal of thought before it occurred to me that the history of the Irish people has forged something

different here, a people with Celtic or Gaelic roots who have
evolved their own problems rather as another nation evolves
its mythology. Everything about Ireland has a reason, but
not all the reasons make sense to the outsider. Therefore you
have to ignore the reason and accept the situation. Or go
mad, of course.

I slept like a log that night, worn out with a long walk, a
good dinner, and a certain amount of Billy's whiskey, and
woke up to another warm day. Where was all this rain
people talk about? All was bustle at the B & B, for Billy and
Norrie were off to a horse show, and although a bit stiff, I
was off down the road for Limavady. Every other house in
this part of Ireland seems to have a horse or two in the
paddock and a horse box in the yard, so they were both up
and doing and eager to be off. First though, an Ulster Fry.

The Ulster Fry is an Irish institution. It consists of a couple
of eggs, a few rashers of bacon, two or three slices of fried
bread, a sausage or two, maybe three – a chop, soda bread
soaked in fat, and anything else that happens to be lying out
in the kitchen and can find its way into the frying pan. This
concoction is referred to locally, and with reason, as a 'heart
attack on a plate'. I persuaded myself that a huge breakfast
was necessary for my long day's flog to Limavady, some 15
miles away, and worked my way stolidly through a vast
plateful before heaving my rucksack out into the yard and
getting ready for the off.

It was one of those hazy mornings, but clearing by the
minute, and Billy showed me around and pointed out the
local landmarks.

'That's the Mussenden temple up there on the coast,' he
said, pointing to a small domed structure. 'It was built by the
Bishop but the National Trust owns it now. It's right on the
edge of the cliff and every gale looks like sweeping it away,
but it stays there. Beyond that, across Lough Foyle, those
hills are in Donegal, in the Republic . . . let's have a look at

your map. You see … the Republic is actually north of Northern Ireland over there. We do it to confuse you.'

They succeed. Since I was two miles north of the town and every step in the wrong direction was one wasted, Billy volunteered to drive me back to my route and drop me off on the 'Murder-Hole Road.'

'Don't be anxious,' he said, catching the look on my face. 'It's not recent. Some highwayman used to hide there two hundred years ago. In fact, they call it something else nowadays, but everyone around here still calls it the Murder-Hole Road. Follow that and it will take you into Limavady.'

When we got to the Murder-Hole Road, just south of Coleraine, Billy got out of the cat and helped me on with the rucksack. Then he shook me by the hand and gave me a poke in the shoulder. 'Remember now, Robbie, when you write that book, be sure to tell them we're not all murdering maniacs over here. Will you do that? And come and see us again?'

'I will, Billy. I will.'

I stood by the side of the road, waiting and waving until he drove off out of sight. It was Sunday morning and people were driving past on their way to church, every driver lifting a hand to acknowledge me. Four young men in a very battered car screeched to a stop and asked me the way, and I was so relaxed by now I hardly flinched. There was enough shade to keep me from the full effect of the sun and a fair day's walk ahead. For the moment I needed nothing more.

I am not very fond of road walking but when the road arrows directly to where you are going, it seems foolish not to use it. This road to Limavady rolls gently up and over a moorland between the humps of the Round Knowe to the north and the Keady Mountain to the south, and since my night-stop lay to the south of Limavady I thought I would get off the main road after a few miles and walk around or over the Keady Mountain – an Irish mountain this, 1,093 ft high – and so to my destination.

The Murder-Hole Road rolls out of Coleraine, west across the moors between the vast fir tree plantations. At the roadside of the Grange Park Wood is a small cottage marked 'Murder Hole', and I could turn off there.

Up to this point I had still not tumbled to the fact that cross-country marching in Ireland is not easy, even where it is possible. I thought I could walk to the end of the track in the wood and then just keep going across country. There was not even the sign of a footpath or a trail, just open moor. Easy. It was another beautiful morning and the gardens of the neat houses and cottages beside the road were ablaze with flowers and shrubs, so it was no hardship just to plod along the main road, nodding at the church-bound locals for a few miles or so to the ruin of the Murder-Hole Cottage.

A local footpad or highwayman had used this to hide his loot and dispose of his victims in the last century, and it is now a ruin. I doubt if the name will improve the prospect for sale and renovation, but since there is nothing to see or remark on I turned off down the lane, along the Curly river, to Bolea, turning off again where a track ran off to my left towards the distant glinting roofs of Limavady. With a bit of luck and effort I could be there by noon.

My tarmac lane duly turned into a track and then into a footpath of sorts, which petered out by a chainlink fence. There was nothing to head for on the horizon ahead so I consulted the compass, fixed a bearing to Limavady, hopped over the fence and sank knee-deep into a bog. I got out of the bog, splashed across a stream and sank into another bog. This went on for some time. The snag is that in Ireland bogs are unavoidable. They can even be found on the tops of hills. The trouble is that most of Ireland, North or South, is just a great big sponge. If Finn O'Cool squeezed Ireland in his mighty hand and got all the water out, sea levels would rise in Australia. It began to dawn on me that this might be a problem.

The best place to walk, and I use the word 'best' with reluctance, is along the sides of the hills, where the water may have drained down into the valley from the peat bogs on the tops. The snag is that walking on a slope is very hard on the ankles. I hobbled along a sheep track around the slopes of the Keady Mountain, which took me off track, since Limavady now lay to my right, but also gave me a clear view of the numerous streams and ponds and other obstacles which lay between me and the whitewashed houses of Limavady. Eventually I gave up the attempt at pin-point navigation round the Keady Mountain and squelched off past a quarry and through various lanes and then down into the town. It was now well into Sunday afternoon and everyone but me was in their Sunday best. I felt very much out of it in my wet and muddy clothing, trudging through the streets under my heavy pack.

The cure for a state like this is tea, and I found an open teashop where I became the object of general interest. Curiously enough, unlike Spain, no one in Ireland thought I was crazy. If the locals had the time for a good walk they would probably take it. 'Good luck to you,' they said, 'and have a good time.'

'Did you hear the story of the three Cardinals discussing the meaning of Time?' I was asked. 'No? Well, the Italian Cardinal said that the word "*Domani*" was a lovely word, meaning not just tomorrow, but sometime when they could get round to it. Then the Spanish Cardinal said, "*Mañana*" was much the same, and when someone said "I'll do it *mañana*" you knew he wouldn't do it at all. Then they looked at the Irish Cardinal and he said his country didn't have any words which had the same sense of urgency.'

Once again my B & B lay outside the town and it took some time to find. Since it lay on my route for the next day I didn't mind so much, and it was hot and teatime by the time I got there. I was not a pretty sight when I rang the bell, and all things considered Robin McCormick, my host, took it very well when he found me on the doorstep. I was red in the face, dripping with sweat and muddy to the waist, but he seemed not to notice.

'Come along in,' he said, without batting an eye, 'and have a cup of tea.'

Limavady is a nice little town. It has some fine Georgian buildings and some small claims to fame. Ulster has had more than its fair share of famous men, mostly the sons of Catholic dissidents who left Ireland in the early years of the 18th century. Five of the men who signed the American Declaration of Independence came from Ulster and the Declaration was printed by John Dunlop, who was born in Londonderry. Twelve American Presidents, including Andrew Jackson and Woodrow Wilson, have Ulster ancestry, as did Sam Houston, founder of Texas, and the astronaut Neil Armstrong, the First Man on the Moon ... and that is without such luminaries as John F. Kennedy and Ronald Reagan, who came from other parts of Ireland. One of the sights of the town is a monument to William Massey, Prime Minister of New Zealand from 1912 to 1925, who was born in Limavady.

More than that though, there is culture. It was here in Limavady in 1851 that Jane Ross heard a blind Irish fiddler playing the tune that is now known as the 'Londonderry Air', though it is even better known as 'Danny Boy'. There is a plaque to this event on the wall of Miss Ross's house in Main Street.

My hosts, the McCormicks, are Catholic. They have several pretty daughters and a lot of religious insignia around the walls, so I could work that out for myself. They were also instantly hospitable to the muddy heathen. My socks went to be washed, there was the tea and the scones in the parlour, and Robin McCormick had a suggestion for the evening.

'We are off to Mass,' he said, 'but we have fixed you a dinner at a restaurant in town. We'll pick you up after that and all go for a drive.' Once again I felt at home, and welcome.

After I had cleaned myself up we all piled into the car with the girls and sped into Limavady, dropping me off at the restaurant for dinner. I might as well say another word here about Irish food. This is from notes written after two days on the trail and things were to pick up later, but I have to say that so far Irish food was terrible. No offence meant, but it is. The basic staple of the Irish diet is still the potato and I was alarmed to learn that the Irish people each get through about 240 lbs of potatoes a year. In the Republic they get through all the potatoes they can grow and import thousands of tons besides.

This might not bother me but these Irish potatoes are not neat Jersey potatoes the size of ping-pong balls, but great heavy King Edwards, huge menacing spuds that lie in wait at every meal, variously disguised. Irish potatoes get served up fried, boiled, mashed, roasted and, for all I know, with custard. They came by the plateful and over the next few weeks played havoc with my hips. With the potato comes overdone lamb or overdone pork with overdone vegetables, all cooked to a pulp. After two days crossing Northern Ireland I would have killed for a salad.

Having given offence, let me add that I understand all this. Many years ago, not long after the war, I worked in the Welsh valleys and the Black Country of England. The tastes of the people there were just the same. They had no time for that fancy arsey-tarsey savoury rubbish the soft Southerners liked. They needed something tasty, something that sticks to the ribs, something a man could go to work on. The solid, heavy Irish meals, the craving for sweet wine, sticky cakes and rich food is a taste nurtured by generations of deprivation. When I remembered that, I still wanted a salad and a few small, firm, Jersey potatoes, but I kept my mouth shut. Caution and common decency compels me to add that as I went on the food picked up no end. I never actually went into my swooning, finger-tip-kissing mode when walking across Ireland, but I got used to it. Besides, hang the food, the people are wonderful.

I might add that apart from being wonderful they are not unaware that cuisine is not their strong point. There is even a certain pride in the knowledge that Northern Ireland has the highest rate of death from heart disease in Europe. Since they are all on a high cholesterol diet, this is hardly surprising.

I had a grand family evening with the McCormicks. We drove to see the house where Jane Ross lived and we went to the Roe Valley Park, a very pretty spot to the south of the town where the engine sheds which first brought electricity to Limavady have been converted into a museum. We took a stroll beside the rock-strewn River Roe and as I also have daughters we talked about bringing up girls. Then we went back for supper and another good 'crack' around the fire. I went to bed stone cold sober but very content.

After the now familiar massive breakfast I got away early. Maud McCormick and her four girls were all there to see me off, with my clothes washed and a packet of sandwiches ready to fend off starvation. There was no sign of Robin, who had already gone off to work, but I had gone only a few miles down the road when he suddenly swept up alongside in his car.

'I couldn't let you leave without wishing you God-speed,' he said, getting out of the car. 'So have a good time now.

Look after yourself, and come back and see us again one day.'

I shook his hand and went away towards the closing loom of the Sperrin Mountains, strangely warmed by this fare-well. Dammit, there are some nice people living in Ulster.

5

Crossing the Sperrins

I am beginning to find out that a man should be forty years in this country and *then* he wouldn't be able to write about it. Who does understand this place? Not the natives certainly, for the two parties so hate each other that neither can view the simplest act of the other without falsifying. And where in all this can the stranger look for truth?

William Makepeace Thackeray, 1842

Some romantic I had talked to in England told me about the Sperrins. He described them in the most lyrical terms: '... the most beautiful part of Ulster, long ridges, rolling hills, deep, open valleys, great for walking ... you'll love it.' They were, he eulogized, the most splendid mountains, of no great height certainly, but with open tops and ridges, the sort of country any real walker longs to put his boots on. I could already see myself striding along ridges, a figure in the landscape, taking great draughts of moorland air, looking down on those green valleys, each a patchwork of well-tilled fields, dotted with whitewashed farmhouses and cottages ... wonderful! I could see the Sperrins dead ahead now, barring the skyline on this warm and misty morning, and I pressed in towards them at my best speed.

His description of these then unheard of mountains sounded idyllic, and up to a point the reality lived up to it. Only on closer inspection did I discover the snags, but since the snags were considerable I will elaborate on them now. It is not entirely fair to say that Ireland has no footpaths. There are a few, here and there, but not very many. The snag at the moment was that all the ridges lay east to west and I was going north to south. There were precious few footpaths leading in my direction, and part of the reason for this shortage goes back to the 'plantings' and beyond.

This process of 'planting' began in Tudor times and went on for generations, and one effect of it was to deny the Irish any rights-of-way over their native land. Footpaths were anyway in short supply hereabouts, for Ireland is too wet and boggy, too full of lakes and streams for people to wander at will as they do in most parts of Britain. Besides, the footpath as a means of getting about never came into the scheme of things at all.

The Romans who conquered Britain and stayed there for 700 years ran out of steam before they could cross the Irish Sea. That road network which the Romans established in Britain, and which remained the basis of English roads until turnpike days, was never established in Ireland. Britain's vast footpath network, in spite of guerrilla warfare from the farming community, is still one of the joys of the English countryside and dates back to the Saxons, and neither the Saxons nor the Danes made much headway in Ireland. Indeed, for most of her history, Ireland had very few roads of any kind. Most Irish roads only date back to the Famines of the last century when road work was offered as a means of providing starving people with money for food. These 'Famine' roads make Ireland a marvellous place for cycling, and were to provide most of my routes on the walk south to Valentia.

The next set of invaders after the Saxons was not interested in footpaths either. The Danish Vikings, the Northmen, started raiding the Irish coast as early as 795 AD. They struck first at the abbey on Lambay Island near what is now Dublin and their raids continued to ravage the Irish Coast for the next generation. As an Irish monk wrote at the time, 'If there were a tongue in every head, they could not recount or enumerate all that we have suffered from these valiant, wrathful, purely pagan people.'

Having harried the Irish Coast into ruin, the Danes began to settle here, as they did in parts of England. Eventually whole armies of Danes arrived to set up proper colonies.

In 837 AD two Danish fleets arrived, bringing settlers who established a Viking city at Dyfflin – the Black pool, or Dublin. Over the next two centuries the Danes established the first real towns in Ireland – Dublin was one and Waterford another, but that was the extent of their settlement. The famous Brian Boru, the King of Munster and High King of Ireland, finally defeated the settler Danes at the Battle of Clontarf in 1014, but Boru was killed in the battle. Although a spent force militarily, the Danes stayed on as seamen and traders until they intermarried with and were absorbed by the native Irish. Ireland absorbs everyone, but bears few signs of their influence – like footpaths, for example.

So it is that any walker attempting to walk across Ireland ends up stuck on the roads. The Irish say, quite correctly, that there is no need to waymark paths today, partly because paths are few and partly because the Irish farmers have no great objection to walkers crossing their fields. All I have to say to that is – try it.

I had already tried a bit of cross-country, off-the-road, on-the-bog walking and found it very hard, wet work. The end result is that I chose to walk on lanes or such tracks as I could find. This added to the distance and played havoc with my feet, but I met more people. This was no real hardship and I walked on happily enough out of Limavady through the hamlets of Ballymore and Moys, along lanes thick with yellow gorse and multi-hued rhododendrons, past gardens still bright with azalea bushes, and along a track into the Loughermore Forest. This was the third day of my walk and the third day of bright sunshine, so I had hoped that the countryside would dry out. It was already hot by mid-morning when I climbed over a fence – with commendable agility for a portly gent like myself – and promptly sank in a bog.

I have to say I found it rather frightening. I kept going down, with no apparent bottom under my boots, and only stopped sinking when my rucksack splashed into the water. Then followed some Houdini-like contortions to hook the handle of my stick back into the wire of the fence, and then to wriggle out of the rucksack straps. Then, by lying on the rucksack and pulling on the stick, I could slowly haul myself from the sucking embrace of the bog. By the time I had climbed back over the fence I was exhausted and not a little shaken. After that I became a bit more careful crossing open country.

There is a certain trick to bog-trotting. You have to avoid pools of water and the bright green vegetation, which always seemed to give way under my boots. It is possible, though very hard work, to hop across a bog from tussock to tussock, or to sweep the feet sideways through the grass and put the weight on the mattress of grass thus created. On open, flat, blanket bog, the going, if squishy and wet, is rather easier. The sensation is very springy, rather like walking on a water-bed. It is possible to follow sheep tracks through the bogs, for the sheep seem to have the knack of finding a way across, but most sheep are lighter than I am and their weight is more evenly distributed. Bog-trotting, however you try it, is usually hard, wet work.

I sat around on the track beside this bog for about half an hour, pouring evil black water from my boots and changing my socks before I decided to try again. This time I took care to pick my way gingerly from tussock to tussock, carefully avoiding the bright green patches. I slowly gained a little height up the slightly inclined slopes of Glenconway Hill. From higher up I could see that various tracks ran across the hill apart from the single one running west, shown on my map but which I could not find. None of them seemed to go in my required direction.

I therefore headed across the moor on a compass bearing, making towards the rise of Altahullion Hill. What with climbing in and out of peat hags, the wide trenches cut by the peat gatherers, and falling into yet another patch of bog, I was soaking wet, very thirsty and covered in mud before I reached the far southern slope of the hill, from where I could look down on the Foreglen and the Foreglen river.

I could also see the white walls of a chapel in the valley which, if that was indeed the chapel at Ballymoney, meant that I had come out dead on track. Making your way directly across country by map and compass and coming out just where you intend to is one of the pleasures of long-distance walking, and this little success quite cheered me up. There is a knack to cross-country navigation, and I was glad I still had it. In fact, considering the terrain I felt rather smug about it.

I made my way directly down the hillside, bouncing lightly over the blanket bog, only falling in half-a-dozen times, and came out over some farmland and through the back of a garage yard just beside the Dungivan to London-derry road. The garage proprietor, who was standing with his head half-buried in an engine, was startled at my appearance and not very pleased to see me.

'Where in the . . . where the hell did you spring from? Are you with the soldiers?'

I suppose that in my wet Rohan clothes and humping a dark green rucksack, this mistake was understandable, but it seemed to need a quick denial.

I shook my head. 'I'm just on a walk. I've come down from Limavady over the moor ... and could I have a glass of water, please?'

The man still seemed perplexed, but he at once became much more friendly. 'It's nothing against you, you understand, but the soldiers come crashing down through here in their bloody trucks, with guns and everything. Last week they damned near ran over one of my children. Anyway, you're very welcome ... you'll be from the Mainland, I take it ... we don't see many of you over here ... and you have good weather ... that's fine, fine ...' He went away to get me that glass of water.

Instead of water I was given a fridge-cold quart of Coke; nectar and ambrosia in my current state of thirst. Did I mention that it was a very hot day? I also borrowed the garage hose and cleaned myself up, hosing off the mud and peat with the help of the children who had the time of their lives washing me down. Since it was hot and I was pretty wet anyway, I didn't mind this a bit. Meanwhile, their father grumbled on about the soldiers who, it seems, are not popular hereabouts. This done, and steaming gently, I set off up the road towards Londonderry and my next B & B, a mile or two up the road. It was now around four in the afternoon, so if I was lucky I would get there just in time for tea.

I have to say that Mrs Hayes took my arrival very well. Cecilia Hayes used to be a nurse in Belfast, so she is probably used to terrible sights, but whatever the reason, she had a good laugh and then went to put the kettle on. I managed to remove my boots and peel off my socks at the door and pad into the bathroom in bare feet. Then the Ulster hospitality took over. I went into the shower, and my stained, wet clothes went into the washing machine. There was then more padding about, draped coyly in a towel until I found something dry to wear, while the tea and scones went into the sitting room. One of the other guests in there was Dr John, also from Belfast, who was young and thin and visibly harassed.

'I'm a locum,' he explained through a mouthful of scone. 'Just filling in here while the local MD is on holiday. It's a good place to stay because, having been a nurse, Cecilia can take the calls and she can work out what's wrong with the patient. Seeing if they really need a call or whatever. It's all go, y'know but I'll try not to disturb you if I'm in and out during the night.' At this point the phone rang, there was a flurry of conversation from the hall and Dr John hurriedly departed on a call, though not before putting his head round the door to say, 'I'll be in for dinner and we'll have a good crack.'

The 'crack' that night was interesting. With the aid of some wine, rather a lot of wine actually, plus my emergency supplies of Bushmills, we had some interesting conversation. There were five of us at the table; a chatty young accountant from Dublin, a taciturn carpenter who was working on a new shopping mall in Derry, Dr John from Belfast, Cecilia and myself. They talked and I listened, mostly to Dr John, who had done his training at the Royal Victoria Hospital in Belfast and seen more than his share of the sharp end of the Troubles. It was a vivid example of what the Troubles can mean to the people on the ground.

'When a man comes in, say, hit in the head by a high velocity bullet, it's a terrible thing, because there is not much you can do ... his brains are on the stretcher. The kneecapping? Well, that depends on how it is done. They don't shoot you through the front of the knee, you know. They do it from the back, so if the victim struggles a bit and the Provo bastards use a low velocity pistol and miss the patella – the kneecap – then the poor eejit might get away with something fairly minor – an in-and-out in the thigh or calf. Otherwise he's a cripple and probably will need a stick or be on crutches for life. We do what we can but it's a terrible wound. It's not as bad as it once was though. We might only get two or three cappings a month these days.'

That seemed an awful lot to me but people here seem to take such matters almost in their stride – if that is the right term to employ about knee-capping. The Derry man even had a knee-capping tale that was almost funny. Almost.

'You know that they tell you you'll be done, so they do? Drug pushers or joy-riders or people that get too pally with the soldiers? Well, there was this fella . . . I don't know what he'd done, but they rang him and said, "Right, boyo, you're for a capping. Be at the corner of the street tomorrow morning and we'll see to you."

'Well,' went on the Derry man, 'he was so worried he went and got drunk and when he woke up next day with a terrible head on, the time for his capping was long gone.' Imagine! So he went rushing about the street looking for the hard men and hoping they'd not be too rough on him. He found someone to pass the word and they gave him another appointment. That afternoon he went off for his 'capping, quite relieved.'

I thought that was terrible. 'You mean they don't just pick you up, drag you away and do it?' I asked. 'They tell you about it so you can worry yourself sick all night? And then you have to turn yourself over for it.'

They nodded all together, as if surprised that I didn't know how things were done on the great housing estates of Northern Ireland.

'That's disgusting,' I said. 'Terrible. I'd run away.'

'I'll tell you what's terrible,' said Dr John suddenly. 'What's really terrible. You'll be having a cup of tea in the back of Casualty, and someone runs in to say, "Come quick, they're bringing in a man." And you wonder – you may not ask but you always wonder as you're running down the corridor – is it a Catholic or a Protestant? It doesn't *matter*. I know it doesn't matter, but you still ask yourself.'

'It shouldn't matter,' said the Derry man, nodding, 'but it does.'

'It'll never end,' said Cecilia, sadly, 'as long as we're all like that.'

It would be wrong to imply that the Troubles are the only topic of conversation around an Irish dinner table. You talk about everything but as the lone Brit and one willing to listen, I found myself the focus of explanations, of the need to explain how it is here, of attempts to get me to see what it is like and try to understand. I can only say that I tried. A little history certainly helps, especially here in County Londonderry, a few miles from the city itself.

The siege of Londonderry in 1688–89 is one of the most heroic, or one of the most tragic, events in Irish history. It depends on your point of view, but the facts are as follows.

James II of England, brother of Charles II, was a Catholic. He tried to fudge the fact but the fact remained and his people would not have a Catholic on the Throne. They had been through all that with Charles I. The Duke of Monmouth, an illegitimate but Protestant son of Charles II, soon raised a rebellion in the West of England. When it failed the King cut off Monmouth's head, but even that did not deter the English Puritans. James II had to go, and when he was deposed he went to Ireland.

James II had dealt kindly with the Irish people. He had given Irish Catholics high offices in the Irish Government and repealed several Acts inflicted on the Irish people by Cromwell. He might have done more but in 1688 the English threw him out and replaced him with William of Orange. Ireland then split over the issue of whether to support the legitimate but Protestant King William of Orange, or the Catholic 'Pretender', King James II. Matters came to a head in Londonderry in the autum of 1688 when, after a series of sectarian riots, news arrived that James was sending in a Catholic regiment, 'Lord Antrim's Redshanks', to replace the existing garrison.

The mainly Protestant population was worried about letting in a large Catholic force, but even the Protestant Bishop felt it would be difficult to keep them out. The regiment was within sight of the city on 7 December 1688 when thirteen apprentice boys seized the city keys and slammed the city gates in the faces of King James's soldiers.

From that act much has followed. Every December the Protestant Orange Orders assemble in Londonderry to celebrate the actions of the Apprentice Boys 300 years ago by parading through mainly Catholic Derry – as the Catholics call it – with fife and drum. 'No Surrender' – the defiant shout of the Apprentice Boys – echoes down the history of Ulster, a total rejection of Catholic or Republican rule.

The siege of Londonderry did not actually start until the April of 1689 and only lasted about six weeks. Food stocks were short at the end of the winter and the population was soon reduced to eating cats and rats to avoid starvation. A convoy of English troops from William's army soon arrived on the River Foyle, but their ships failed to break the boom and they withdrew again. The townspeople somehow held on, close to starvation, right through the spring and early summer of 1689, until the boom was broken in July and relief supplies finally reached the city.

That long, hard summer has never been forgotten by the Protestants of Ulster. It gave them the slogan of 'No Surrender', which is scrawled on their walls to this day, usually above a picture of King Billy on his prancing charger. It also taught them that their security in the face of the Catholic Irish nation depended on maintaining the British or Unionist connection.

The Protestants of Ulster gave King William the gift of time; time to gather his forces, time to seize the Throne of England and come to Ireland with a trained professional army. King William landed at Carrickfergus in 1690 and smashed the armies of King James at the Battle of the Boyne. In 1691 the remnants of the Catholic armies in Ireland surrendered to King William at Limerick. and thousands of Irish soldiers went abroad under their commander Patrick Sarsfield. These were 'The Wild Geese', the first of those tens of thousands of Irishmen who fought for Ireland in the armies of France and Spain.

Well, all that may seem a long time ago to a visitor from the Mainland, but in Ireland the past is only prologue. The present reality is the curse of the IRA. The IRA is by no means the only terrorist or paramilitary group operating in Northern Ireland. There are several groups on the Protestant side as well, all largely engaged in sectarian killing. The 'Provos', the men of the Provisional IRA, will kill anyone: police, soldiers, informers – or touts – politicians, people they consider undesirable, anyone who gets in the way; but neither side has a monopoly of violence.

'They can't always kill who they want,' said Dr John, 'so they kill who they can.'

It should not be imagined that the good people of Northern Ireland – and that means most of them – get out of bed every morning and set out for a hard day's terrorism. That is left to the PIRA or the UVF or a handful of other groups, but most especially the 'Provos', who are still hard at work in the Good Old Cause of Irish unity.

Mao-Tse-Tung wrote that the terrorist swims among the local population like a fish in the sea. While no one – but no one – approves of the killings, the bombings, or the kneecappings, there are still enough people, North and South of the Border, who are either nursing bitter memories of Ireland's long suffering at English hands or scared enough to provide the hard men with aid and protection. That is why my walk through Ireland became so involved with Irish history. If you don't know the history, you cannot know Ireland.

6

On to Glenelly

I had rather have a fool to make me merry than
experience to make me sad; and to travel for it
too.

William Shakespeare,
As You Like It, IV.i

We had a real wallow in Irish history that night, sitting
round the table with the whiskey and the wine, and maybe
that's the way to get into it. The long story of Ireland's woes
must be told gradually because although it has a common
thread there are endless knots and tangles. The thread is the
eight centuries of alien rule that began with Strongbow and
the attempts of the Irish to shake it off. The current tangle
is the IRA.

The largely Catholic IRA can be traced back to the years
before Partition, but long before that there was the Orange
Order, a Protestant organization created in Ulster during the
18th century to resist Home Rule. I had already seen signs
of Orange activity and these multiplied near the border.

Ambling down one of the side roads I had passed a bus-
shelter totally decorated inside with a large mural depicting
King Billy on his horse supported by the marching band of

the local Orange Lodge. I had already heard the tapping of drums and the squealing of pipes on this journey, for all over Northern Ireland at the start of summer the marching bands of the Orange Order tune up for their July Parades.

With a little luck I would be out of Ulster before these parades took place. I had seen them often enough on television, gaudily clad bands led by baton-twirling youths in front of long columns of men in bowler hats, wearing Orange sashes and marching along with umbrellas. What they were doing I hardly knew, except that many of the marches seem to go through Catholic areas and lead to violence. The time had come to find out a little more about this curious institution before I went on through Ireland.

The Orange Order was formed as the Orange Society as long ago as 1791. It took its name from King Billy, Prince of the Netherland House of Orange, who ruled in England as William III. The Society probably arose out of another secret organization, then called 'The Peep O' Day Boys' who spent their spare time terrorizing local Catholics. The 'Peep O' Day Boys' were the first to introduce the practice of kneecapping, which has been used here most barbarously ever since.

This side of Orange Order activities then did no more to endear Orangemen to the Protestants than the activities of the IRA find approval with the majority of decent Catholics today. Like the IRA, they were either an evil that must be ended, or in some cases tolerated by their co-religious brothers as being on the 'right' side when it finally came down to it. The Orangemen were also useful politically in fending off bids for Home Rule, right up to the foundation of the Free State, by making it clear they would resist it violently and vigorously.

The 'Orange Card' was played by many British politicians down the years, and the Orange Order lives on today because if push ever comes to shove, the members can be relied upon to take to the streets. They can, and have, halted in its tracks, any move towards a Catholic or Republican domination of the North.

When Northern Ireland had its own Parliament at Stormont, the Prime Minister would be an Orangeman, and to give just one example, Sir James Craig, Prime Minister of Northern Ireland just before the last war, told the members of Stormont that he '. . . prized his office of Grand Master of the Orange Order in County Down far more than that of being Prime Minister of Northern Ireland. I am an Orangeman first and a politician second.' This attitude was common well into the 1960s when the then Prime Minister, Sir Basil Brooke, was proud to boast that he did not have a single Catholic in his employ.

I can recall talking to some Royal Marine friends who had just returned from serving in Northern Ireland in the early days of the Troubles. They had already served in Malaya, Cyprus, Aden, Borneo and half a dozen trouble spots in Britain's crumbling Empire, and they were shocked to discover that in their own country – for the Northern Irish have always claimed to be part of the United Kingdom and they can't have it both ways – discrimination was being openly practised by one set of their fellow citizens on another set, with the tacit support of elected politicians and paid civil servants.

Catholics had virtually no say in the governance of Northern Ireland. They suffered discrimination in housing, schools, jobs, and public life, and there is no excuse for it. The only reason is a fear of a political solution, backed by religious and social prejudice, and twenty-five years into the present round of Troubles, not a great deal has changed. The Orange Order has done little to ease the tension between the communities over the past quarter-century.

By the end of the last century the Orange Order was so powerful that Lord Randolph Churchill, Winston's father, was able to state in 1886, that if the Liberals went for Home Rule all the Tories had to do to defeat it was 'to play the Orange Card' and so bring the Government down. That 1886 attempt at Home Rule duly failed but Home Rule was high on the political agenda again in 1912. The Orange Card was duly played again, this time by Sir Edward Carson, the Protestant leader in the North.

Sir Edward was an interesting man. Born in Dublin, he was a famous and skilful barrister, the man who had destroyed Oscar Wilde when the latter chose to sue 'Bosie's' father for libel. Carson is best known for his part in the Archer-Shee case, which was later used as the basis for Rattigan's play, *The Winslow Boy*. When Home Rule again came up on the Parliamentary agenda in 1912 Sir Edward proclaimed the 'Ulster Covenant' which declared the total opposition of all Ulster Protestants to Home Rule. Nearly half a million Protestants signed his Covenant, some in their own blood.

To give muscle to their pledges Sir Edward then raised the Ulster Volunteers, 100,000 men pledged to fight Home Rule and defend the Union. In March 1914 it was made clear by the Curragh Mutiny that the British Army might not act to suppress the Volunteers, and in April 1914 these Volunteers imported arms, including 35,000 rifles. These munitions were landed openly at Larne without the Police or Army making any attempt to interfere.

There is a little point here concerning the democratic principle of majority rule. The democratic ideal says that the interests of the majority must prevail but the rights of the minority must be respected. This is the case for continuing the Union in the North – because the Protestant majority want it that way.

Back in 1914 Northern Ireland did not exist. The Catholic majority of the Irish population wanted Home Rule but the Protestant minority were determined they

should not have it, and the British Government was reluctant or too afraid to enforce it. The solution was Partition
– which it all comes back to in the end.

The Catholic Republican response to Carson's Volunteers
was to set up the Southern Volunteers in October 1913. The
Southern Volunteers were largely raised from members of
another pro-Home Rule organization, the Irish Republican
Brotherhood or IRB, which in turn can be traced back to the
Fenian Movement which was started in the mid-1800s. The
aim of the Fenians was to establish an Irish Republic.

It was the Southern Volunteers who staged the famous
Easter Rising in Dublin in 1916, of which more anon. After
that was bloodily suppressed by the British Army, support
for the Independence of Ireland grew even more solid. Under
the leadership of another legendary figure, Michael Collins,
the IRA played a prominent part in the brief Anglo–Irish
War that led to the Government of Ireland Act of May 1920
and the Anglo–Irish Treaty which established the Free State.
So we go round the Mulberry bush yet again, wading
through the blood of the past.

You can get any number of reasons for the present
Troubles in Ireland. It was getting into my head that the root
cause of the problem was Partition, but not everyone agrees
with that. There are those who say, with good reason, that
the aim of the Marxist IRA is to overthrow the Government
of Ireland and establish a Marxist State, to which end the
dispute over the Border is useful to the terrorists. It gives
legitimacy to their cause and an excuse for their brutality.
After a while you tire of reasons and yearn for solutions.

The present violence that began in 1968 and continues to
this day, is by no means the first IRA insurrection, though it
is by far the longest lasting and most bloody. All Irish
movements seem to splinter in the end and the IRA is no
exception, least because it has split the Republican movement down the middle. Sinn Fein, the 'political wing' of the

IRA, decided to recognize the 'Partition Parliaments' of
Dublin, Westminster and Stormont in 1969, but this news
was met with outrage by the more hard line Republicans.
They then set up a Provisional Army Council which led to
the formation of the Provisional IRA or PIRA – the Provos
. . . and so the sad and sorry tale continues and we see no end
to it.

What with one thing and another, it was quite a heavy night.
When I went in for the usual heart-stopping breakfast next
morning, neat in my clean, pressed clothes, all the others
were long gone and a stiff walk now lay before me. My
route lay over the next range of the Sperrins, from the
Foreglen river, a tributary of the River Faughan which flows
into the Foyle north of Londonderry and over to the
Glenelly Valley in the heart of the Sperrin Mountains.

The main range of the Sperrins now lay ahead, open-
topped moors, quite glorious to look upon, but hacking
across the tops had already proved unwise, though there
were day-walking routes running into the hills from every
village. What I needed was a trail to the south, but none
existed. It looked as if I was in for another hard day up and
over the hills to the Glenelly river that lay some 20 miles to
the south.

This tramp would take me over the 2,224 ft height of the
Sawel Mountain, the highest peak of the Sperrins, and had
I been walking west to east I could have enjoyed a pleasant
ridge walk along a series of rounded tops. As it was, I had
an up and down day ahead, with two ranges to get over and
20 miles to cover. Oh well!

The best answer to a long day is an early start. I therefore
left fairly late, and full of tea, at around 9.30. Even so, once
I shook out the stiffness and the aches from my muscles, I
made good time along the lanes to Kilculmagrandal and
round a hill to the long bridge at Tirglassan and then round

Straid Hill into the village of Park. This trek took most of the morning. It was pleasant walking on empty lanes, weaving around a series of steep little rounded hills, all at around the 300m (984ft) mark, and by the time I got to Park I was ready for a half or two in the pub and an hour out of the boots. That done, I set off on the long, steep haul up the hill over the open moors to the Sawel mountain, and then down to the Glenelly valley. On the way I had a curious encounter with a sheep.

There are a lot of sheep in these parts, black-faced Scots sheep for the most part, hardy enough to survive out on the wet moors. Since sheep are not the most winsome creatures, I had paid little attention to them, and they generally got up and trotted off when I came close. I was trudging along a lane, thinking of something else, and miles away mentally, when an insistent bleating drew my attention to the field beside the road.

There, just inside the wire fence, was a lamb. It was trotting along to match my pace and bleating loudly. I stopped for a closer look, at which the lamb, a teenage lamb, very woolly and about the size of a spaniel, tried to climb through the fence towards me. After scratching his woolly head, I had some trouble pushing him back. Everyone likes lambs, and this one seemed very friendly.

'You stay in there, little fellow,' I said firmly. 'Come out here and you'll get run over.'

'Baah!' said the lamb. 'BAAAAH!' It was a remarkably noisy lamb. His last bleat was like a trumpet call. There came a drumming of hooves and a score of sheep, a mixture of big ewes and small lambs, appeared behind him, lining the grassy bank above the lane. Standing there together they proceeded to bleat the place down.

'Baah ... Baaah ... Baaaa ... BAAAAH ... AAH!' When the Sheep Choir gets into full voice the din is tremendous. I put my hands to my ears and flinched. The row intensified.

'For God's sake, shut up,' I cried. 'I'm not hurting him.'

'Baah . . .' went the lamb, piteously.

'BAAH . . .' went the assembled sheep. 'BAA-stard . . . Lamb-napper. BAAH.'

I stood there over the lamb while the assembled sheep went demented. I even tried yelling at them, but the noise continued until I could stand it no more. I legged it up the road, as fast as my heavy rucksack would let me, as if to escape a lynching. This was a mistake. The lamb and the flock followed, and 50 yards up the road there was a gate. The lamb sprawled itself down and under the gate and came clattering up the road after me on his little black hooves, still bleating piteously, still followed by the other sheep raging inside the fence.

'Now look,' I said to the lamb. 'This can't go on. Go back.'

'Baaah,' said the lamb.

There is a limit to how much aggravation human flesh and blood can stand. I picked up the lamb, tucked it under one arm, carried it back to the chorus line of sheep and tipped him into the field.

Let no one tell me sheep are stupid. Two minutes later he was up the fence, under the gate, back in the road and clattering after me again. I picked the lamb up and put him back in the field. Quick as a flash he shot back out again. This went on for some time.

'Sod you then,' I said at last, quite worn out. 'I've got other things to do with my time than mess about with you. If you get run over it's your own bloody fault.'

'Baa . . .ah,' said the lamb, happily.

So off we went along the lane, the lamb and I, striding along together for half a mile or so, while the bleats of protest faded into the distance. We might have been together now had not a farm tractor appeared ahead, filling the lane from side to side and trundling fast towards me. Here was

an opportunity. I picked the lamb up and stood in the
tractor's path until it stopped.

'Is this your lamb?' I asked the driver. 'He comes from a
field about a mile back and he won't leave me alone.'

The driver switched off the engine, pushed his cap back
and studied us both for a moment, nodding. 'He thinks
you're his Daddy, so he does,' he said at last.

'Well, I'm not his bloody Daddy,' I said. 'Can you take
him back where he came from?'

'I'll sell him to you,' said the farmer suddenly. 'Since
you've taken to each other.'

'What??'

'I can see the little fella's take a fancy to you. Call it £25
... cash, mind.'

Are these people mad? He then came down to £20, which
may have been a bargain. For a second I wondered how a
book called *Travels with my Sheep* would sell, but then I
came to my senses. I declined the offer, handed up the lamb
and fled. When I reached a turn in the road and looked
back, I could see that anxious little white face peering over
the farmer's shoulder, bleating after me above the noise of
the engine, as if its little heart would break. I pressed on up
the road feeling like a real swine.

Getting to the top of the Sawel Pass over the main ridge of
the Sperrins was a good, hard, uphill walk, on one of those
narrow mountain roads that climbs and climbs and never
seems to end until you suddenly reach the col. The road was
quite empty and the moors quiet except for the sound of
skylarks and water tinkling in the streams. This is what
walking is all about, a good trail with peace and quiet on
either side and great views at the top. I took a breather for
half an hour at the col, sitting on my rucksack to soak up the
sun.

Then I plunged down the hill for the Glenelly Valley and

the village of Cranagh. Give or take a sheep or two, I had not met more than a handful of people all day and now I needed somewhere to stay and rest before another long day on the morrow, when I must march all the way south to Omagh. There was also something wrong with my feet but I preferred not to check on them until I was settled for the night. The pub at Cranagh was shut, which is most unlike an Irish pub, and the only man about was a roadsweeper. He seemed quite pleased to see me and was even delighted when he heard my voice. We sat on a pile of gravel at the edge of the road and had a chat.

'You're from England,' he said. 'I can tell. And where abouts in England are you from?'

'A village near Marlow,' I said. 'It's on the River Thames, west of London . . . just a little place.'

'And is it pretty?'

'It is,' I said. 'Well, quite pretty.'

'As pretty as this?'

'Almost. No . . . not as pretty as this at all.'

Sitting on the gravel heap, dashing sweat from my eyebrows, I had a good chance to look around me. The Glenelly Valley really is very pretty. Like a lot of these Sperrin valleys, it falls into two parts, with rich bottom lands along the banks of the river, split into neat fields and farms, and then half way up the hillside the open moors begin. The sun was just starting down to the west, sending big shadows over the fields, and when we stopped chatting a deep stillness fell across the scene. I could have sat there quietly for hours, just enjoying it.

'Well, you're very welcome,' said my new friend, springing up and seizing my hand, 'and I hope the people here are good to you. Billy Conway's place is just down the road, and if you fancy a bit of a crack later, we could have a drink in the pub here tonight?'

I can't get over the friendliness of these people. The

roadman pointed the way to the next B & B, where the lady of the house was busy in her garden. Billy Conway, my host for the evening, keeps sheep on his smallholding next door, a task to go with his job in the nearby town. I suspect that Billy keeps sheep because he is a farmer at heart and he soon put me right about the lamb I had met on the road.

'That would be a house-lamb,' he said. 'His mother wouldn't feed him so they'll have taken him into the house and given him the bottle. Now he doesn't think he is a sheep at all, and when he sees you . . . you're it. Now, while you are here and if your feet will stand it, why don't we take a little walk down the road after tea and try a little panning for gold?'

7

The Road To Enniskillen

Irelande is with strange warr possest like an
Ague: now raging, now at rest, which time will
cure: yet it must do her good if she were purged
and her head wayne let blood.

John Donne, 1594

I was more than a little surprised to find goldfields in
Ireland, let alone on the green slopes of the Sperrins, but sure
enough, gold panning was one of the options at the Sperrin
Heritage Centre, a mile down the road from my B & B, half
way down the Glenelly Valley. The Centre itself has the
usual folklore displays including one concerning the distill-
ing of poteen, the raw Irish whiskey, but they also provide
a pan with which you can sift sand for gold in the nearby
stream. It was wet work but I was used to that by now.

There has always been gold mining in the Sperrins.
Prospectors can find it in small amounts, but recent esti-
mates have it that there is some 300,000 ozs of gold
hereabouts, ready for extraction, which at $400 an ounce is
serious money. The thought that some Anglo–American
company will now tear these green hills apart and ravage the
land for profit has brought the conservationists into the fray,
but for the moment swilling sand and stream water about in

my pan, I thought that gold prospecting was a rather
pleasant pastime. Mind you, I found nothing, not a glint or
glimmer, not a trace of colour. Wet to the elbows I gave up
and went back for tea.

When I got back from the goldfields, I took off my boots
in the bedroom and made an alarming discovery. In the last
twelve hours I had collected an impressive array of blisters.
There were five on one foot and four on the other, most of
them raw. Thus does constant road walking, interspersed
with wetting the feet in bogs, take its toll of the lower
extremities. I sat there wincing, and wondered what to do
now.

Give or take a wince, I don't really mind blisters. Walkers
get used to them and I usually just pad them up and press
on. They heal themselves in time. The snag was that I still
had a lot more road walking ahead unless I could find a
footpath. Here I was lucky, for my map revealed that the
Ulster Way, which had so far proved elusive, ran across the
top of the long east-to-west ridge across the valley which I
could see from my bedroom window. A long-distance
footpath was finally going the way I wanted to go and by
following the Ulster Way to Gortin I would, with luck, have
12 miles or so of soft hill path, half a day at least of gentle
walking on the following day. My feet were ready for it.

The Ulster Way Footpath is the longest trail in Ireland,
circling the entire province and broken into five main
sections, each a footpath in its own right. The Skerry Trail
runs from Portballintrae to Castlerock, 21 miles along the
Antrim Coast, and ends up with the North Sperrin Trail, a
36-mile route from Castlerock to Dungiven, which lay to the
north-east. Then came the Glenelly Trail which ran before
me and led west, all 34 miles of it to Gortin. That was
followed by a 10-mile trail to the Ulster Folk Park and
Omagh. The Trail then led on to the border with County
Fermanagh, which I must cross on my way west to

Enniskillen. All I had to do tomorrow was cross the river and turn right, then follow the Ulster Way all the way to Gortin and beyond – perfect.

My second bit of luck came that evening over dinner, when Billy mentioned that he was going into Omagh next day and would take my heavy rucksack in for me. I try not to be a purist in these matters. It's the walking that counts, not the lugging of heavy weights. When I walked across France, quite a few hoteliers had offered to drive my rucksack 20 miles up the road to the next night-stop, and I leapt at the offer every time. Anyone who has ever tried a long-distance walk with a heavy pack will know the feeling of relief when you take the damned thing off. Free of weight, on a footpath, with hills ahead ... I went to bed that night anticipating a long, light, easy day tomorrow.

I began the day with an early start, after I had eaten the daily Fry and phoned the hotel in Omagh to describe my rucksack and assure the staff that Billy wasn't bringing them a bomb. He then departed for Omagh and I set off across the Glenelly river for the 1,257 ft top of Corratary Hill, just across the way. Halfway up the hill all my fine ideas ran onto the tarmac. The Ulster Way no longer ran along the top of the ridge – path erosion had forced a diversion down to the road through Corramore. I was back on the hard stuff again and I could have wept.

Well, at least I didn't have a 50lb pack crushing my feet flat. That was a bonus. It was also another beautiful sunny day, so I strolled along happily enough, pining for the crest to my left, but cutting through the Sperrins at the road fork by the Eagle's Nest to the Barnes Gap. Here the Ulster Way ran off the road and I was able to divert onto it for the last mile or so into Gortin. I came into Gortin just after mid-day, crossing over the beautiful Owenkillew river and past the grounds of Beltrim Castle, once the residence of the Houston family whose son Sam founded the State of Texas.

Gortin is one of those pretty Irish towns with a main street wide enough for a cattle market and three small pubs. Gortin is an old town, dating back to the time of St Patrick in the 5th century AD, and it must once have been bigger and more important than it is today, when it lives by the river fishing and as a forestry centre. Since it was now very hot and the middle of the day, I found my way into a cool, shady pub and a curious conversation.

It can sometimes take up to a minute for a total stranger to meet an old friend in any Irish bar, but here it took rather less. Irish pubs are endowed with tall bar-stools and I had hardly disentangled myself from my glasses and camera straps, and climbed onto a stool to claw for my pint of Smithwicks, before the man on a nearby bar stool had discovered my name, occupation, place of residence and current activity. Well, two can play at that game.

'And yourself, sir,' I said. 'What do you do yourself?'

I should have known better.

'I, sir,' he said proudly, 'am the finest pig-smuggler in Monaghan.'

The other customers, just visible in the gloom along the bar, nodded their heads together in agreement.

'He is so,' they said in unison, rather like a Greek chorus.

In the next half-hour or so, I learned more about pig-smuggling than any law-abiding Englishman should know. It appears that the European Community try to level off commodity prices by paying a subsidy to Irish farmers who ship pigs into the North. It might be the other way round but that's the gist of it. You heave a few porkers into the transit van, get your import form stamped at the Border and in due course you get a fat cheque from the EEC, making up the difference between the low Northern Irish price and the lower one available in the Republic . . . or that too might be the other way round. What you don't do is sell the pigs.

'Oh no,' said the Finest Pig Smuggler in Monaghan. 'You

never sell the pigs. You'd have to buy more and then where's the profit?'

'You don't sell the pigs, so you don't,' echoed the other drinkers from the gloom.

'But . . .?' I said. 'What . . .?'

'What you do,' said the Finest Pig Smuggler (as to an eejit), 'is having left the Border you drive back into the Republic, down one of the unpatrolled roads, and you repeat the process a day or two later.'

So it goes on, the pigs circling through the Customs Posts like the ball in a roulette wheel, picking up money all the time. Some pigs have crossed more frontiers than an airline stewardess, and since pigs are very intelligent animals they could probably find their own way to and fro without any help from the farmer. As to the 'eejit', that's the Irish for 'idiot', and I soon got used to people nodding in my direction and pointing out the big 'eejit' with the rucksack. Eejit I may be, but I know how to listen to a good tale.

'It's a fine business, so it is,' said the Finest Pig Smuggler in Monaghan. '. . . and your glass is empty.'

Strange though it may seem, I know a bit about pigs. My great-aunt Isabella had a pet pig called Barbara, which was a very intelligent pig indeed. The only snag was that Barbara did not know she was a pig. Barbara thought she was a person. This was during the last war, when I spent my school holidays on my great aunt's ramshackle farm in Wiltshire. Half the farmhouse had been taken over as a Mess by the US Army Air Force, and a family story goes that the American billeting officer was a little concerned to discover that his lustful young airmen would be sharing their accommodation with my two nubile young cousins.

'Don't worry, young man,' said my aunt, tapping her forehead. 'My two girls have got it up here.'

'Wherever they've got it, Ma'am, my men will find it,' said the officer grimly.

But for Barbara his fears might have been justified. Fortunately, when life got boring of an evening Barbara would leap from her sty and come into the house. She could trip the latch with her snout and if you shot the bolt she simply body-charged the door and took it off its hinges, frame and all. Here are the lovers, curled up on the sofa in the wee small hours, the atmosphere ripe with possibilities, when the door flies open and a large Wessex Saddleback sow trots into the room grunting happily, and settles down on the rug in front of the fire. Not even Casanova could survive such an intrusion. Barbara eventually went over to the American Air Force, probably because the swill was better, and got promoted to the rank of Pfc (Pig, First Class). I think they ate her in the end.

I fell out onto the bright streets of Gortin about half-past two and soon found a Trail out, a real footpath this time, that led up to the top of the next ridge. This was a pretty path running beside a stream, a delightful walk, but I was drawn on by sounds of gunfire. When I emerged at the top I saw a rifle range to my left, with lines of soldiers sprinting down from point to point. I was taking all this in when a soldier of the Ulster Defence Regiment suddenly appeared at my side and asked me a few questions.

There were other soldiers dotted here and there among the undergrowth, acting as picquets for their comrades on the range. This one was in full camouflage gear, complete with helmet and rifle, and he checked me over carefully. He was polite enough and asked the usual questions: Where was I from and where was I going? Since I had never met a UDR soldier before I wanted to talk to him, and once he discovered I was harmless he was happy to talk. He was a part-time soldier, if working sixty to seventy hours a week can really be called part-time.

'That's a hell of a lot of hours,' I said, 'even in my day. How do you manage that and a job?'

'Well, I'm unemployed at the moment,' he explained. 'Were you ever a soldier over here yourself, Sir?'

I shook my head. 'I was a soldier, but not over here, thank God.'

'What were you in then, Sir?'

'45 Commando . . . Royal Marines.'

This was clearly a recommendation. Other soldiers were summoned from the undergrowth to say hello and sing the praises of my old Commando, which clearly has earned golden opinions in the Province.

'45 Commando, eh? That's a hard unit . . . take no bloody nonsense at all, so they don't. Kick them cheeky bastards up the arse . . . Tough bastards . . .'

It's nice to hear the old regiment so well spoken of. I stood there in the sunshine chatting with the soldiers, while a few cars roared south for Omagh. Then their range practice was over and everyone was climbing back into their civvies for the drive home. I was almost sorry to leave this bunch of lads and flog on south through the woods of the Gortin Glen, but it was better in there under the trees, hilly enough but cool and shady, the path soft under my sensitive feet. There are said to be deer here, for siska deer have escaped from the reserve at Baronscourt, but I saw nothing as I plodded on. Then, about five o'clock, I emerged onto the road at the Ulster–American Folk Park.

As a rule I am not all that interested in museums. In fact, I hold the All-Comers record for seeing the essential sights of the Paris Louvre; eleven minutes flat including the *Mona Lisa* and *The Raft of the Medusa*, which I put in because of the sharks.

The Ulster–American Folk Park was still worth a stop, mostly because I was dying for a cup of tea. It also helps to explain the strong links which still exist between Ireland and the USA and pre-date the time of the Great Famine. All that apart, it's a very good museum. The Ulster–American Folk Park is a little bit of Americana imported back to the Auld Sod, set around the cottage where Thomas Mellon was born in 1813.

Mellon went to America and made his fortune as a steel magnate. His family virtually created the town of Pittsburgh, and both the Golden Gate Bridge of San Francisco and the lock gates of the Panama Canal were made of Mellon steel. Like a lot of Irishmen – the Kennedy family is another which immediately springs to mind – they prospered greatly but never forgot their roots.

The Folk Park tells the story of how the Irish people were forced to migrate to the New World. It shows the state of poverty and deprivation they fled from and the hard times they met across the ocean. There is even a Conestoga waggon – a 'prairie schooner' – dating from the end of the 18th century, as well as log cabins and schoolhouses. I bought an ice-cream and enjoyed the visit. Then I had to get on south again, for Omagh.

Fortunately, the distance from the Folk Park to the town of Omagh is not very far, and beyond the Folk Park the land flattened out. I tottered on in the early evening, very tired now, finally limping across the River Strule into Omagh where, as Billy had promised, my rucksack was waiting at the Royal Arms Hotel. They even took pity on me and carried it up to my room and sent me up a pot of tea.

I must have been getting fitter because after half an hour groaning on my bed I was able to get up and limp down to the bar. Bars are useful at the end of the day, because I get drunk from the feet up and after a while my feet stopped hurting. Therefore, I had a drink or two and went out to look around the town, which is rather pretty. The centre is the usual Control Zone, where cars cannot be parked, but the rest of the town is set along the hill above the River Strule and although quite small it has a couple of impressive churches and some lighthearted claims to fame.

This is the birthplace of Jimmy Kennedy who wrote *The Teddy Bears' Picnic*, and I liked one shop sign advertising 'O'Kane Brothers – Estate Agents and Undertakers'. The local paper is *The Tyrone Constitution*, first published in 1844, just before the Great Famine, but I was too late to go in and look at the early editions, which is something I usually do on my travels.

My feet were in a rather poor condition for too much strolling about after a very long day, so I soothed them again with several Bushmills after dinner and limped upstairs to bed.

At Omagh I left the Sperrins behind. I was sorry about that because even when the walker is largely restricted to trails and lanes there is something about hills and mountains that seems right. This is where the walker ought to be; the plains are not his place. Plains are for cyclists and horsemen but the footman comes into his own in the hills, across the moors and tracks. Irish mountains are not very high and the bogs make walking on them difficult, but they are a marvellous backdrop to the scenery. I wanted to get back to the hills as soon as possible, and to do that I had to get away fast to the west and into the Republic.

Stretched out on my bed that night, my feet simmering gently, I took a good look at the map. I soon decided that I had bitten off more than I could chew if I was to get to Enniskillen in two days. I had already decided to allow three days to the Border beyond Enniskillen, but that was clearly not enough either. The snag was not the distance, which could just about be done if I pushed it, but the state of my feet. My feet were now endowed with open blisters, the result of a week of walking on hot roads under a heavy pack. My choice now was to rest up, slow down, or hack on.

Resting up had no appeal. If you set out on one of these trips you soon become infected with the 'Something Lost Behind the Ranges' syndrome, with the need to get on and see what lies over the next hill. Slowing down wasn't an option either. The miles you don't do today go into the pot to be drawn out tomorrow. That left bashing on and my feet were voting against that. Decisions, decisions . . .

I have to say that I rather enjoy this sort of thing. Bill Tilman once said, 'There is no point in setting out for anywhere you are certain to reach,' and I agree with that. If everything worked out as planned there would be no reason for attempting it. Things go wrong; that's life. What matters then is how you can think your way round the problem without too much compromise.

Fortunately, there was a fourth option. The problem was not just the distance and the roads, but the weight. I had already found that walking without a heavy pack was a joy, and also that much of my cargo was superfluous. I had a full range of camping gear in there and I clearly did not need it.

I have this theory that there is a solution to everything if you will simply apply your mind to it. Well, not the Troubles perhaps, but most things. All you have to do is identify the problem and work out how to solve it, and then see if that solution is available. I carried out some radical surgery on my feet, cutting off flaps of skin and padding up the rest, and then whimpered my way into my trainers and limped round to the bus station. It only hurts for a little while.

There was good and bad news at the bus station – yes, they would take my rucksack to Enniskillen, but I would have to go with it. It was the bombs, y'see. Accepting a parcel or carrying a piece of luggage without a passenger was just not on – had I not heard of Lockerbie? I hauled out the maps again, explained my predicament and we pondered while I chewed my fingernails. While we were looking at the map the man relented. If I would come a bit of the way and they could have a good peek inside the rucksack, then the driver would – might – take it on a bit for me. We settled for a ride to Dromore and I limped off back to bed. Dromore was not much of a distance but it would save my feet and I could settle for that.

When I woke up next day it was pissing down with rain. This was the first rain in a week but when it rains in Ireland it does so with a skill born of long practice. After seven days of sunshine it was raining as if St Patrick and all the Saints were up there twiddling taps. I put on the Rohans but by the time I got to the bus station I was drenched. I stood in a widening pool of water while the driver took a cursory poke about inside my rucksack and carried it on board the bus for me.

'You don't look like a tearaway to me,' he said, 'and that's a fine limp you have there. How are the feet?'

Just pulling on the boots that morning had made my eyes water, but you have to be brave. 'Don't ask,' I told him. 'They'll probably be better when they warm up.'

'Well ... You can come all the way, you know – to Enniskillen. Or I'll take the bag on to Irvingstown and leave it for you at the Post Office.'

I looked at the rain tipping down, felt a twinge in my feet and thought, 'Sod it ... what am I trying to prove here anyway,' and climbed on board the bus.

Once I had crossed the moral divide I could see there is an advantage in hopping on a bus now and then. Even when the rain isn't streaming down the windows you get to meet the local people who come climbing aboard to commute to their jobs. With my rucksack as a conversation piece the 'crack' was soon going strong.

'Things are quite good here,' said one man, to a background of nods from the rest. 'Or they would be if it wasn't for those bastards.... We get some trouble happening around here about once a month, but if you're not in the Police or the Army you'll have no trouble.'

Most of the people here, like most of the other people I had met so far on this journey had long since learned to live with the Troubles. Unemployment, the current curse of Ireland, was also dismissed in a very Irish fashion.

'I know plenty of fellows who are drawing the dole on this side of the Border and then nipping off to jobs in the Republic,' said one man. The chorus of nods was less complete at this; there were vigorous nods from those who agreed, but none from those who were probably heading across the Border. I told them about meeting the Finest Pig Smuggler in Monaghan, which produced a general agreement that the European Community was a great device for recycling the taxpayers' money into the pockets of rogues. So, chatting the time away, we came to Dromore, where I heaved myself out of the bus and into the rain. The rucksack went on to Irvingstown, and nobody worried at all.

By getting a bus to Dromore I had put Enniskillen just within my reach that day, but while conscience made me get off, honesty compels me to add that I would have done just as well to stay on the bus. The day was just another road walk south and west through the village of Trellick and after that, somehow or other, I got gloriously lost. The rain was tipping down, the visibility almost zero and all the sensible people were in the pub. I picked up my rucksack at Irvingstown but by about four in the afternoon it was clear that I would never make Enniskillen that day. This proved correct, for when I finally worked out where I was, I was near Killadeas, on Lough Erne, which was not too bad. I had a provisional booking in a B & B at Killadeas and though I had let this booking go, if the room was still vacant I could use it.

* * *

Mrs Flood was somewhat surprised to find that her English guest was a drowned rat with a rucksack. and I left a pool of water in her beautifully decorated hallway, but she was hospitality itself and rushed off to fetch the tea.

I ought to say a word about these Irish B & Bs, because if I had known about them before, I could have spared myself a lot of effort. Bed and Breakfast accommodation is widely available in Ireland, and not just in rooms left empty after the children leave home but in proper small hotels. I came to think of them as 'half-hotels', for you have your own room and bath, often in an extension, and are welcome to join the family in the kitchen or sitting room for dinner or tea or a drink. They are marvellous, well-kept and very hospitable. I became a complete devotee of the Irish B & B.

Once I was under cover at Mrs Flood's, the rain stopped. Life is like that. I ventured out for the evening limp down the road to see the fine church at Killadeas and a scramble through the woods to the shores of Lough Erne, but that was enough for one day. I had used up a lot of energy in the last week and the pace was starting to tell.

Next morning I made my way south beside the northern arm of Lough Erne, down the road into Enniskillen. The road comes into town just by the War Memorial, where the IRA exploded a bomb during the November Armistice Service of 1987, killing eleven people. A long brass strip on the memorial records this atrocity with the names of the victims, one of the few War Memorials to record the names of civilian victims of a terrorist campaign.

Here for the first time I ran into a mixed patrol of the RUC and the British Army, who were manning a checkpoint at the entrance to the town. The RUC were friendly enough, commenting on the place and telling me where to find a hotel, but the soldiers were sullen and wary, the infantry deployed on either side of the road, a chatter of contact coming from the radio in the back of their Armoured

Personnel Carrier. I nodded my way past and went to find a pub.

By now I had a little routine going for my arrival at any town, where I would limp along to the first bar and turn in the door. So it was here, but I had been at the counter perhaps thirty seconds and had barely dropped the rucksack on the floor when a man was at my elbow with a question.

'What are you doing here?'

It was not a friendly question. Nor was it an easy one to answer, and even the fact that it was asked made me nervous. This had not happened before. Irish bars are not often small but this one was very small, very quiet and very full of people. All of them were looking at me.

'What are you doing here?' asked the man again. When I said I was simply getting a drink, if that was all right and if he had no objection, that didn't deflect him at all. Maybe it was my accent. I got a grilling about where I had come from that day and where I was going. Only when he had hefted the rucksack off the floor did he nod, shrug, and vanish out the back. I had walked into a Republican bar where strangers, and especially English strangers, and even more, English strangers with rucksacks, are not made very welcome ... at least to begin with.

'When are you Brits going to hand back the Six Counties?' asked the barman, passing over my pint. A dozen faces turned to await the answer, and it always pays to be diplomatic.

'Well, if it was up to me, you could have them back tomorrow,' I said, 'and I'd wish you joy of it ... as it is, it's up to you. I think you'd better sort that out among yourselves.'

Frankly, Enniskillen isn't the place where Republicans have much to boast or complain about, not with that Memorial down the road. There was a bit of a silence and I tried not to drink my beer too fast. Then someone offered to refill the glass and things were suddenly back to normal. We spread the map on the counter and discussed the route and the bogs and the 'Finest Pig Smuggler in Monaghan'.

Then it was my turn to buy a round and one thing led to another. I had walked across Northern Ireland and knocked a hole in this journey. More than that, I had enjoyed myself. As the beer got to work, my feet stopped hurting and the upshot was that I stayed in there for hours. I think there was singing.

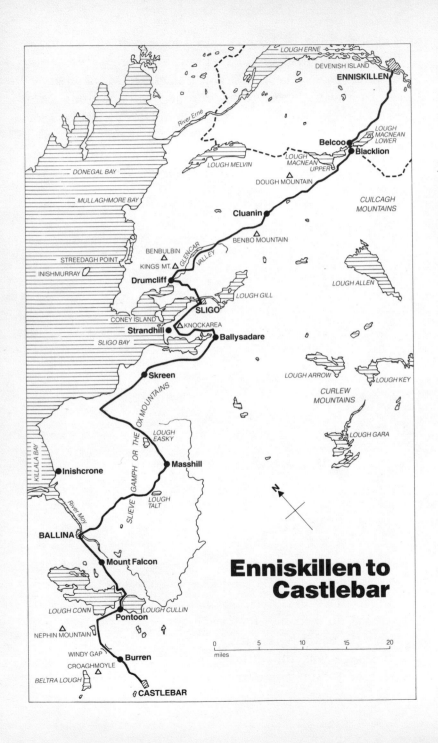

Enniskillen to Castlebar

LOUGH ERNE

DEVENISH ISLAND

ENNISKILLEN

River Erne

LOUGH MACNEAN LOWER

Belcoo **Blacklion**

DONEGAL BAY

LOUGH MELVIN

LOUGH MACNEAN UPPER

DOUGH MOUNTAIN

CUILCAGH MOUNTAINS

MULLAGHMORE BAY

Cluanin

BENBO MOUNTAIN

STREEDAGH POINT

BENBULBIN
KINGS MT.

GLENCAR VALLEY

LOUGH ALLEN

INISHMURRAY

Drumcliff

LOUGH GILL

CONEY ISLAND

SLIGO

KNOCKAREA

Strandhill

Ballysadare

SLIGO BAY

LOUGH ARROW

LOUGH KEY

Skreen

CURLEW MOUNTAINS

SLIEVE GAMPH OR THE OX MOUNTAINS

LOUGH EASKY

LOUGH GARA

KILLALA BAY

Inishcrone

Masshill

LOUGH TALT

River Moy

BALLINA

Mount Falcon

LOUGH CONN

LOUGH CULLIN

Pontoon

NEPHIN MOUNTAIN

WINDY GAP

Burren

CROAGHMOYLE

BELTRA LOUGH

CASTLEBAR

0   5   10   15   20
miles

8

Crossing Sligo

> Travel, in the younger sort, is a part of education:
> in the older a part of experience.
>
> Francis Bacon,
>
> *Essays*

I took two days off at Enniskillen. This was partly to rest my feet, partly to look around and partly to recover from the welcome party. Even on foot I seemed to have been rushing it and I needed time to relax and get myself sorted out. This is what happens on a walk. Your body starts to act like a brake on the mind and your senses start to slow down as the pressure comes off. It can feel a little strange to begin with but the end result is delightful. The pressures of modern life take a toll of everyone and one way to release the pressure is to go for a good long walk. I think stress is caused by impatience, by the self-inflicted need to get somewhere in half the time or do ten things at once. On a walk, you can't get anywhere faster than your legs will carry you and getting there becomes an end in itself. The advantage is that after a few days life becomes far more sane. Even so, I was quite glad of the rest.

Besides, it was still raining as the Irish climate tried to make up for the hot sunshine of the previous week. In addition there is a lot to see in Enniskillen, all of it within easy reach, but there was also another reason. I had been very taken with Northern Ireland and I didn't really want to leave.

One of the advantages of travel is that you can sort matters out. Complicated issues make more sense when your feet are quite literally on the ground. I had long since come to agree with Billy's dictum that 'We're not all murdering maniacs over here.' I had begun to feel some empathy with these good people, caught as they are in some terrible time-warp, unable to escape from their past, as if they were entangled in a web which was no less dangerous for being virtually invisible. One might not see or sense danger in this Province but it was there all the same. Step too far out of line in either direction and something would come at you like a train. Even so, I liked the place and the people and I liked Eniskillen, even in the rain. What I needed now was the time to get it and myself in perspective. Enniskillen was easy.

Enniskillen is the capital of County Fermanagh, the lakeland country of Ulster. The county is divided by the River Erne which, like the River Shannon, flows so slowly through relatively flat country that it has widened north and south of the town into two great loughs. There is the Irish touch in that Lower Lough Erne lies to the north, which is downstream and fair enough, though North always seems up somehow. Enniskillen stands like a sentry in the narrow throat of land between the two loughs, with the historic Watergate guarding the town astride the road out to Sligo and the West of Ireland.

The Watergate was the only fortress in Fermanagh to escape destruction during the wars of the 17th century, and since I like old fortresses I hurried there on the first morning.

Long before the English got this far west, Fermanagh was a stronghold for the powerful Maguire clan, who held on until the Puritan 'planting' in the early part of the 17th century. The Maguires took a leading role in the rebellion of 1641, when the Catholics retook Enniskillen for King Charles. By 1689, however, Enniskillen was a strongly Protestant town and the Protestants held the town for King William against Jacobite forces serving King James. The town today still retains a Protestant bias, which may account for the periodic attentions of the ungodly.

I took myself off along the river to see the old Watergate, which is part of the former Enniskillen Castle. As castles go this one is quite small, but rather splendid. It was begun in the 15th century by Hugh Maguire but contains elements of an earlier keep erected in the 13th century by a lord with the marvellous name of Hugh the Hospitable. It was rebuilt after the 1641 rebellion, when the Watergate was added to the medieval keep. The Cole family lived in the castle for 200 years until they moved to Florence Court, a rather splendid country house outside Enniskillen which is now owned by The National Trust.

Today the Watergate contains a Heritage Centre which told me about the Maguires and a very fine military museum celebrating the history of two local regiments, the Royal Enniskillen Fusiliers and the Royal Enniskillen Dragoon Guards, the famous 'Skins', now, alas, disbanded. All their regalia is there, from Waterloo guidons to Great War VCs, and I spent a happy morning examining the displays while the rain streamed down outside. One of the most famous Enniskillen officers was the gallant Captain Oates, who left Scott's doomed Antarctic expedition in 1912 with the words, 'I'm just going outside. I may be some time,' and walked to his death in the blizzard. There is a memorial to Captain Oates in the Town Hall, one of many to these gallant Irish soldiers.

Other famous sons of Enniskillen include Oscar Wilde and Samuel Beckett who both went to school here. Enniskillen must still be a pleasant place for schoolboys, with a wealth of lakes and woodlands to roam about in. When the rain slackened in the afternoon that is what I did, taking a boat excursion up the Lower Lough to Devenish Island. This used to contain a monastery founded in the 6th century by St Molaise, one of those Celtic saints that abounded hereabouts at the time. The buildings are in ruins except for the tall round tower, about 85 ft high, which looks for all the world like a lighthouse but was built, like all these monastic round towers, to protect the community from marauding Danes.

Many Irish monasteries contain round towers – there is an excellent one at Glendalough in County Wicklow – and they are a fine example of passive resistance set in stone. The monks simply shinned up into the Round Tower, which had a door well up the wall, hauled up the ladder and made faces at the Danes until they went away. Most of the islands on Lough Erne support a church or a priory, while the lake itself pokes up towards the border of Donegal like a long blue boomerang, and supports a great fleet of cabin cruisers. I could have stood a little lake cruising, which is very restful for the feet, but instead I went back to Enniskillen and got ready for the next stage of my journey over the Border into Sligo.

I left Enniskillen and Northern Ireland with considerable regret. Nine days on foot across Northern Ireland had entirely changed my preconceptions of the place and the people, altering views distorted by twenty years of seeing Northern Ireland only through the eye of the television news. Maybe the fine weather helped; it usually does.

Try as I might to arrive with an open mind I had imagined a country crammed with whey-faced, ranting bigots where, under a steady downpour, men in black balaclavas shot it out with the military, while priests and women in pinafores raised their hands for God's justice, or wept. Wherever it came from, this is a bleak picture to carry in the mind, and one which is largely false.

Yes, that sort of thing certainly happens in Northern Ireland, but that is not all of it. Northern Ireland is my kind of place, beautiful, interesting, friendly, and historic, while the people are quite marvellous. Maybe the walking helps. It certainly reduces the barriers and provides a ready excuse for conversation. When the walker reels into the pub or the B & B, saying 'Hello' is superfluous. Even assuming that the Irish need an excuse for conversation, which seems unlikely, my expedition opened a lot of doors. The Troubles are certainly there, and most pub or evening conversations come round to that subject in the end, but what I took away with me as I walked west past the Watergate was the memory of the open-hearted people I had met along the way.

People apart, the weather had been glorious. I was now sporting a considerable tan and the feet were healing nicely in some soft, newly-purchased, loop-stitched socks. I was just telling myself in the mirror that all handsome men are slightly suntanned, when it started to rain again, copiously. I put on my state-of-the-art 'Sprayway' raingear feeling like a child in his new school uniform, and set off in a steady downpour for the West of Ireland.

The way West, out of Enniskillen, leads along the river and past the Watergate. This was crowned with a flagpole from which fluttered the defiant cross of St George. Once that had faded from view there was nothing for it but to put my head down and march hard for the border of the Republic at Belcoo. There was no footpath so this was simply a bash down the main road on a verge wide enough to avoid most of the traffic. By staying on the verge I could avoid the spray but there was nothing else to recommend it. It was a dreary day. Clouds sat on the tops of the hills, my head was tucked deeply into the hood of my anorak and the rain swept relentlessly down.

At Belcoo the road did a left and then a right dog-leg turn, first past the fortified British Army–RUC guard post and then past a lone Garda constable. Suddenly, there I was in the Republic, with the first stage of my journey finally completed and only about 300 miles to go. No one asked to look at my passport and the traffic at the frontier hardly slowed down. If this was the Border, it all seemed far too easy.

There were signs here pointing to the Cavan Way, the first of the Republic's long-distance footpaths, but the map told me that it would take me south and in the wrong direction. I was heading fast for the West Coast, but I stopped just across the Border that night in the village of Blacklion, fairly wet on arrival but otherwise well contented. My feet seemed to be definitely on the mend and the rain could not last for ever. I had a lot to learn about Irish rain as I began to plod my way across Sligo.

As far as I could gather from the books I had read, some people feel that Sligo is overshadowed by the beauty of Mayo and Connemara. If so, that was a cheerful prospect because, even in the rain, Sligo looked good enough to me. This is a region of lakes and mountains, and most of the mountains have delightful names, like the Ox Mountains and the Curlew Mountains, and a target on my walk next day, the splendid heap of Benbulben, which hung above the village church at Drumcliff, the resting place of the poet William Butler Yeats. That too had been a place marked on my original plan as somewhere I had to see and to get there I had only to walk due west, along the deep glacial valley of Glencar. This was a long walk, a full day of 25 miles at least, but the country was beautiful and the road flat.

The country begins to change west of Enniskillen. Round-topped hills began to appear through the gusting drifts of rain, taller than anything I had seen so far. Ulster is beautiful but the scale of the country increases in the west, and with it the beauty of the landscape. The hills are higher and steeper, the valleys deeper, the lakes more frequent and more blue. The great clouds sweeping in from the Atlantic are cloud castles, deep and dramatic. What with one thing and another, I took to this region at once.

There was even a range of considerable hills away to the south, which I could identify from my map as the Cuilcagh Mountains. My original route had gone right across these hills, but that route meant missing Drumcliff, so here I was on a tarmac road again. The Cuilcaghs are Irish mountains and since, technically at least, a mountain has to be over 2,000 feet, they were actually no more than hills, but if the local people call them mountains, that's good enough for me. Besides, the prospect ahead was delightful ... a good walk on a level road with splendid scenery on either side and W.B. Yeats at the end of it.

I like poetry. Plenty of people do. I therefore fail to understand why other people think people who like poetry are either odd or effeminate or simply poseurs. I found this out fairly early on in life when I was in the Royal Marines. One dismal day I was flopped out with some other NCOs on one side of a truck while our merry men lay like heaps of puppies on the other side, grumbling, sharing cigarettes and running us down. From under the axles came the following conversation:

'Ooo you wiv then?'

'I'm wiv Terry Brown's section.'

'Oh yeah ... wot's ee like then?'

'A' right ... not bad. Wot about you?'

'I'm wiv Robbie Neillands.'

'Oh 'im. . . . any good?' A long ghastly pause followed.

'All right, I su'pose ... reads poetry.'

Then came an even longer and more ghastly pause while

the other Marines digested this information. Then a third voice enquired, 'Not a poove, is he?'

I know that listeners rarely hear good of themselves but it took me years to live that down.

The fact is that poetry is useful for a traveller, especially one who reads fast like I do, for I cannot keep myself in books. I therefore take a fat book of poetry along on my journey, preferably in paperback. That way I never run out of something to read, and can entertain myself as I travel. Besides, W.B. Yeats is one of my favourite poets, and I wanted to see his grave, that's all.

I was out early next day, forging west down a valley which grew in beauty by the mile, between the Dough Mountain and the Southern hills. A great escarpment threaded with silver waterfalls rose like a wall to the north, the road was lined with tall trees and clumps of purple fuchsia, and some miles beyond the village of Cluainin, or Manorhamilton, a long lake lay below me, filling the bottom of the valley. This was Lough Glencar, out of which flowed, as near as I could tell from the tiny print on my tiny map, the Drumcliff river which led into Drumcliff Bay.

I could have swerved off south after Mounthamilton and taken the track over Benbo mountain to Lough Gill and Yeats' 'Lake Isle of Innisfree', but when you are on foot your options are limited, and I was finding it difficult enough just reading the map.

On crossing the Border I had changed from the bearable British 1:50,000 scale to the Irish 1½": 1 mile or 1:126.720 scale, which is barely adequate for walking. The names of places were in such tiny script I could hardly read them and gauging where I was from the map became one of my main preoccupations in the weeks ahead. I seemed to be moving much slower because the scale had changed, and here was another problem added to the lack of footpaths.

The Irish maps have not been fully revised for decades. As

any walker knows, up-to-date, large-scale maps are a prerequisite for accurate cross-country navigation. This is especially true when a country has no footpaths. It occurred to me somewhere along this road that apart from those on the Ulster Way, I had not seen a footpath sign, a fingerpost or even a stile for nearly two weeks. Well, you can get used to anything, and I could cope here as I had coped in Spain. All I had to do was turn south at the West Coast and I would eventually get to Valentia. I was in no particular hurry to do that.

Anyway, there was no need to fret at the moment. My destination lay somewhere ahead in the eye of the tilting sun and if I just kept going west I would get there. Meanwhile, there was the scenery to enjoy. The Glencar valley fell away steeply to my right, then rose on the far side in a steep escarpment threaded with those ribbon-like silver waterfalls cascading down the emerald-green face of the cliff. The air was soft and clear, so that all the colours stood out quite sharply. I strolled along at a good pace, marvelling at the great clumps of purple fuchsia beside the road.

When the valley widened before the jut of the King's Mountain, I came down off the main road and crossed the Drumcliff river. From there I made my way on a minor road towards Drumcliff Bay and the church at Drumcliff. I saw the church tower from a mile away and diverted towards it and there, inside the gate and just to the left of the church door, stood a plain grey slab bearing the words I had come so far to see.

> *Cast a cold eye,*
> *On life, on death,*
> *Horseman pass by.*

The grave of William Butler Yeats, Nobel Prizewinner, Irish patriot, last of the Romantic poets. All that apart, it is this epitaph that brings people to Drumcliff. I suspect that is why Yeats chose it.

The Irish are wonderful with words. They are fluent in poetry, song and drama and this seems to be their main cultural gift. They are much less interested in, say, architecture or visual beauty; or at least they seem to be. Give or take a Georgian square or two in Dublin, the towns are not attractive and since the Irish are given to using vivid paints and plastic sheeting, the buildings are often positively gaudy. They have an ear for beauty though in words and music, and few countries in the world have produced so many writers, playwrights or poets. I can think of a dozen without much effort, from Shaw to Behan, but my favourite of them all is Yeats.

William Butler Yeats was born into a Protestant family at Sandymount, outside Dublin in 1865. He died in the South of France in 1939, so his life spanned the most turbulent years of modern Irish history from before Charles Parnell's death in 1891, through the Great War and the Easter Rising to the setting up of the Republic. He spent his youth shuttling between London and Dublin and did not marry until he was fifty-two, while his approach to life was, to say the least, unusual.

Yeats belonged to that class of Protestant gentry known as the Anglo-Irish ascendancy. The great love of his life was Maud Gonne who, though the daughter of a colonel in the British Army, was an active Republican. Yeats pursued Maud for many years but in 1903 she married the patriot Republican, John MacBride, and Yeats was desolate. He abandoned revolutionary politics for a while and took up the theatre; Yeats was General Manager of the Abbey Theatre in Dublin from 1904 to 1910, though he continued to write poetry and pine for Mrs MacBride. Then came the Easter Rising of 1916, after which John MacBride, who was one of the leaders of the Rising, was tried and shot by the British.

Yeats then proposed marriage to the widow who had, anyway, separated from MacBride some time before his death, but he was again rejected. He then promptly proposed to Maud's adopted daughter Iseult, who also rejected him. He finally married Georgie Hyde-Lees and was, somewhat to his surprise, very happy. This was in 1917, a scant year after the Easter Rising, an event which affected him far more than the current slaughter then taking place on the Western Front. I doubt if Yeats had much time for the Great War poets, but when he turned his pen to the problems of Ireland, he made it very clear where his sympathies lay. In 'An Irish Airman Foresees His Death' he writes:

> My country is Kiltartan Cross,
> My countrymen Kiltartan's poor,
> No likely end could bring them loss,
> Or leave them happier than before . . .

– while in 'Easter 1916' he writes about the effects of the Rising. 'A terrible beauty is born' – though this was not written until 1921 when the Irish people were tearing themselves apart.

Yeats' grandfather had been the Rector of Drumcliff and Yeats expressed a wish to be buried here, 'Under bare Benbulben's head'. Yeats first came to Sligo in his youth to stay with his relatives, the Pollexfens, who were shipowners in Sligo. William's brother Jack was a fine landscape painter, and his works are displayed in the County Museum in Sligo along with a lot of W.B. Yeats' memorabilia, including first editions and early manuscripts.

W.B. Yeats became a Free State Senator, and was active in the Dail for some years, though he continued to write and was eventually awarded the Nobel Prize for Poetry in 1923.

One of the things that surprised me was how recently the

Yeats brothers had lived. Jack Yeats died only in 1957 and
W.B. Yeats died at Roquebrune in 1939. After the war an
Irish warship was sent to collect his remains which were
then buried as he wished – 'Under bare Benbulben's head' in
1948.

The local people are rightly proud of the Yeats' connection,
so much so that the Tourist Board often refers to Sligo as
'The Yeats Country', clearly with considerable success.
People were pouring into this quiet churchyard throughout
my visit, photographing the headstone and touring the
church. Yeats has become an industry. It is certainly a
very pretty spot, tranquil but for the roar of passing traffic,
and I sat on the wall at the back of the churchyard for
quite a while, resting my feet and looking out across the
valley to Benbulben, which is only 1,730 ft high but still
a most impressive mountain and set in some breathtaking
scenery.

Another haunt of the *literati* hereabouts is Cuildreven,
scene of the famous Battle of the Books in 561 AD, between
St Columba and St Finian. St Finian had loaned St Columba
a psalter and St Columba copied it without his permission.
St Finian then demanded the copy back, St Columba refused
and the dispute ended up before the High King of Tara, who
gave judgement in favour of St Finian. 'To every cow its
calf,' he said. 'To every book its copy.' St Columba was
furious and took himself off to Iona in a huff.

I was considering walking north for a while, past Streedagh Point where three Armada galleons came to grief in
1588, for a look at Mullaghmore Bay where Lord Louis
Mountbatten and members of his family were blown to
pieces by the IRA in 1979, but I had more than enough of
the IRA by now. Instead I turned west for Rosses Point and
my first real climb of the trip, up the hill of Knocknarea. I
could see Knocknarea ahead now, a most distinctive hill, just

1,076 ft high, with what looked like a nipple on top. I would keep that for tomorrow, for the evening was drawing on and I had walked a long way that day.

Like most of the other visitors I spoke to hereabouts, I was quite overwhelmed by the sheer beauty of the Sligo landscape. This is a mixture of coast and lake and mountain, of rushing river and tumbling waterfall. Sligo is both dramatic and breathtaking, an almost theatrical display of scenery, a stage-set draped from time to time with curtains of rain. It rained a fair bit for the rest of my trip but to be honest, in the West of Ireland the rain hardly matters.

You can even see the rain sweeping in from far out in the Atlantic, masking the offshore islands as it comes, picked out with great rainbows which trail a path across the clouds, adding still more drama to a landscape that is never less than striking. I became fascinated by the clouds and cloud formations of the West of Ireland, great billowing pillows of white, so unlike the flat grey skies of England.

I took a drink out onto the hotel terrace before dinner and sat there sniffing the evening air, which was mild and moist and tinged with the smell of the sea. I stayed there, looking around at the surrounding hills, the map across my knees, thinking of the way I must go tomorrow, on across the hills and into Mayo.

The mountains of Sligo are not very high but they are very old. The Ox Mountains, or Slieve Gamph, which I must cross tomorrow or the next day, are said to be the oldest mountains in Ireland, 600 million years old, or more. Time has worn them down into long, rolling ridges, green and beguiling to look on but carpeted from top to bottom with blanket bog. These Irish hills look more gentle at a distance than they actually are. They look like easy walking, but when you get onto them the ground is quite rough and seamed with streams and eroded gullies. All this I had yet to discover; for the moment I was content to sit on the terrace and admire the view.

Future problems hardly matter when you are sitting in the soft Irish light, looking at a rainbow arcing over the dark hills across the Bay. Tomorrow I would shin up Knocknarea and take a quick look at Sligo town. Then I would march as hard as I could for the town of Ballina and really get stuck into this beautiful part of Ireland.

That decided, I limped back to the bar. The bar was being propped up by a bride, clad in the full wedding regimentals of flowing white dress and veil, her bridal bouquet resting on the bar. So far, so normal, but she had at her elbow, instead of a flute of champagne, a pint of Guinness. There was no sign of the bridegroom, and the bride and the barman were deep in conversation. I listened hard – why not admit it? – and could hardly understand a word they were saying. Only weeks later did I realize that whenever I stayed in an Irish hotel there seemed to be a wedding going on and a bride in the bar. For the moment I ordered a large Blackbush, toasted the bride by raising my glass and was rewarded with a big smile.

More and more people drifted in, clearly the wedding party, some with buttonholes and slicked-down hair, and the atmosphere became steadily more convivial. This was the main bar, not a private function room and I was soon drawn into the party. I found my glass being refilled as if by magic, and was soon deep in conversation with the Best Man.

'What day is it?' I asked.

'It's ... lemme see.... sure, it's Sunday. No ... it's Friday.'

I nodded. 'I only asked, because in England people usually get married on a Saturday.'

He seemed surprised. 'If we tried that here, the priest

Carrick-a-Rede bridge.

The Ulster Way (*above*) leads to the Owenkillew river (*below*) at Gortin.

At the Giant's Causeway.

above: The Watergate, Enniskillen.

right: W.B. Yeats' grave, Drumcliff, near Sligo.

Benbulben.

right: The hills and moors of Mayo.

above: Westport.

left: John MacBride's
bronze bust, Westport.

left: Approaching the summit of Croagh Patrick.

right:
Climbing Croagh Patrick.

The view from Croagh Patrick.

The chapel on the summit.

could never pack them all in, so he couldn't. Eileen here got the afternoon off from the tourist shop, and we hired the band, and away we go.'

Away we went indeed. Weddings are riotous affairs everywhere these days, and Irish weddings are no exception. When I was a lad people got married at two o'clock on a Saturday afternoon, returned to the bride's home for a slice of cake and a glass of champagne and about an hour later, after a spot of confetti hurling, the happy couple flew off to Mallorca and the guests sloped off to the pub. Halcyon days.

No wedding seems complete nowadays without a two-day rave. After observing a number of weddings over the next few weeks, I blame the Irish for this modern and expensive development. Later that night – much later that night – I was back in the bar with Eamon, while the guests danced on in the ballroom. Everyone was in there. I have never seen a priest doing the Twist before, but he did it very well. The whole hotel vibrated slightly for most of the night and there seemed no point in going to bed.

I remembered that evening in fragments next morning as my hangover and I flogged round to Sligo town in the rain. Sligo town sits snugly astride the Garavogue estuary, the Garavogue river draining Lough Gill. By local standards Sligo is quite a large town with a population of some 16,000, who inhabit the usual mixture of narrow streets lined with terraced houses, pubs and small shops. There is a harbour, now only half full of fishing boats, but this was once a great immigrant port through which the local people fled to America during and after the Great Famine of the 1840s. Long before that Sligo was the capital for the Fitzgerald family, a Norman brood who came across with the mighty Strongbow at the end of the 12th century.

Sir Maurice Fitzgerald founded Sligo Abbey in 1252 but

this was destroyed by a Puritan general during the rebellion of 1641, when the native Irish rose against the English landlords. The ruins by the river are quite impressive, even in the drifts of rain, and I spent a little time there before going into town.

Shafts of pale sunlight were drying the streets as I went to the Sligo Museum. This contains paintings by Jack Yeats and a lot of W.B. Yeats' memorabilia, and I had a cup of coffee and a small 'crack' in a coffee shop while another flurry sent the rain streaming down the windows. After that storm passed I set out at a smart clip for the hill of Knocknarea.

Knocknarea is a small hill, only 1,076 ft high, but most of the people who visit Sligo make the time to climb it. I found that out when I couldn't find the path from the road to the summit and banged on the door of a small cottage. Before I could open my mouth, the lady who opened the door said, 'It's half a mile up on the left.' When twenty people a day come knocking on your door you don't have to bother with the question, and sure enough, half a mile up the road a track led up to Knocknarea. This track had been turned into a fair-sized stream by the regular morning rainstorms, but for once it was a definite footpath, not a road or a country lane, and I thoroughly enjoyed it.

There were even walkers on it. I had a long chat while sheltering in a gully with two lady walkers, both called Moira, who were up here on holiday from Dublin. Moira One confirmed that there were very few footpaths in Ireland and since she had just been walking the Inca Trail in the Andes, she spoke with some authority. Moira Two said that the Irish preferred their mountains in 'their natural state' (a phrase I came to dread), and added that Irish parents tend not to take their children walking anyway, so local footpaths would never get used. Then the rain came sheeting down again, and we pressed on uphill for the Cairn.

The top of Knocknarea is flat and open but crowned with that massive nipple-shaped Cairn I had seen from Drumcliff the day before. This is actually a prehistoric burial chamber, and like most such things in Ireland, a source of legend. I met a man huddled on the leeward side who told me the Cairn was the burial place of Queen Maeve, ruler of Connaught in the 1st century AD and that she had been buried upright, ready to spring to life at the Last Trump.

This Queen Maeve appears frequently in Irish folklore, especially in a saga, the 'Tain bo Cuailgne', the Cattle Drive of Cooley, which relates how the warriors of Ulster, led by the Knights of the Red Branch, defended the North against an invasion by Queen Maeve and the armies of Ireland. This cairn is one of the biggest burial mounds in Ireland and has yet to be fully excavated. I hate to spoil a good story but it is more probably a passage grave, and a good deal earlier than the 1st century AD. Either way, it certainly is a most impressive cairn, 630 ft in circumference and 80 ft high, and visible for miles around. Scrambling to the top I had vast views in all directions, to the Ox Mountains which barred my route to the south, up the Sligo coast, and well out to sea, where the great clouds and rainstorms were marching towards me in an orderly fashion. It was all quite beautiful.

There to the north lay Yeats' mountain, Benbulben. Just below lay the tiny beach at Strandhill, and out in Sligo Bay I could see the green hump of Coney Island. This takes its name from the fact that it was once infested with rabbits, or coneys, and gave its name across the Atlantic to Coney Island near New York City and so, carried in the cramped holds of the immigrant ships, did memories of Ireland slip across to the New World. At a guess I could enjoy views over a hundred miles of coast and country that morning, so I turned west and took a good look at the Ox Mountains, which lay across my route to Ballina and Mayo. I decided to set off without delay, but coming off the hill I was advised by another walker not to leave Knocknarea without visiting 'The Glen'.

I found 'The Glen' with some difficulty, tucked away at the end of a muddy path, halfway down the mountain. It is actually a narrow ravine slashed into the rock, only 30 ft wide but nearly a mile long and somewhat eerie. There was no sound there but the patter of the rain and lush green vegetation sprouting from every nook and cranny of the rock. This was worth seeing, but it all took time so I by-passed Strandhill and struck out fast for the Ox Mountains.

One of the few advantages of road walking is that you make very good time. This narrow moorland road to the west had attractive views and the day was made lively by the constant rainstorms and the rainbows which seemed to come with them. At one time there were four of them around me, each a brilliant arc of colour set against the dark clouds and the dull red-brown of the hills. I plodded on into the village of Skreen, from where I got a lift from a man in a pub to the point where the main road across the Ox Mountains, the Slieve Gamph, heads south over the moor towards Lough Easky.

The Ox Mountains are not very high, running up to some 1,600 ft, but they are very open and wet and quite without shelter, not unlike Dartmoor. The main spine of the Ox Mountains actually straddled the road, but lay to my right for the first few miles. After that I came over a low rise and skirted the eastern shore of Easky Lough, a great expanse of empty, wind-ruffled water. I trudged along happily enough across this empty moonscape, ducking into my rainhood when the storms swept past, quite content to be out here on my own.

A mile or so past Easky Lough I turned off across the moor by the hamlet of Masshill and began to climb a little.

The road quickly deteriorated into a track, but the going was good enough towards the next lough, Lough Talt, which came into sight suddenly, tucked away behind a small hill. Apart from shinning up Knocknarea, I had now been on the road all day and was definitely starting to flag. I came onto the main road to Ballina at the foot of the shallow pass that led over the Ox Mountains and west towards Ballina, but that was still six miles away. Enough was enough. I found a wayside B & B, took off my boots on the doormat and hopped my way in towards the tea and scones.

9

Ballina to Castlebar

The moment the very name of Ireland is mentioned, the English seem to bid adieu to common
feeling, common sense, and to act with the
barbarity of the tyrants and the fatuity of idiots.

Sydney Smith, 1940

Two weeks into the walk and I was getting into my stride.
There is a wonderful sense of space out here on the West
Coast of Ireland and I like that. The valleys are wide and the
hills not too high, so the whole place feels spacious. I am not
a great lover of the mountain ranges, not because I dislike
the heights but because they make me feel hemmed in.
Ireland is just about right, with enough hills to make the
scenery interesting but plenty of wide and glorious views.

To keep saying that the country is beautiful is to dull the
senses with repetition, but few countries in the world can
offer such varied scenery or such a gloriously empty country.
Nowadays the world seems over-full with people. It is
difficult to walk three paces in a straight line down any high
street without bumping into somebody, but walking here in
the west of Ireland, I often hardly met a soul all day.

Once across the Ox Mountains I descended gently on a

124

bright, fresh morning to the great green limestone plain that surrounds Ballina. The town, the largest in County Mayo, straddles the narrow estuary of the River Moy that runs back for six miles from the exit to the sea by Inniscrone on Killala Bay. Sleepy Ballina is a pleasant little place, a large village rather than a town, with a population of about 6,000. The main street is the usual mixture of small shops, cafés, and pubs, so I had a lunchtime drink and a look at the map in a pub in the High Street, and with nothing left to detain me, set off south again towards Castlebar. Before I got there though, I made a stop at Mount Falcon.

The walker has the time to pick up rumours, and one that grew with proximity as I walked west, was the one about the Mount Falcon Hotel. The Mount Falcon lies just off the road between Lough Conn and the River Moy, a few miles south of Ballina. Here, or so rumour had it, the owner was a character, a real card, a gem, a National Treasure. If I was stopping anywhere in Mayo, they all said, then I had to stop at the Mount Falcon and meet Mrs Constance Aldridge, but I had better hurry because Mrs Aldridge had been eighty-six for as long as anyone could remember, and you never knew, did you? I therefore hurried down beside the Moy at my best speed, and was soon crunching up the gravel drive to the door of the Mount Falcon, which lies some miles south of Ballina.

I could see at a glance that this hotel was not as other hotels. The car park was full of cows placidly licking the raindrops off the bonnets and wings of the assembled vehicles. Then a battered white van held together mainly with string started up and came lurching round the cows towards me. The cows scattered quickly into the flowerbeds and stood there munching the hydrangeas. The van was jammed to the roof with small girls in jodhpurs, who gave me a collective shriek of welcome as the van sped by. So I dodged the van, skirted the cows, opened the front door and was instantly submerged in a flood of puppies. For about five minutes I stood in the porch in danger of being licked to death.

Mrs Aldridge, who was waiting within, told me later that she was '. . . very good at puppies', and this indeed seemed to be the case. The litter now leaping all over me belonged to Bonnie, a very lovable Springer bitch, who climbed onto my lap whenever I sat down, and stayed there, quivering with pleasure.

Mrs Aldridge is a small, capable woman, one of those people who were once the great props of the Empire. She would probably look right as a fairy godmother, but she runs her hotel, staff and guests together, with a big smile and a will of iron.

Mrs Aldridge has lived in Mayo since the 1930s, when her husband left the Army and they decided to open an hotel. They took their time looking about and eventually bought the entire Mount Falcon estate, fields and herd, river fishing and large house, all for just £4,000. Mind you, £4,000 was a fair piece of change in 1932.

'We set up as a fishing hotel,' she said, 'and we only wanted fishermen. Their wives could come if they could fish, but no children. Of course we have children now, if they behave, and we get a lot of foreigners, Italians, French, German, some Americans, but not so much to fish because some idiot dredged the Moy and the fishing is not what it was. I do wish some people would leave things alone, don't you?'

I do. If I am any judge, only a fool would tamper with Mrs Aldridge's fishing. The Mount Falcon still has the feel of a fishing hotel. Behind the heavy front door lies a vast hall off which lead various rooms full of comfortable furniture, though every chair is occupied by a spaniel. The bedrooms have unusual names: there is 'The Brigadier's', the 'Over the Kitchen', the 'Yellow Carpet', and the 'Far Corridor'. The honeymoon suite is 'Above the Dining Room'. I suddenly remembered a hotel I had visited in Canada where the brochure advertised: 'Our honeymoon suite; with ensuite bathroom and lake view, just $150 a night. (Accommodates up to three.)', but thought I had better not mention it.

The wide hall at the Mount Falcon is a litter of green wellies, Barbour jackets and wet puppies, while antlered heads of long-shot stags gloom down from the rafters. The 'Help-Yourself-on-an-Honours-System' bar is in the larder and all the guests dine together around a long refectory table with Mrs Aldridge as the matriarch sitting at the top. We dined very well that night on roast beef, which Mrs Aldridge carved at the sideboard, knives flashing. Everyone was very careful to keep their elbows off the table and clear their plates. That apart, we had some good conversation, far better than you can get at most hotels.

One gentleman from Dublin was an Oscar Wilde fan and kept up a steady flow of Wilde impressions, ranging from Wilde's dinner in – Leadville, Colorado – 'Three courses, whisky, whisky and whisky' – to his comment on British cooks, '... who should be turned into that pillar of salt they never know how to use.'

Another gentleman, from Belfast, who was also in the pig-smuggling trade, told me that actually moving real live pigs about was quite unnecessary. All you needed was a van full of manure and a tape of pig squeals to play on the radio outside the Customs office; I think he was having me on. Halfway through dinner there came a tremendous crash from above, and a thud which shook the ceiling. Apart from muttering 'Honeymooners!' Mrs Aldridge made no comment.

I spent a very cosy evening at the Mount Falcon, moving puppies off chairs, being licked by Bonnie, dipping into books and talking to the other guests. Most of them were here for the fishing and had come back for the umpteenth time. When I went to bed well after midnight, Mrs Aldridge was still going strong and rounding up the guests for a game of cards. Just before I dropped off there came another crash as the honeymooners' bed fell apart again.

Next morning all was bustle. The cows were chased out of the porch and a litter of puppies raced out the door and fled yelping across the lawns. The hall was full of people gearing up for a hard day's touring or going fishing, packing up their picnics and Thermos flasks, selecting flies, debating on the certainty of rain. Mrs Aldridge stood in the middle of all this, sturdy as a tree, giving orders and advice, sweeping down upon me like a ship in full sail.

'You must go there. I insist. You cannot miss it. Not there, you silly girl ... there, in his lunch. I've put in some hard-boiled eggs. Catch that dog ... too late! Are you off? Well, you should stay two nights. It takes two nights to get used to this place. Well, if you must ... come again, but do try to book in advance .... I'll always fit you in but you must be more responsible.'

Duly chastened and quite determined to become more responsible, I slunk off into the rain. I felt exhausted by the time I got out the door ... but I will go back again. Mrs Aldridge and her hotel are living treasures, tremendous value and worth closer inspection.

By staying at the Mount Falcon I had already gained some distance on that day's walk towards Castlebar and it was easy walking to the south, down first to the breezy shores of Lough Conn, a long lake backed by the Nephin Beg mountains across the water, and then south across the bridge and islands by Pontoon that run like a causeway between Lough Conn and the small, pretty Lough Cullin. Once across the causeway, and after a stop for a dry-out in the village of Pontoon, there was a choice. I could go south, directly along the main road and into Castlebar, or head north-west, around the shore of Lough Conn and up Glen Nephin for the narrow track that climbs towards Castlebar through Windy Gap. This last was a bit longer but a lot more picturesque, and since Windy Gap is mentioned in a poem by Yeats, there was really no contest at all.

> As I came over Windy Gap
> They threw a halfpenny into my cap,
> For I am Running to Paradise.

So west it was, Running to Paradise, my head turned into the rain flurries to look across the glen at the smooth round bulk of the splendid Nephin mountain, which lay far away across the green valley floor and filled my eyes for most of the day. I slogged up the empty winding road to Windy Gap, which the wind came roaring through to buffet me about. Bowed under the pack, I made my way up the hill and round the stone cross on the col and was soon out in open country.

This was another beautiful route between the hills with the top of Croagmoyle lying to my right, and a river cascading along to my left, and not a car passed as I made my way down the far side of the hill, past the village of Burren and over the pond- and stream-littered plain towards that day's destination, Castlebar.

Castlebar is the county town of Mayo and about the same size as Ballina, which is to say it is really a rather large village. Even so, this is a place of some style and significance. There is a fine big church at the top end of the High Street and a great open park in the centre, the celebrated Castlebar Mall.

This Mall contains the grave of John Moore who was the Provisional President of the Republic of Connaught in 1798. This was at the time when a force of a thousand troops from Revolutionary France, under General Humbert, landed at Killala Bay and defeated the troops of the English General

Lake – a rout that has gone down in Irish history as 'The Races of Castlebar'.

This event threw a great panic into the English who had always thought of Ireland as a hotbed of sedition. Although General Humbert was eventually defeated, this invasion proved the decisive factor in prompting the Act of Union between Ireland and Great Britain in 1800, which put an end to the Irish Parliament and set Independence back a hundred years. It also saw the end of one of the great heroes of the Irish Independence struggle, Wolfe Tone.

With all it promised in the shape of liberty, the French Revolution had an instant appeal in Ireland. The Irish Parliament, though subservient to English rule, had been in existence for centuries and during the 18th century the Irish Protestant Ascendancy was edging towards Independence. In 1782 their leader, Henry Gratton, won a declaration from the Westminister Parliament which, at least in theory, would prevent England legislating about Irish affairs. The idea was to create two separate but equal states linked by the Crown. It should be pointed out though that the members of both Parliaments were Protestants. A hundred years after the Battle of the Boyne, the Protestants were still keeping a very firm grip on the levers of power on both sides of the Irish Sea.

The Irish Parliament had managed to repeal many of the discriminating laws passed against the Catholics, but for some this drift to Independence was still too slow. One of these impatient patriots was Wolfe Tone, a Dublin Protestant, who founded the United Irishmen in 1791.

This was a secret organization, dedicated to making Britain grant Irish Independence, but also, as the name implied, to uniting all the Irish people, Catholic, Protestant or Dissenter, into this common cause. Thousands of United Irishmen went to join Humbert's small army but the result was total disaster. After Humbert's defeat, the French survivors were shipped back to France, but all the captured Irishmen were hanged as traitors. A British squadron also captured a French frigate with Wolfe Tone aboard and he cut his throat in prison rather than die on the gallows. He remains one of the great Irish patriots, and his aim of replacing Catholic and Protestant with the single name of 'Irishman' is one that should be revived.

Castlebar had been marked on my map early on as a place I wanted to see because it has associations with the Bingham family, better known as the Earls of Lucan. One Lord Lucan, the third Earl, was involved in that famous disaster which befell the British Cavalry when the Light Brigade charged the Russian guns at the Battle of Balaclava during the Crimean War. Lord Lucan was commanding the Cavalry Division with an admirable incompetence matched only by that of his much detested brother-in-law, Lord Cardigan, who commanded the Light Brigade.

Lord Cardigan actually led the famous and fatal charge of the Light Brigade down the 'Valley of Death' towards the enemy guns, but this antipathy towards his superior officer and brother-in-law played a part in the disaster. This may seem a tenuous reason for putting Castlebar on my itinerary, but it is people and events rather than architecture that make most towns worth visiting. Irish towns, with some few exceptions, are not very pretty.

Besides, there was another reason, a more serious one. Castlebar was one of the many places stricken by the Irish Potato Famine – the Great Hunger – of 1845–47, an event which explains better than any other why the Irish people knew they had to separate from Britain and run their own affairs. God knows, when disaster struck in 1845, they could hardly have done worse than the British managed to do.

The British visitor today, learning about the Hunger in the

place where it actually happened, discovers the full extent of the tragedy with a terrible and shameful impact. The tumbledown, roofless cottages, the shuttered, abandoned hamlets, the sheer loneliness of the countryside through which I passed recently and was to pass through in the weeks ahead, can all be traced directly back to the Hunger. In Castlebar it can be traced to the actions of the third Earl of Lucan.

The Hunger cannot be taken in at one attempt. The story has to grow on you and the place where it began to grow on me was in the quiet Sunday streets of Castlebar. To look at this tragedy through the actions of one man in one place makes the story more human but no less tragic or terrible.

The career of Charles Bingham, third Earl of Lucan, provides a glimpse of the power a landlord could wield in Ireland in the middle decades of the last century. It was a marvellous thing to be an English mi'lord anywhere in Europe at that time, but to be a lord in Ireland was to be practically a god.

George Charles Bingham, Third Earl of Lucan, was born in 1800, the year of the Act of Union. He is recorded by Cecil Woodham Smith as being, 'a Byronic hero, dark, passionate, romantic'. Like his brother-in-law, Lord Cardigan, he was a professional soldier, or as professional as any soldier needed to be in the decades after the Napoleonic Wars, which is to say he knew and cared far more about parades and pretty uniforms than the management of men. He had joined the Army at the age of sixteen as an ensign in the 6th Foot. By a series of purchases he had become Lieutenant-Colonel commanding one of the smartest Cavalry Regiments in the British Army, the 17th Lancers – 'Bingham's Dandies' – by the age of twenty-six.

Lord Lucan's military duties, such as they were, diverted him from concern with the running of his ancestral estates in Ireland, where the family had made their mark as soldiers in the days of Queen Elizabeth I. They had since acquired the baronetcy at Castlebar in the wilder part of Mayo, but like many others, the Lucans were absentee landlords. They kept an agent in Castlebar whose task was to wring as much money as possible out of the hapless tenants and send it to England where the Binghams kept up a considerable state. The Binghams themselves rarely ventured across the Irish Sea.

In the same year that he purchased the command of the 17th Lancers, Lord Lucan was returned as the Member of Parliament for Mayo. Here again there was little need to stand for election, campaign for votes or present a manifesto. For all their pratings about honour and breeding, the aristocracy of the day got what they wanted by cash, power and coercion. Their abilities, if any, had little to do with it. It soon transpired that Lucan's election had been gained with the aid of votes in the gift of another landowner, a Major Fitzgerald. The gallant major had been offered a 'comfortable appointment in a good climate' as his reward for polling his tenants' votes in Lucan's favour.

The Irish have always had a somewhat cavalier attitude to the role of the vote in the exercise of democracy. To this day, it is necessary to issue warnings before Polling Day against 'personation', the practice of appearing at a polling booth under various names or at different polling booths under the same name to cast several votes for one's favourite candidate. How they get away with it, beats me, but one of the sayings in Ireland as Polling Day approaches is a reminder to 'Vote Early and Vote Often'. Sometimes, however, parties to the fraud fall out.

When the 'comfortable appointment' was not forthcoming, Major Fitzgerald blew the gaff to Parliament and then rather foolishly challenged Lord Lucan to a duel. What followed was rather comic. With all his faults, Lucan was no coward. Lucan left his regiment and hurried to Ostend, where the major was residing, and arrived at Fitzgerald's door in the middle of the night. He offered to fight the major then and there, by moonlight on the beach. The major demurred, claiming to have mislaid his pistols, but Lucan would not wait. He offered the loan of his own pistols and said that the major must put up or shut up, fight or apologize. Wisely, the major apologized.

Ten years later, in 1837, Lucan relinquished his command of the long-suffering 17th Lancers and retired on half-pay to his estates in Ireland. He was the first member of his family to go there for years, but the move was necessary. Revenues from rents had fallen steeply in the last ten years and clearly something had to be done. Since the turn of the century the family agents at Castlebar had been the O'Malley family, the post descending from father to son, but Lucan was not at all satisfied that the O'Malleys were up to their duties or paying over all that they collected. He also suspected that the O'Malleys had got too big for their boots, were hunting on his land, shooting over his fields and giving parties at his house.

In all this Lord Lucan was quite correct. The estate was a visible shambles and heavily in debt. The accounts reluctantly provided by the O'Malleys were both confused and inaccurate, so after a short pause while Lucan investigated this situation, the O'Malleys were sacked. All hell then broke loose in Castlebar.

The O'Malleys were related to half the population and the new Earl – for Bingham succeeded to the title on his father's death in 1839 – was already vastly unpopular. The younger O'Malley, St-Clair, even offered to fight a duel with the Earl, an offer which was scornfully rejected, but the O'Malleys continued to shoot and hunt over the Lucan estates until Lord Lucan had the younger O'Malley arrested for poaching. The case was tried at the Sessions Court in Castlebar and must have been one of the few occasions in legal history when both the plaintiff and the defendant not only appeared in the Court but also sat on the Bench to hear the case.

Both were magistrates and neither would leave the Bench and the result was a violent and undignified public row in the Courthouse, while a host of spectators watched and listened, open-mouthed, from the public gallery. Both men were eventually removed from the Bench for Contempt of Court, after Lord Lucan called his fellow magistrate a blackguard and O'Malley had threatened to break every bone in the Earl's body the next time they met in the Castlebar Mall. It was all most enthralling.

Although defeated for the moment, Lord Lucan was not yet at the end of his resources. He decided to revive the medieval Manorial Court granted to his distant ancestors and try the O'Malleys himself. Lord Lucan was then further aggrieved and greatly disappointed when his lawyers told him that Manorial Courts no longer existed. None of this might have mattered too much. It could all have provided an amusing incident in rural Irish life, but the situation on Lord Lucan's estate was anything but amusing, and a major disaster was about to descend on all the hapless Irish tenantry.

It is hard for anyone to conceive how, fifty full years after the Act of Union, which supposedly made England and Ireland one country, the British Government could have allowed the country people of Ireland to suffer as they did. Reading about it now, generations after the time of the Great Hunger, the situation of Ireland in the middle decades of the last century induces a sense of shock, then anger, then – if you are British – shame.

Put simply, in the middle decades of the last century, the Irish peasantry were little better than slaves. Outside Ulster they had no legal rights to their land, or to tenure, or even to decent treatment. No one protected them or was remotely interested in their welfare. They were, to all intents and purposes, a bloody and sometimes rebellious nuisance. This was not, after all, such a long time ago. My grandmother, who brought me up, was born in 1870, just thirty years after the events I am about to describe, when most of the people who survived the Famine were still alive and most of the people responsible for Ireland's suffering were both alive and in power.

The poverty and ignorance of the Irish peasantry beggars description. In the Bingham fief of Castlebar in 1845 only seven people could read. Hardly anyone could afford shoes. Barefoot men and women stood ankle-deep in mud on the Mall when Lord Lucan rode by with his hounds. There were few schools outside the main towns, a lack of good roads, no system of trade or distribution, hardly any shops. Work for wages was rare, subsistence farming the common lot, and very poor subsistence at that. If he could not pay his rent the landlord threw the tenant and his family out to starve.

Even paying the rent was no security. If a tenant improved his farm, the landlord might evict him without compensation in favour of another farmer who could pay a higher rent. Only in Ulster, where the Protestants held sway, did the – mainly Protestant – tenants have any rights at all.

'Not a bit of bread have I had since I was born,' said one Irish tenant in 1845. 'We never taste meat of any kind, or bacon. Our common fare is potatoes in pepper and water.' The average Irish peasant ate 14lb of potatoes every day, and nothing else.

The state of Ireland in the 1840s was that of a disaster sliding inexorably into a catastrophe. There were very few towns, and those that existed were, as I had already seen in Ballina, small and unimportant. There were no major industries to provide regular employment, few trades outside the linen mills of Ulster. The destitution of the ordinary people was absolute and yet the population was soaring. In the 1840s the population exceeded 8 million people, nearly 60 per cent more than Ireland supports today. The bulk of these people were tenant farmers, living on a few acres of field and bog.

The peasants lived by their fields, in cabins or mud huts or even in holes dug out of the bogs. Their ramshackle huts contained a peat fire for warmth and cooking, but they had rarely more furniture than a stool and a bed on the mud floor. In this squalid habitation large families lived with their animals, sleeping side by side with the pigs. A German traveller who passed through Ireland in 1843 wrote that he had 'never seen such deprivation, not even among the Letts or the Finns'.

The Irish peasantry were subsistence farmers, living on what they could grow, selling any surplus to pay the rent, but as the population increased, as it did in the 1830s and 1840s, the cultivated land began to run out. Here again, the landlords were largely responsible. They could have drained the bogs, created more pasture and invested money in improved methods of cultivation. They did neither. If the Irish peasant took matters into his own hands and tried to improve his lot, the landlords either took the profit or sold his improved smallholding to a wealthier tenant.

The landlord had all the rights and used them like a rod of iron against the tenantry, evicting at will and often on a whim. There is the story of Lord Leitrim, who noticed that one of his tenants had the audacity to build a new cabin for his family. Lord Leitrim promptly sent his agent to evict the man and his family and pull the cabin down. God only knows why he did it, but he could do it, so he did. What happened to the homeless family thereafter bothered Lord Leitrim not a jot.

The answer to the pressure on the land was that employed

in other agricultural nations; to gather up the small subsistence farms into larger, more economic units which would produce crops for money while providing work for wages. This, in short, was collectivization, but where were the surplus people to go once turned off their land? The landlords simply did not care, and the Government of the day was committed to the economic doctrine known as *laissez-faire*, under which doctrine of non-interference the men of business could do what they wished.

As the Irish dilemma steadily increased, a new style of terror arose, that of the 'consolidating landlord', and the leader of these consolidating landlords was the Third Earl of Lucan. In the 1840s Lucan began to evict his tenants and combined their holdings to create larger farms around his home at Castlebar, on the wild moors of Mayo.

There was no thought of compensation. The Earl simply evicted his tenants, men and women, children, babes-in-arms, old folk; he threw them onto the streets to starve. Distrustful of the Irish peasants, he brought in Scots farmers to take over the unoccupied land and sent hired gangs of men called 'crowbar gangs' about the country to pull down any hovels his late tenants might have managed to put up for shelter. No one interfered with this action. Indeed, honours were heaped on Lucan's head. In 1840 he became a Representative Peer for Ireland; in 1843 he was restored to the Magistrates Bench. In 1845 he even became the Lord Lieutenant of Mayo, the county he was tearing to pieces.

Ten thousand people were evicted from the Lucan estates alone, and on the 15,000 acres thus cleared, Scots farmers came to till the land and create more acreage where the villages had been levelled and the houses pulled down. There was no work for the local people and the new Scots tenants of Lord Lucan were anyway forbidden to employ them. They had to go, and where they went was not the Earl's concern. Those who could fled to the slums of Britain or

America. Thousands died, of cold or neglect or simply of broken hearts, all the spirit beaten out of them by their harsh treatment.

The curious thing is that Lord Lucan himself saw no wrong in this. The land could not support the people, therefore the people had to go. Where they went, whether they lived or died, was not his business. He was not responsible, he had broken no laws, he was simply protecting his interests. Indeed, he felt somewhat aggrieved that his efforts were not fully appreciated by his peers and fellow countrymen. He was pouring money into his estates, building farms and importing machinery and taking out very little in rents. Indeed, such was the spirit of the time that Lord Lucan's actions were considered almost enlightened. Other landowners simply evicted their tenants and leased the land to anyone with more money and made no improvements at all.

By the mid-1840s then, rural Ireland was a countryside in terror. In every county the hapless peasantry were being hounded from their homes to starve in the open or die in the ditches. They lived where they could and how they could and they kept themselves alive on the potato. Then, in the summer of 1845, the potato crop failed.

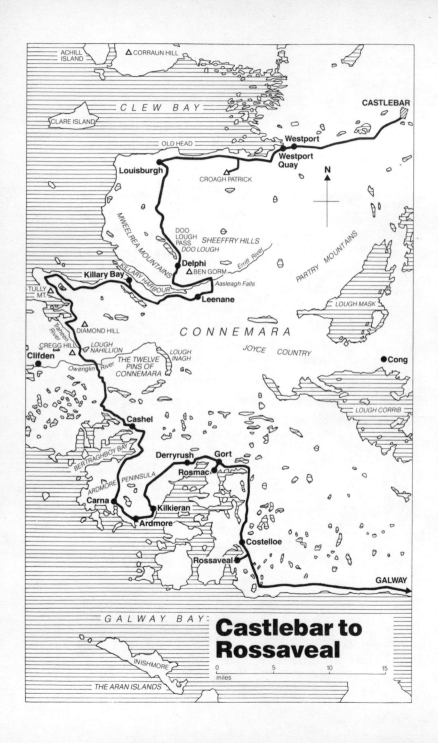

Castlebar to Rossaveal

0   5   10   15
miles

10

Climbing Croagh Patrick

> Above all, young travellers, take my advice and
> never be such a fool as to go up a mountain ...
> I have tried it. Men still ascend eminences and on
> coming down say they have enjoyed it, but they
> lie. Keep you down and have breakfast while the
> rest go up the hill.
>
> William Makepeace Thackeray, 1856

I left Castlebar, on another of those bright and blustery mornings, for the short 12-mile walk down the main road to Westport. I have been rather dismissive about Irish towns so far, so to add a little balance let me say that Westport is a rather pretty town set in splendid country on the shores of Clew Bay. Clew Bay is a vast inlet, a picturesque and beautiful natural harbour, one of the largest on the West Coast, a sheltered anchorage set behind the bulk of Achill Island.

The entrance to the inner bay is protected by another beautiful island, Clare Island, which lies out in the bay off Corraun Hill to the north, while the whole bay is overlooked to the south by the shark-fin peak of Croagh Patrick, the Holy Mountain. The climb up Croagh Patrick is one of the great excursions through Ireland, for this mountain is a place of pilgrimage for the Irish people. The ascent of Croagh Patrick is not an experience any visitor should miss, and it had been listed in my initial itinerary as something I had to do. Now the time had come to do it but the snag, as ever, was the weather.

I needed a good day for my climb up Croagh Patrick and the weather was, well, spasmodic; clouds and rain one minute, sun and wind the next. I was in Westport by noon and by two I was out on the Louisburgh road, looking up at the peak of the mountain. There were people up there on the path, walking up and down the path and creeping up the steep rocky slope to the summit. The clouds had parted and the afternoon, though windy, was bright and clear, so what the hell, I decided to go for it.

As I was to discover, everyone and anyone who can climbs Croagh Patrick, at least if they are Irish. There are a lot of pilgrim sites in Ireland of which the pilgrimage to Knock is the most recent, and the pilgrimage to St Patrick's Purgatory, an island on Lough Derg in Donegal, is the most rigorous. On the Purgatory Pilgrimage the pilgrims have to spend three days barefoot, fasting on the island, and take part in an all-night vigil. This is to reproduce a measure of St Patrick's sufferings, for he fasted on the island for forty days and nights. He did the same on Croagh Patrick, but modern pilgrims get up and down in hours.

The pilgrims to Croagh Patrick today only have to climb a 2,500 ft mountain and say a number of 'Hail Marys' and Creeds at three Stations along the way. Many people climb it barefoot though the path is steep and rough and, for the last hundred metres or so up the sheer scree to the summit, positively dangerous. It would not do to slip up there and the rocks must be cruel to soft feet.

At the top of the mountain is a small chapel where Mass is celebrated every Sunday, and a pilgrim summit cross all hung about with rosaries. As for the reason behind this pilgrimage, it is said that having climbed up here, far above the western shore, St Patrick first prayed and fasted for forty days and nights. Then, at his command, when he rang his bell, all the snakes and venomous creatures in Ireland flung themselves off the southern precipice – the one below the scree. It may be so. The precipice is certainly there and there are no snakes in Ireland. True or false, this story attracts some thirty thousand Irish pilgrims of every age and state of health to climb the mountain on Garland Day, the last Sunday in July. Heaven knows how they all fit on the narrow track to the col and get up that sheer and hazardous slippery slope to the final summit, but somehow they do.

The afternoon seemed fair and after carefully lacing up my boots and stuffing the raingear hurriedly into my rucksack, I grasped my walking stick and set out for the top, jaw set and ready for anything in my stout boots and Rohan jacket. I felt quite heroic. After about 10 yards I passed a lady coming down who said she had taken three hours up and down to the summit. She was wearing knee-high fashion boots with 2-inch heels and carrying a Yorkshire terrier. Some people have no idea.

A lot of Irish mountains are not really mountains at all, at least in the technical sense, but at 2,510 ft, Croagh Patrick is well over the lower mountain limit, and since it rises directly from the seashore you get to enjoy or suffer every inch of it. There are three Pilgrim Stations on the way up, where pilgrims must stop and circle each Station several times reciting the Creed or 'Hail Marys'. About halfway up there is even a substantial stone-built lavatory, presumably to cater for the crowds who arrive on pilgrim days. On this day there were only about fifty people on the mountain, most of them – thank God and St Patrick – more than willing to stop for a chat and a breather while I leaned over my stick and fought for breath. I am really getting too old for this sort of caper, but the views were worth it . . .

For a while the path up Croagh Patrick follows a rushing brook. Then it gets very steep and rocky, climbing up an obvious and well-eroded track about 10 ft wide which leads to the centre col. Here the track turns west and the steep south-east face of the peak comes suddenly into focus. When I got to that point I stopped in my tracks, for the sight before me was awesome.

The peak of Croagh Patrick was a most amazing sight. The summit of Croagh Patrick is a spectacular mountain, soaring up steeply to a rounded shark-fin tip, the rocks glittering white against the blue sky. Seen from the col, it also looked exceedingly hazardous. The scree rises steeply to the summit with no visible path up and nothing to stop you falling all the way to the valley far below if you should happen to slip. On this silver granite scree-slope, looking like so many ants on a pile of sugar, I could see the black specks of people, slowly making their way up and down. I have no great love of heights and this final ascent did not appeal to me at all. However, having come this far I could hardly go back.

I got my breath back trudging across the flat part of the col, and exchanged a few words with an elderly couple who had been to the top for Mass. Then I had a chat with the priest, who climbs this mountain several mornings a week to hold a service at the summit. I wondered if this was some form of penance imposed by his Bishop, but I decided not to ask. Trudging on slowly I was soon on the lower edges of the final slope, trying to find some path to the summit. Since I could not even see the summit and there was this awesome yawning void to my left, I made my way up by climbing gingerly across the jumbled scree towards anyone who I could see on the slope above. One of these was a lady in a yellow anorak, who was sitting on a rock smoking a cigarette.

'How far is it?' I panted, trying not to look down to my left.

She took a few puffs while considering the point. and then waved her hand vaguely over her head. 'Oh, just keep going . . . it's there, it's there. This is my third time up and my last, you know. Enough's enough you know, isn't it?'

I didn't know at all but this question clearly required some comment. 'This is my first time, and my last,' I said. 'I'm getting too old for this sort of thing.'

'Ah well, you see, I have my reasons,' she said, pausing significantly. 'I wouldn't be here otherwise.'

The Irish are like that. Give them half a chance and they settle down for a crack, even on the side of a sheer slope and in the teeth of a howling wind. Did I mention the wind? Sparks were pouring from the lady's cigarette and the wind was trying to tug me off the rock. I didn't like it. Irish winds are strong but when they stop blowing the clouds rush in and the rain comes down. You can't have it both ways.

Later that day I met a man with a little girl in tears, and he told me he had sat her on a wall to take her photograph and the wind had blown her off. I could well believe it. Meanwhile, back on the mountain, the lady was waiting for the question. You only have to play the game a little, so I went first.

'Why is that?' I asked. 'What reason can it be?'

'Well, you see, Himself always wanted a boy. We had the girls but we wanted a boy and I thought I'll try anything. I was that desperate, so we made the pilgrimage to St Patrick last year and sure enough we had boy . . . he's nearly ten months old now.'

'Well done,' I said. What else could I say? At least I was getting my breath back.

'Now then, Himself said we should come up again for Mass, to thank St Patrick . . . well it seemed only fair. So we did . . . we came up in May – the whole family.'

'How many children do you have?' I asked.

'Five. Four girls and now a boy.' She got up off the rock

and began to look about her for a safe way past me. 'He's below in the car with his eldest sister, and I must be away to him. So have a good day, and take care of yourself up here.'

She had gone a few steps when a thought struck me and I had to shout after her. 'You said this is the *third* time ... are you wanting another boy?'

She stopped again with a rattle of scree and edged round to look back up at me. 'God, no! This is to tire the man out ... five children is enough for anyone. He's up there, lying in a heap. You can't miss him. Tell him to hurry along.'

'I see.' Another thought occurred to me. 'And what did you call the boy?'

She gave me one of those great wide Irish grins, her hair blowing wildly about her face. 'Patrick, of course.' she said. 'What else?'

Patrick of course; what else? St Patrick is as much a symbol in himself as the Patron Saint of Ireland, for Ireland is a place where a name can be a statement. In the North, for example, if you meet a man named Pat and another named Billy, you don't need to ask which one is the Catholic and which is the Protestant. St Patrick is a famous man who has done a lot for the unity of the Irish people, and that is good of him because he first came to Ireland as a slave.

We know quite a bit about St Patrick. He was born when Britain was still under the rule of the Roman Empire, some time around 400 AD. When he was about sixteen he was captured by Irish pirates and remained a slave for ten years before he managed to escape to Brittany. Some time during his captivity he got the idea of bringing Christianity to the pagan Irish – or perhaps he just got on well with them – so, after studying theology at Tours and Auxerre, he returned to Ireland as a missionary in 432 AD. The Irish were then devoted to the Druidic religion but the Druids seem to have put up no great resistance to Christianity and the Irish kings were interested.

There were few martyrs here as the new religion spread and by 444 AD St Patrick had founded the first diocese and built the first cathedral at Armagh, a town which is still the centre for the Catholic Church in Ireland. By the time he died in 461 AD the entire country was Christian. The Christian religion was so strongly established in Ireland that it was here, on the western fringe of Europe, that Christianity survived the various pagan invasions which swept away the Roman Empire during the fifth and sixth centuries. Thanks to St Patrick and the Irish monks and saints, clinging on in remote abbeys and on lonely rocks, Christianity survived. Even civilization survived, at least according to Sir Kenneth Clarke, and from Ireland it eventually spread back across the barbarous lands to the East.

The Irish, or Celtic Church, which had by then spread to Scotland and Northumbria, then found itself in dispute with the Church of Rome, most notably over the date of Easter, but after that matter was settled by the Synod of Whitby in 664 AD, the Irish Church slipped under Roman rule and has remained there to this day, the longest serving member of the Christian faith. No wonder the Reformation failed to take root here, and no wonder the Protestants fear the enduring power and influence of the Irish Catholic Church, however unreasonable those fears may be in practice.

Well, enough of this for the moment. Just thinking about St Patrick brought me gasping and panting on a final rush to the summit, though I was overhauled on the last few yards by four fit young men who came swarming up the scree slope like fell-runners. They had, they told me, done it for a bet. One of them, Fergus, was both willing and able to take some photographs with my camera, thus solving one of the main problems of travelling alone – finding someone to take your photo.

I am not particularly vain but a landscape looks better with a figure in it, and I usually ask the people I encounter to take my picture as I pose in a suitably dramatic fashion on some handy crag if only as evidence of effort and to prove that I have actually been there. The trick is to find someone who can operate the aperture and stops, remember to pull back the cocking handle and fiddle with the zoom and the focus, hold the camera straight and not press the trigger with too much force. If I am lucky, about one photo in ten comes out unblurred. Fergus, praise be to St Patrick, knew all about a Nikon's stops and zooms and took some useful snaps.

The views from the summit of Croagh Patrick were simply glorious, though in that wind it seemed wise to stay away from the edge of the drop. The clouds were, as ever, a dramatic backdrop to the scenery but the air itself sparkled, washed clean and bright by the passing rain. I could see the green mass of the Partry Mountains to the south-east, the marvellous greens and blues of Clew Bay far below, and could look across Old Head on the shore to the beckoning bulk of the sharp little hill on Clare Island. Clew Bay is a great litter of small green islands, marvellous to look upon so the five of us sat out of the wind in the lee of the chapel and had a good chat before starting down.

They were students from Dublin, up here for the weekend. They had decided to climb up Croagh Patrick after a few jars in the pub at Westport Quay, and but for running into me they would probably have nipped up and down Croagh Patrick in about 90 minutes. As it was it took us that long just to get down, chatting all the way and picking our way over the scree and the rocks.

My freshly-blistered toes were soon pressing painfully into the front of my boots, and I found it hard to hurry. Even so, I enjoyed coming off the top with these cheerful young men.

The current curse of Ireland lay upon those young men. Not the Ulster Troubles, but unemployment. Ireland has always had a population problem, for the practice of having large families will always mean that a lot of young people will be looking for work. In the past this has been eased, if not solved, by emigration to Britain and America, but the recession of the 1990s is worldwide and severe and unemployment levels in the host countries are currently high. Not quite as high as in Ireland though, where about 20 per cent of the workforce have no jobs or any prospect of jobs.

These four were all well educated, but there was no work for them at home. Therefore, Fergus was leaving for England and another year or so at university, and Patrick was off to South Africa to work for a mining corporation. The other two didn't know what they would do. Their average age was twenty and already life was bleak, but they had that youthful optimism which told them that something would surely turn up.

There was a sadness in this that goes beyond the usual problems of the unemployed. We sat together on the edge of the col, halfway down this dramatic mountain, looking across Clew Bay, blue and beautiful in the evening light. We talked of travel and they asked about some of the places I had seen, but I travel from choice and not necessity, which makes a difference.

The Irish people love Ireland and to leave it, or rather to have to leave it to find work, is a sadness in itself. The lads were up here on the hill today, enjoying themselves like four young men will, sharing jokes, enjoying each other's company. Next year they would be far from home and from each other. No amount of cheerful chat could conceal the fact that having to leave your home and friends is a sad reason for travel.

We got down to the car park in great good humour, having knocked off another of the challenges dotted along my route. There was some talk then of going to the pub, but they had a long drive back across Ireland to Dublin and Irish roads are not the sort you can hurry on. They came roaring past as I was walking into Westport and a great blast on their car horn ushered me into town.

The site of Doo Lough.

The Pins of Connemara.

A mountain-top near Galway.

The coast of Inishmore, Aran Islands.

right: A painted wall in Ballyvaughan.

left: The central roadsign of Ballyvaughan.

A Celtic cross, Kilfenora.

An effigy, the Abbey, Kilfenora.

On the Burren.

above: A dolmen on the Burren.

above: A sight of
the Reeks.

right: The path to
Carrantuohill.

The view from the Devil's Ladder.

The summit of Carrantuohill.

With Mickey Dore the ferryman at Reenard Point.

Journey's end.

11

Walking West

There are few things in the world more delightful than an evening among the mountains and lakes of Connemara. A friend of mine describes the air as like breathing champagne.

Harriet Martineau,
Letters from Ireland, 1852

It was quite late in the evening when I got back to Westport and I had to hurry because I had an appointment in the bar of the Clew Bay Hotel with one of the local heroes, Matt Molloy.

Matt is a famous chap in Westport, partly because he and his wife own the 'Matt Molloy's' pub in the main street, but mostly because Matt is a member of Ireland's leading folk group, The Chieftains. I had brought along a tape recorder to make a programme on my walk for the BBC, and since Irish pubs and Irish music are a great part of Irish life, they can hardly be excluded, and few pubs in Ireland are livelier than Matt Molloy's on a Saturday night. I also thought that an interview with a celebrity would suit the producer very nicely. I forgot to remember that I am not very good at names. In fact I am bloody awful at names.

Matt Molloy is a most amiable, unpretentious and long-suffering fellow, so we got a glass or two and retired with the tape recorder to a quiet corner of the bar. We were about five minutes into the interview when he could stand it no longer. Then he leaned forward and tapped me on the knee.

'Rob ... er ... my name's Matt.'

'Yes? So ...?'

'Well, it's just that you keep calling me Mac ... and my name's not Mac, it's Matt.'

'Oh ... sorry – er – Matt. Let's see ... can we start again?'

'And, another thing, Rob ... I don't play the guitar.'

'You don't?' Somehow or other I had the idea that all folk singers played the guitar, but Matt soon punctured that belief.

'I have never played the guitar,' he said. 'I play the flute. I wouldn't mention it, but you keep asking about how I learned to play the guitar, y'see ....'

'Oh dear ... silly me. Sorry ... er ... Matt. Can we go again?'

'Of course ... of course.'

Sounds of tape rewinding, controls clicking, cassette ejecting, foul language, throat clearing, etc ... and then ... 'Well,' I began brightly, 'I am sitting with Mick Molloy of The Chieftains in the small Irish town of ... sorry, Matt ... but where the hell are we?'

Matt has lived in Westport for several years, where his wife runs their large and flourishing pub and holds the fort while he is off touring with The Chieftains. Their pub is a real pub, with food and music and a good 'crack' always available, and mercifully without such modern gimmicks as slot-machines and piped music.

'What would we want a slot-machine for? It would only cost money better spent on Guinness, and if they want music we have that from about nine or ten every evening. We have some good local musicians and anyone can sit in and play – if they're not actually quite awful that is.'

'And do you play there yourself, Matt?'

'I do, yes, of course. It keeps me from working behind the bar. I draw the line at that.'

Irish music is a feature of most Irish pubs, certainly in the countryside. The Irish are a very musical people and produce a great many skilful musicians, enough to provide most of the country pubs with a resident group. The basic instruments are the fiddle and the flute and the accordion and concertina, backed up by the *bodhran*, which is a shallow drum not unlike a tambourine, with goatskin on one side and played with a small drumstick. The harp which, with the shamrock, is a great symbol of Ireland, is apparently quite popular but I never saw one. Folk groups, however, can be heard everywhere, playing away for hours every evening if provided periodically with glasses of Guinness. The music tends to be of the lilting repetitive kind that jogs along in a heartwarming way, and it adds a great touch of gaiety to any evening in the Irish countryside, broken up with singing.

The singing, on the other hand, tends to be doleful. Most of the songs concern people who are dead or drowned or gone away, and there is always the danger that the stranger will be asked to join in a chorus or even get up and entertain the company with a song of his own.

The only small danger in Irish pubs is the drunks. Irish drunks are Irishmen writ very large and very friendly, but it can make life difficult if you are trying to record some conversation and your interviewee says, 'Fuck', or is that 'Fook', every couple of minutes. The F-word is the most popular expletive in Ireland, where everyone swears like a trooper and you can't blame that on the Guinness.

I can't say I don't like Guinness because I have never tried it, but if the Irish need lubrication, Guinness fits the bill. I suspect that half the attraction of a pint of Guinness is the ritual that goes with it. Just to begin with, you don't pour a pint of Guinness, you 'build it', pouring in more of the dark brown nectar as the white foam collar creeps slowly up the glass. This can take ages, so committed Guinness drinkers will order their 'pints of plain' well ahead, like a special dish on a fancy menu. Then everyone sits around with foam on their upper lips, telling each other how Shamus or Eamon pulls the best pint of plain in town.

Westport is a very fine little town and, unlike most Irish towns, quite pretty. The Carrowbeg river flows through the town centre and under a couple of bridges along a tree-lined promenade known as the Mall. The Mall is endowed with a bronze bust of the Major John MacBride of the IRA, who was shot for his part in the Easter Rising of 1916, another significant event in Irish history which we might now consider.

It will be recalled that when the Home Rule Bill was finally passed in 1914, the implementation of the Act was deferred until the Great War ended. This deferment found no favour with a number of Irish politicians and by 1916, with no end to the war in sight, some leaders of the Irish Volunteers, including Patrick Pearse, Joseph Plunkett, John MacBride, James Connolly and Tom Clarke, great names now in Irish history, decided to implement the Act immediately. They also went not just for Home Rule but for the full Republican States. Another Irish patriot, and incidentally a Protestant, Sir Roger Casement, was then in Germany arranging for a shipment of arms, and a plan was struck to seize Dublin and declare the Irish Republic, on Easter Monday 1916.

It all went terribly wrong. Erin MacNeill, the actual Commander of the Irish – or Southern – Volunteers, the

South's answer to Carson's Protestant Ulster Volunteers, was not informed but got wind of the Rising and put notices in the paper cancelling any 'manoeuvre' planned for the Easter weekend. Sir Roger Casement was captured almost as soon as he set foot in Ireland and the shipment of essential arms never reached Dublin.

Even so, the Rising went ahead. By Monday morning the Volunteers had captured all the important buildings in Dublin and set up their HQ in the General Post Office. They then fired on a cavalry patrol, and fighting gradually spread across the city. The British Army promptly moved in and during five days of fighting the heart of Dublin was severely damaged. Artillery was deployed in the city streets and Royal Navy gunboats sailed up the Liffey to bombard the General Post Office.

On the Friday, Patrick Pearse surrendered at the General Post Office and the other strongpoints fell shortly afterwards. The defenders then discovered, much to their surprise, that their actions met with the general disapproval of the Dublin citizens. Most of the Irish people saw the Rising as a blow against Home Rule and, even worse, as a betrayal of those Irishmen then fighting Germany on the Western Front. This disapproval disappeared when the British Military gave sixteen of the leaders, Pearse, MacBride and the rest, a rapid court martial and had them all shot. The wave of sympathy for these men has never quite died away. When the Republican political party, Sinn Fein, put up candidates for the 'Khaki Election' of 1918, they swept the board.

John MacBride, the husband of Yeats' unrequited love, Maud Gonne, whose bronze bust glares out defiantly at passers by along the Westport Mall was rather unlucky to be shot. He had only taken a minor part in the Easter Rising, but he had fought on the side of the Boers against the British during the South African War and that was enough to tilt the balance against him. As for the executions, they were, as so often happens, rather more than a crime. They were a serious political blunder. They turned the thoughts of the Irish people away from the actions of the conspirators, actions which had led to the destruction of the centre of Dublin, and onto what was seen at the time, and since, as a brutal act of repression and intimidation by an occupying power. The plot against the Government in time of war has long since been forgotten; the shooting of the patriots will always be remembered.

The conspirators knew the risks they were taking. They had raised rebellion and allied themselves with Germany, an enemy power, at a time when tens of thousands of their fellow countrymen were fighting that enemy in France. Even so, when tempers cooled, most of the other rebels were quietly released and it would have been much better for Ireland and England if the main conspirators had simply been detained until the war ended and then released in their turn. As Churchill was to remark, 'The grass never grows on the scaffold site,' and this was certainly the case in Ireland where wrongs inflicted, though forgiven, are never forgotten.

I had another good day in pretty Westport, a fine little town with a lot of Georgian buildings, though I didn't actually do much. I mooched about the shops, ate lunch, had a few beers, read a book on a seat by the river when the sun was out, and generally rested up after that hard day shinning up Croagh Patrick. Next day though, I was off again, heading west along the coast for the wild country of Connemara.

On every journey I have ever undertaken, there is one place, one part of the country, that remains in my mind as superior to any other. Thinking of other journeys I can remember the volcanic hills of the Auvergne, of the pilgrim town of Guadaloupe in Extremadura, of the golden deserts in Syria north of Damascus, of the tiny but beautiful

Waterton Park in Southern Alberta, as places which remain in my memory when the rest of these journeys have become little more than a blur. On this journey through Ireland the one place that matches or exceeds any of these is the beautiful lake and mountain country of Connemara.

Summer was getting well into its stride as I came to Connemara. The first purple flush of heather was beginning to appear on the hillsides, the gorse was flaring in the hollows out of the wind, and the lanes were heavy with drooping fuchsia and the bright orange montbretia. Even the bogs were looking their best with a thatch of golden grass covering each one like a blanket. All this stood out against a lush emerald-green backcloth and the loom of purple mountains. But for all that, Connemara is a gradual land, a place that steals up on you. It was only after a few days, as I was sitting late one afternoon on a wet hillside somewhere south of the Twelve Pins, that I suddenly said aloud, 'This-is-bloody-marvellous,' and marvellous it is.

I run ahead of myself; first I had to get to Connemara, and that took a day or two. Part of the attraction here in the West of Ireland is the desolation, and the road to Connemara is almost empty of people. I passed a hundred ruined cottages and picked my way through a dozen empty, roofless hamlets as I made my way south to Galway Bay. The Hunger had come this way and taken the people with it.

I made good time along the coast road from Westport past Old Head on another breezy morning, looking up to cloud-capped Croagh Patrick. The road rolls gently up and down beside the sea and leads on to Louisburgh, a pretty little town, or large village of the West, which was once notorious as the home of the 16th-century Pirate Queen, Grace O'Malley, who became a friend and confidant of Queen Elizabeth I.

Grace O'Malley, or Grainne Uaile, is an interesting

woman. Out here in the West of Ireland she kept her own estate as Chieftain of the Western Isles and successfully ignored the English rule for decades. She built a castle out on Clare Island and kept a fleet of ships in the bay to do her bidding, which meant preying on English shipping. If she needed laws she had the old Irish law – the Celtic 'Brèhon' law – to fall back on. This was a code of ethics, very suitable to Irish life, for it was based not on the edicts of a central power but on the wishes and needs of the community and the family. It covered sanctions against the fostering of disorder and made provision for the settling of disputes by arbitration, all of which seems very sensible. It also permitted divorce at will; Henry VIII would have greatly enjoyed the tenets of the Brèhon laws. Grace O'Malley married several times and usually managed to retain the joint property after divorcing her husbands. Women held a high status under the Brèhon laws and this gave Grace enough confidence to deal as an equal with the imperious English Queen, Elizabeth I, when the Queen complained about the O'Malley pirates.

Anyway, Elizabeth knew a bit about pirates; her favourite sailors, Drake and Hawkins and the rest, were little better than pirates, and slavers to boot when they got the chance. Grace O'Malley's castle at Louisburgh is now in ruins, but the tale goes that after years of feuding, seizing English ships and pursuit by English admirals, Grace eventually sailed up the Thames to parley with the Queen at Westminster. They struck a deal, by which Grace would hunt down pirates off the coast of Clare as the price for keeping her lands. Grace is buried at the abbey on Clare Island but her castle in Louisburgh still does duty as the Gardai Station. I stayed a night in Louisburgh before setting off across the moors for Leenane at the head of Killary harbour.

My view south to the Twelve Pins of Connemara from the top of Croagh Patrick had been blocked by other mountains, by the Mweelrea Mountains to the south and west, and the Sheeffry hills which lie directly south, across the twinkling, waterlogged plain of North Mayo. Away to the east the Partry Mountains blocked the skyline and south of there lay the Joyce Country between Leenane. This is a region of great beauty, but not an easy one to cross, being barred by hill and mountain, river and stream, dotted with lakes and carpeted with blanket bog. As before, I tried a little trek across the squelching moor and returned damply to the road after half an hour.

That left a choice of routes. Both were on roads offering splendid views and fairly empty country, and both led down to Galway Bay, which marks the southern limits of Connemara, which may be roughly defined today as North Galway.

While I was studying the map and brooding over which way to go, I noticed how this part of Ireland, the land between, say, Castlebar in the north and the city of Galway on the great bay, is virtually an island. To the west lies the Atlantic Coast, and beyond that, America, while to the east all the roads and all the rest of Ireland is barred by two great long loughs, Lough Mask which lies north of Coney and Lough Corrib which lies north of Galway City.

In the 17th century these two loughs and their tributary rivers at first protected Connemara from the full fetch of the Cromwellian invasion, and they still protect this part of Ireland from the debilitating effect of the English language. Over here, in the West of Ireland, lies the 'Gaeltacht' – the land of the Gael – where Irish, or Erse, is still, though only just, the common tongue of the country people. The Celts came to Ireland in the 7th century BC and spread out from there to establish Celtic communities in the western parts of England and Scotland, where Welsh, Cornish and Scots Gaelic had their roots in the Celtic tongue.

Elizabeth I and her successors, right down to Cromwell,

made strenuous efforts to stamp out the Irish tongue, though without the success currently enjoyed by radio and television today. Irish, or Erse, was adopted as the national language after Independence in 1921, but without any great success. The best current estimate is that fewer than 100,000 Irish people still use Irish at home or socially, but strenuous efforts are being made to teach the language in schools and to use it in public on signs and documents. Where the language does hang on is out here in the West, where many of the people are descendants of those who were forced to flee here in the 17th century when the stark choice before them was flight or death, to 'Hell or Connaught'.

Oliver Cromwell, Lord Protector of England from 1649–1660, was a man of war. Cromwell was probably the most implacable general who ever bore arms. That he was a military genius is undisputed, but he lacked common humanity and his military talents were bolstered by his unswerving belief in both the Parliamentary cause and the Puritan religion. After Cromwell had defeated and beheaded King Charles I, he turned his attention to the rebellious Catholics of Ireland. By 1649 the English had spent 500 years trying to cow the Irish people without success. Cromwell had a more radical solution. He decided to remove them altogether.

It will be recalled that at the end of the previous century, during the Tudor 'planting' period, the native Gael had already been driven off the best land in Ulster and the east of Ireland. The 'plantings' were extensive, especially in the counties of Donegal, Armagh and Antrim, where the native Irish had been largely replaced by English or Scots settlers by the end of the 16th century. In September 1641, the dispossessed Irish peasants rose against their oppressors, first forming a league known as the Confederation of Kilkenny.

By 1641 the bulk of the 'settlers' were in Ulster and most

of them were Scots Presbyterians. Most of their tenants or peasant workers were Irish Catholics, the former owners of this land and the fuse for their rebellion only needed a match. The Protestants were greatly outnumbered by the Catholics, and when the 1641 rebellion began they were quickly overwhelmed. There were, inevitably, atrocities, even by the brutal standards of the day. The best re-membered Catholic outrage against the Protestants took place in November 1641, on the bridge at Portadown in Ulster, when 100 Protestants, men, women and children, were hanged from the parapet, flung into the river to drown, or had their brains dashed out as they swam ashore. The Protestants of Ulster still remember this.

The 'Confederation' of Kilkenny had the limited aim of repossessing the 'planted lands', but their confrontation with the current landowners and the subsequent fighting and massacres eventually sucked the Irish Confederates into the English Civil War. Irish troops went to the aid of King Charles and played a major part in all the King's battles, even though Irish soldiers captured by the Parliamentarians were routinely shot. In August 1649, seven months after the King's execution, Cromwell arrived in Ireland. What fol-lowed was so devastating that '*Mallacht Cromail*' – the Curse of Cromwell – is an Irish imprecation to this day.

The litany of English oppression in Ireland rolls on down the centuries, but few acts were so savage and unnecessary as the assault and sacking of Drogheda, with which Crom-well opened his campaign. Drogheda lies in the Boyne Valley, well within the Dublin Pale and the citizens had played no part in the Confederation of Kilkenny. Never-theless, when the town fell to Cromwell's forces, everyone inside was slaughtered or imprisoned.

Those men of the Drogheda garrison who survived the assault were shipped off to slavery in the Barbados but the bulk of the citizens, men, women, children, were simply put to the sword. Irish men and women died by the thousand in the sack of Drogheda while the English losses were just sixty-four men. A few weeks later a similar butchery was perpetuated against the innocent Catholic people of Kilkenny.

By 1652 all Ireland not yet in ruins lay at Cromwell's feet, but he had still not finished with the Irish people. They were hunted across the moors and bogs like wild beasts, or deported or hanged or shot or beaten. Amnesty was eventually granted to Irish men of military age if they left Ireland for ever. Those who chose to remain were to be driven out of their homes and harried west beyond the Shannon into the stark boglands of Connaught – to the present Mayo and Connemara – where they must fend for themselves or starve.

Even today, walking south from the Sheffrey Hills, it is hard to see how anyone can make a living here. The land is stony, the fields small, the soil scanty. Only sheep and goats can survive here and the land is virtually empty of people. Their former lands were taken and sold to pay the cost of Cromwell's campaign, or given to Puritan veterans as a reward for their services.

Legal form was later given to these atrocities by William of Orange. In 1695 he passed a series of 'Penal Laws', all designed to further harry and persecute the Irish people. These were enacted by the newly-established Irish Parliament in Dublin, a totally Protestant assembly, but aimed solely at the Catholic community.

Catholics were denied rights of assembly or schooling. They could not hold any public office, or serve in the Army, or hold land on a lease of more than thirty years. If a Catholic died his land had to be divided among all his children, unless one of them turned Protestant, in which case he inherited everything. This repression had a continuing effect and by the end of the 18th century less than 5 per cent of the land in Ireland belonged to Catholics. An Irishman could not own a horse worth more than £5. If a Protestant offered him more than that for his beast, the Catholic had to sell it. These laws were not fully repealed until 1829, and even if most of them slowly fell out of use, they remained a thorn in the side of the Irish people.

There was nothing hole-in-the-corner about the forced migration of the Irish people in the 1650s. The usual excuse for an atrocity, that no one knew anything about it, just won't wash. In 1653 an Act was promulgated at Westminster 'For the speedy satisfaction of the Adventurers of Ireland and for Arrears due to the Soldiery and for the Encouragement of the Protestants to Plant and Inhabit Ireland.' What was happening to the Irish people was done with the knowledge and consent of the Westminster Parliament.

The first basic requirement was to drive the entire population west of the Shannon where, said the Act, 'Connaught and Clare shall be set aside for the habitants of the Irish nation to which they must transplant themselves with their wives, children and such servants as will go with them before May 1st 1654.' This order was directed at Irish tenants and landlords but more specifically at anyone who had fought or aided and abetted the Catholics in the recent struggle against the Parliamentary forces. Those peasants without land, or with property valued at £10 or less could either go beyond the Shannon with their masters or remain as servants of the new landlords.

This order sent a wave of fear across Ireland. To comply meant that the migration had to be completed during the six months of winter and there was nowhere in Clare or Connaught for the people to go. There were no huts or habitations, no towns or villages, no shelter of any kind. The people could stay and die or go and starve. Nobody cared, one way or the other Connaught was, and is, the most unfertile of all the Irish provinces. Its present beauty cannot conceal the fact that it still provides a very thin living for the local farmers. Even so, the transplanting of the people went ahead.

Property, houses, barns, crops and cattle, were all confiscated. The people were driven off their own land and herded west like cattle, driven out by the soldiers. Those who resisted were killed or imprisoned and then sent into bondage to the Barbados. It was even a crime for a native Irishman to be found inside the walls of cities like Dublin and Cork.

To be fair, all this was not done without some opposition from liberal Englishmen. A number of Puritans and Parliamentarians argued that not only was it inhuman to transplant the entire Irish population, it was also, in practical terms, impossible. Moreover, they argued, even if it could be done, surely it would only result in a large and hostile population being established just beyond the frontiers of the fertile land, which was what the English hoped to avoid. By 1655 public feeling in England was just swinging against the transplantings when there came the news of Catholic massacres in the Duchy of Savoie, and popular feeling swung the other way. The Irish had to go 'to hell or Connaught'. In June 1658, the Venetian Ambassador to England wrote to the Doge: 'This Government has one object, to root out the Catholic faith from Ireland and instal Protestants in every part of it.'

The Government almost succeeded. The great exodus to the West began, and long lines of refugees were soon filing along the muddy tracks across the Shannon Valley. Where were they to go? It was said at the time that in County Clare there were not '... trees enough to hang a man, water to drown him, or earth to bury him.' So it was, but so it went on. Although many of the Irish people slipped back to the East, or fled abroad or emigrated to Spain or the Americas, the Cromwellian transplantations were added to the long list of Irish grievances.

When Charles II returned to the Throne of England in 1660, the Irish people hoped that he would review the Cromwellian edicts and reward their constant loyalty, but they were to be disappointed. Charles stood in too much need of Parliamentary support to spare a thought for his father's Irish allies. James II scarcely stayed on the Throne long enough to make any difference and his successor, William of Orange – King Billy – was no friend to the Catholics. As for the people who took that trail of tears to Connaught, they simply vanished. Some, perhaps most of them, eventually filtered back across the Shannon, but tens of thousands simply disappeared, swallowed up in the moors and mists of this beautiful, desolate and tragic countryside.

12

Crossing Connemara

I don't know how it is but the men and the landscapes seem to be one and the same, ragged, ruined and cheerful.

William Makepeace Thackeray, 1842

From Louisburgh it is a good day's walk south to Leenane, a small fishing port at the end of Killary Harbour. Killary Harbour is really just a 10-mile long inlet off the West Coast with a few curraghs, the traditional Irish punts or canoes, drawn up on the pebble strand. I walked south to Leenane by the pass through the Sheffry Hills and the Mweelrea Mountains, past Lough Doo and Delphi. When I reached the harbour, I swung inland, up to the head of the sea lough to where the River Erriff comes spilling into the sea over the Aasleagh Falls.

This is a spectacular route and stunningly beautiful, with tall emerald-green mountains rearing up ahead and the road rising and falling towards them across a golden-yellow open moor littered with small lakes and streams. I walked south towards the Pass for most of the morning, undisturbed by the few cars swishing past, and the mountains grew steadily closer. These are real mountains, tall and jagged, lush-green from the rain-nourished moss but thickly dotted with sheep. To say that the setting is stunning is to state the obvious; nowhere I had reached so far could match this place for beauty. So, gaping about me, I entered the Doo Lough Pass.

About halfway down the Pass, a small stone beside the road marks the site of the Doo Lough tragedy of 1845, when a whole community was wiped out and dispersed by the Famine. No one lives here now in this great glen between the mountains, and nothing moves on the hillsides but the grazing sheep. If Ireland does not have a Glencoe, then this Pass by Doo Lake is the nearest I came to one. Most of this desolation can be traced back to that wet summer of 1845, when the potato crop finally failed.

Even today the Irish eat a lot of potatoes. Not for nothing are the members of Ireland's largest clan, the Murphys, usually nicknamed 'Spud'. The potato tuber was brought to Ireland in the 16th century by Sir Walter Raleigh, who had large estates here, and in that mild climate and fertile soil the potato flourished. The potato suited the Irish people in many ways. The potato does not require a lot of labour and when mixed with milk and bran it can provide an acceptable diet. Such a diet is not adequate, but the Irish peasants, if malnourished, could still survive. With his subsistence thus taken care of, the peasant could grow other crops to pay his rent. So it developed, the potato for subsistence, other crops for a little money to pay the rent. Then in 1845 the potato crop failed and starvation began to stalk this beautiful land in earnest.

The cause of the crop failure was a blight caused by a fungus, *phystophthora infestans*. This blight had struck the potato crop before but in 1845, and then year after year until 1849, the crop failure was total. In those four years the population of Ireland fell by 2 million people, about 25 per cent. The Great Hunger of 1845–49 was a Celtic Holocaust.

Previous blights and recurrent food shortages should have revealed to those in authority how fragile was Ireland's food supplies. The country people lived solely on the potato and what other crops they could grow had to be sold to pay their rent. They could not eat their cash crops because if they could not pay the rent they were turned out to starve. Even if they had money there was nothing to buy. Anyway, work for wages was virtually unknown in Ireland. Most of the small holdings in the south and west had no need of labour beyond that supplied by the peasant and his family. This was subsistence farming at the most basic level, with no margin for catastrophe at all.

Outside the main towns there were few roads, no system of distribution, no shops. Even in a good year the country people lived on the edge of famine. 'There never was a place,' wrote the Duke of Wellington in 1843, 'in which poverty ever existed to the extent that it exists in Ireland.' The Duke of Wellington was himself an Irishman and a man of great influence in British affairs, but there is little evidence that he did much to help his fellow countrymen when disaster struck in 1845.

The potato blight was first reported in America in 1844. In Ireland in 1845 the first indications for the potato harvest promised a most abundant crop, but when the first potatoes were dug in September 1845 it was soon evident that the blight had arrived there too. Potatoes were dug up rotten and stinking, or rotted away swiftly after being dug, sinking swiftly into a black mess of corruption. Reports of this disaster began to pour into England, but little was done to anticipate the catastrophe that such an event must mean. The Prime Minister, Sir Robert Peel, replied to the news with the dismissive opinion that the Irish always had a tendency to exaggerate. By the winter of 1845 half the population of Ireland were starving and that was no exaggeration at all. Before long famine was wiping out whole families and entire communities.

Accounts written at the time, many of them published in English newspapers, make horrifying reading. Mr Cummings, a Cork magistrate, wrote to *The Times* in December 1846:

> On entering a deserted hamlet I went into some hovels to discover the cause. The scenes presented cannot adequately be described. In the first, six famished ghastly skeletons were huddled in a corner, four children, a woman, and what had been a man. All had fever. Within minutes in that village I was surrounded by at least 200 such phantoms. My clothes were nearly torn off by this throng and in a nearby house the police found two frozen corpses, half devoured by rats. In a field lay the body of a girl of 12, dead of starvation, half covered by stones.

The streets of Westport were '... crowded with gaunt wanderers', those of Galway '... full of walking skeletons, the children crying with the pain of hunger, the women too weak to stand.'

The Inspecting Officer in County Clare wrote in his report:

> I am not a man easily moved but I find myself shaken by the extent of the suffering I have to witness, especially among the women and little children, who scatter across the turnip field like a flock of famished crows, the women half-naked and shivering in the streets, their children screaming with hunger. I can handle anything else but this I cannot stand, so when may we look for relief?

* * *

Relief measures were put in train but too little, too late, and for too short a time. When the facts began to emerge in Britain there was a wave of public sympathy for the Irish people and large sums of money were swiftly raised for the relief. The first contributor was Queen Victoria who gave the then huge sum of £2,000, and her gift was followed by large sums from the Rothschilds and the City. Shiploads of Indian corn were sent across to replace the potato, soup kitchens set up, work on the roads for wages was offered, accommodation in workhouses was provided for the destitute. None of this did more than scratch the surface of the problem, for nobody but a few officials actually working in Ireland seemed to grasp the full extent of the tragedy.

Charity did little to alleviate the suffering. The Government was reluctant to spend the vast sums required and such aid as was sent was periodically cut off. In spite of pleas by the administrators that starving people were dying in the streets and must be fed, distribution of corn was also restricted. The Government was reluctant to spend public money and even more reluctant to take any action which might undermine the Corn Laws and the price of grain. The litany of reported horrors from Ireland rivals anything produced a century later at Belsen or Dachau. There were authenticated tales and confused reports of cannibalism, of children dying in the streets or being eaten by rats, of boatloads of skeletons rowing out to vessels off Killary, begging for food.

The Killaries, which lie south and west of Doo Lough, were particularly hard hit. In June 1845, the revenue cutter *Eliza* encountered a boatload of starving people drifting off Killary harbour. One man, reported the Captain, was lying in the bottom of the boat unable to stand, while all the others were skin and bone and staring eyeballs, in an advanced state of starvation. Coastguards taking vessels to

Clifden and the Killaries reported people dying in the streets from '... a total absence of food.' Requests for food to feed these people were rejected as 'irritating' by Mr Lister, who was responsible for the County Commissariat at Westport.

Underpinning this latest tragedy was the fact that while the potato blight was nobody's fault, the resultant suffering and the lack of resources to ease it, was aggravated by centuries of neglect and indifference both to the state of Ireland and the Irish people. Even where the sufferings were recognized, little was or could be done to help because the country was without the necessary infrastructure. The roads, the railways, the methods of distribution to get food out to where it was needed, simply did not exist. Whole communities, like the one here at Doo Lough, just disappeared.

The landlords did little to help. Since the peasants had nothing to eat but their cash crops, they could not pay their rents. Some landlords certainly remitted the rents or allowed their tenants more time to pay. Others – a few – went even further and spent their own money lavishly to help their tenants survive. Many more, perhaps the majority, simply proceeded as before. When their rents were not paid they threw their tenants into the streets. Even this did not unduly disturb the Government.

Lord Brougham, speaking in the House of Lords, said:

> It is the landlord's right to do as he pleases. If he abstains from exercising his right he confers a favour and an act of kindness. Otherwise tenants must be taught the law of the land. Property would be valueless and capital would not be invested in cultivation if the landlord were not allowed to do what he wants.

The callous arrogance of this speech is breathtaking.

So, while the Irish starved the evictions continued. In March 1846, 300 starving people were evicted from their homes at Ballinglass in Galway so that their fields could be consolidated into a farm. This action was carried out by the Police and the Army, though it is reported that the soldiers from the 72nd Highlanders were disgusted and gave the people money.

Even where food could be found, prices were high and the people had no money. Those who could get away emigrated in search of work, but by 1846 another scourge had appeared; typhus. The emaciated men and women arriving at English ports brought with them a deadly fever which thrived in the crowded tenements where they were forced to live and the Irish were now on the move in considerable numbers. Over 300,000 arrived at Liverpool alone in the first five months of 1846, at a time when the resident population of Liverpool was less than 250,000 people.

Before long, Irish immigrant ships and ferries were being turned away from British ports. Tens of thousands more took flight across the Atlantic to Canada and the USA, sometimes in ships so ill-found and leaky that they became known as coffin ships. The passengers had to provide their own food and when this ran out, as it frequently did, starvation occurred. Voyages took months rather than weeks and the ill-nourished people were in no state to survive such privation.

Even worse was a shortage of water. Bloody battles took place on the broad Atlantic as thirst-crazed passengers fought the crew to get at the water butts. Shiploads of emaciated and destitute people crawled into ports along the Eastern seaboard to horrify the American and Canadian people.

Here too, many immigrants were already stricken with typhus, so quarantine stations were set up in New York and Boston and along the St Lawrence river where the immigrants had to remain while the fever ran its course. Thousands died before it did so, and for fear of the disease spreading the local people were reluctant to help.

In the spring of 1847 at Grosse Island, the quarantine station near Quebec, there was talk of 'an avalanche of diseased and dying people' in numbers far beyond the capability of the doctors sent to help. By the time the quarantine station here closed six months later in October 1847, over 5,000 people had died.

It was not just the famine and disease that ravaged the Irish people. It was the total lack of care or kindness. People who should have helped, who had the duty of helping, did nothing, or as little as possible. What little they did they did with great reluctance. That many hundreds of people, officials, charity workers, landlords, people of goodwill in many lands did help cannot be disputed, but the Government of Britain, to which Ireland was joined by the 1800 Act of Union, was either indifferent or reluctant to face the multiplying problems in Ireland.

When the figures were added together later it was estimated that at least a million Irish people died of disease or starvation during the Famine years of 1845–49. This must be an underestimate because thousands of deaths were never recorded. People died on the roads or in the fields and rotted away in the bogs or ditches. On the far West Coast whole communities simply disappeared.

Another million people fled abroad, taking with them hard thoughts about the British Government and people who had let their families and neighbours perish. The deep hostility towards Britain still found today in the Irish communities of America and Australia can be traced in large part to the Hungry Years of the 1840s.

* * *

My word, this is a sad tale. Though it must be told and is best told here, for many of the horrors took place hereabouts, I have to add that the land through which I was now passing, through the great Pass to Leenane and Killary, is simply beautiful. After Doo Lough comes Delphi at the southern end of the Pass, an unlikely name in such a setting, a pretty spot with a salmon fishery. After that the road winds between the Mweelrea mountains and Ben Gorm, a 2,303 ft high peak along the Bundaraggah river to the sea lough of Killary Harbour. Here I turned east for Leenane. The road is set well above the sea and there was a seal in the water here, dipping and diving for fish along the shore.

The road takes a hairpin bend round to Leenane, past the wide overspill of the Aasleagh Falls, which mark the point where the Erriff river flows out into the sea. Here is another pretty spot, the river dotted with fishermen winding away into the backdrop of green hills. I had come about 20 miles that day, through a beautiful part of Ireland, and now I needed a drink. I therefore came to a halt at the Rock Café for a much needed pot of tea and a few scones.

The Rock Café is one of those Irish places where you can, within limits, get anything from a glass of beer to tractor parts. The local priest was in there, drinking Guinness and playing dominoes, and while I was drinking my tea two farmers drove up with tractor and trailer. The latter contained a large black-faced ram, which whiled away the wait by butting his head noisily against the door of the trailer, clearly impatient to get in among the ewes for a hard day's tupping. Periodic thuds and crashes from the car park therefore played counterpart to my conversation with the farmers as we sat at the bar and drank some tots of Paddy, the local Irish whiskey mixed with hot water, sugar, lemon and cloves, into a toddy, a fine drink on a bright, soft day like this.

'That's a fine ram,' I offered as an opener. 'Are you taking him up to the hill, and would you gentlemen care for a drink, just to keep the cold out?'

'We are, we are,' they agreed. 'And we will, we will . . . very kind of you.'

'What sort of sheep do you run here?' I asked. The green hills of Connemara are full of sheep, which are dotted over the moors or run or rest along the roadsides, or cover the mountains all the way up to the crests, so I was interested to know where they came from.

'We keep Scots Blackface . . . they're very hardy, and you can leave them on the hill whatever the weather.'

'Well, almost,' said the other. 'Unless we have the snow, but we don't have the snow very often.'

'You are not from these parts?' asked the first farmer, signalling the bar-lady for another round of the hard stuff.

'No . . . I'm over from England. Just here for a walk . . . a little holiday.'

I had given up telling people I was walking across Ireland. The Irish are great leg-pullers and most of them would not have believed me anyway. Walkers in the short term they are familiar with, though most of the ones I met were simply hitch-hiking. Besides, it was my origins rather than my purpose which interested the farmers.

'England, is it?' they marvelled. England was a remote place, somewhere men vanished to and never returned, but I gathered that English visitors were rare hereabouts. 'Whereabouts in England is it?'

'Near London.'

'London, is it?' They thought about that for a moment, nodding the idea through before one of them asked, 'Do you keep sheep yourself?'

Did I look as if I kept sheep? Glancing in the mirror behind the bar I took in this wild-haired, wet fellow staring back at me, so yes, probably I did look as if I kept sheep. It was a little hard to explain that sheep-rearing is not a major occupation in London, though I can remember sheep grazing in Hyde Park during the war. I got around that difficulty by discussing the matter of my lamb back on the Sperrin road in Ulster and the price I had been asked for it.

This interested everyone and the bar became animated. The price was difficult; my newfound farmer friends became very cautious over the price. Did I know if it was a ewe lamb or a ram lamb? Well, since I didn't know that, they couldn't tell if it was a fair price or not, and since I didn't have the lamb with me it was even more difficult. However, there was no money in the sheep these days, so I was better off without it. We all agreed on that.

We had another round of Paddy while we thought about sheep, then more thuds and crashes from the ram outside in the trailer reminded them they had to be off. There were some handshakes before they took the ram a-tupping and I went off to find a bed. The fine weather of the morning was breaking up now with great grey rainstorms rushing in from the Atlantic, and I had come quite far enough for the moment.

I walked the last mile or two into Leenane – or Leenaune an Lionan as it is called on my topographic map – and had no trouble finding a B & B. This is a quiet part of Ireland, a place for visiting fishermen and local farmers. The tourists come by in coaches or on bicycles, but they don't seem to stop. By five o'clock Leenane was deserted, silent and peaceful. Later that evening I wandered alone along the foreshore among the black, tarred curraghs, looking out in vain for the seals.

At Leenane I had another of those hard choices. Should I go east to the Joyce Country or out to the West Coast and the town of Clifden, 20 miles away. I had heard that Clifden was a pretty place and as this is the principal town of Connemara I ought to go there. The other choice was to forge directly south across the Twelve Pins to Cashel and Galway. I brooded on the decision over breakfast but it was really no contest. The Twelve Pins – or Twelve Bens – of Connemara were in sight now straight ahead, a barrier and a challenge. The Pins are good mountains which rise to the 2,000–2,300 ft mark, smooth and rounded and dangerously attractive.

I longed to walk across the Twelve Pins but I now knew, from bitter experience, that they were also a wet and springy slough of blanket bog. Even so, I would walk there if I could. There is a long-distance footpath, the Western Way, which is said to run right down the West Coast of Ireland and across the Twelve Pins. Well, it may be there but I never found it. There are even some provisional 1:50,000 scale maps to the Twelve Pins which show a route or two, but in the end I stuck to the road that leads south and skirts the Pins and Lough Inagh.

First though, I went out to Killary Bay for a 'crack' with Michelle Hughes who runs the Killary Adventure Centre and leads walking tours across the Pins.

'The Twelve Pins or the Bens, it's the same thing,' she said. 'We do a four-day expedition, walking about six or seven hours a day, and we can take in most of the Twelve Pins in that time, walking on the open mountain. We do have these new 1:50,000 maps and that's real luxury. How you have come this far on the $1\frac{1}{2}$" to the mile beats me. They make the navigation very difficult.'

'I've mostly stayed on roads and tracks,' I admitted. 'The bogs scare me and I don't find the open tops easy going.'

'They're not,' Michelle agreed, 'but I like doing the navigation. It has to be spot-on when the cloud or mist comes down and you can get four seasons here in one day, you know. Mind you, when the sun does come out it is really beautiful.'

Michelle was right there. Over the next few days the weather was fine, a mixture of sunshine and rainstorms as

I wandered south, sometimes on bog, sometimes on tracks, mostly on roads. The countryside was simply stunning. I was in no hurry now, for my pace had slowed to an amble over the past weeks. As they say in Ireland, when God made time he made plenty of it, and I could still do my three miles an hour over most terrain and so clock up twenty miles on a good day.

While that may sound easy, it was still a long way to my next aiming point at Cashel Bay. This was how I did it, butting my way across Ireland on the best route I could find, from one aiming point to the next. Had the terrain been less challenging, well provided with footpaths, or even with roads across the mountain tops, I could have walked across Ireland in half the time it actually took. As it was, I gave up all attempts to sort out a programme for time and distance, and just did the best I could each day. I tried, and not for the first or even the hundredth time, to hack directly across country by compass, if only to cut corners and reduce the overall distance, but the Irish terrain is not really suitable for cross-country walking.

Connemara is all rock and stream and blanket bog, as springy as a mattress, bouncing under your boots as you pass over it with water squirting up at every stride. This is fun for a little while but you can't do the distance that way. Once off the road my feet were wet within twenty paces. Within a hundred yards I had sunk in to my knees, and I discovered, not for the first time, that boots with those fancy cutaway shock-absorbing heels are less than useful on wet, boggy slopes. I practically skied down some of the slopes, sliding on my heels to end up on my back in a bog. After half a mile of that I would crawl back to the road, cursing, wet and weary, where I would change my wet socks for a dry pair and set off once more for the south. That was a small inconvenience and did nothing to spoil the walk. I was almost alone out here in the wild, with just the occasional car and the solitary fisherman to share this beauty with me and the sheep, and I liked it that way.

As I went south – pardon me now if I rave – the countryside of Connemara became, if possible, even more beautiful. How people make a living here beats me, but by God, it's lovely. I passed a few fishermen from Britain or Germany, say one every three or four miles, but otherwise there was not a soul to be seen in this empty landscape. The wind blows in constantly from the ocean, so there are few trees, and another result of this incessant breeze is that the gorse, instead of growing up into tall bushes and thickets, survives here as ground cover, a yellow carpet clinging closely to the soil. It was now the end of July but the land was already a tapestry of autumn colours; purple heather, golden gorse, blue lakes and sky, green hills and yellow or red bog-grass, great grey rocks and boulders spattered by green and yellow lichens, all of this picked out in that clear Atlantic light. Quite marvellous.

The air here is translucent and unpolluted, washed clean after crossing three thousand miles of Atlantic Ocean, and crossing Connemara in the late summer was like walking across a massive Persian carpet. I can think of nowhere so beautiful as Connemara at the end of summer.

I got to Cashel on a wandering route from Killary Bay, coming round Tully Mountain and Ballynakill Harbour, then across the small Park at Diamond Hill and up the long track lined with piles of drying peat, and past the old quarry by the Traheen river to Lough Nahillion, and then over the moor by Cregg Hill, working my way around the radio mast on top, the best landmark for miles around, plunging into a stream or two and then passing over the Owenglin river. The Twelve Pins now lay due east, looking marvellous each day against the morning sky.

The Owenglin is a lovely river, fast and shallow but varied, foaming over green rock at one point, dropping into deep, still pools a few yards further on. Like most of these West Coast streams, this is a salmon river, divided into beats, and there were more fishermen here, wading thigh-deep in the water or casting their flies from the banks.

I stopped for tea one afternoon at the Ballynahinch Hotel, where a great salmon lay breathing its last on the scales in the drawing room, and a day later I came slowly round the shore of the inlets off Bertraghboy Bay, round the north shore of Cashel Bay and up the gravel path to the Cashel Bay Hotel. Five days from Louisburgh across this splendid Connemara countryside, and every one a delight.

On a trip like this, just now and again, a chap needs a little luxury. There is actually no need to take the full, hard-hitting backpacking kit on a walking trip through Ireland, and I only carried it now because I had no way of getting rid of it and from the fear that I might get stranded on the moors one dark and stormy night and be very glad of my sleeping bag and tent. Lord knows, they had come in handy enough when I trudged across Spain.

Every other cottage in Ireland seems to be a B & B, and though cottages are few in Connemara I always found somewhere to stay where a bed, a shower and a massive breakfast were available at no great cost. At Cashel Bay though, I went a bit up-market.

The Cashel House Hotel is one of the great country house hotels of Ireland and a very swish place indeed. The Cashel House caters for what my grandmother used to call the 'carriage trade', but fortunately this is swish in the Irish fashion, which is to say they don't mind mud-spattered 'eejits' turning up unannounced and standing in a spreading pool of water in their foyer. Any Spanish hotelier would have summoned his strongest porters and had them throw me into the street, but Irish hoteliers are different. All it takes is money.

In fact, it takes rather a lot of money, but if God had wanted us to be frugal all our lives, He would never have invented plastic. Besides, everyone made me welcome. A porter came to carry my wet, cow-pat stained rucksack to my room as if it was a Vuitton suitcase; for deep down the Irish have a fondness for an 'eejit'. I was assisted from my squelching boots and peeled out of my raingear and allowed to run about the warm corridors in my wet socks. Once these had been swapped for dry socks, my wet ones and anything else that needed a 'once-over-lightly' were sent to the hotel laundry while I was sent a pot of tea and a plate of soda bread and scones. After a wild and windy day on the moors, all this luxury was delightful.

The Cashel House Hotel became famous in Ireland in 1969–70 when the French ex-President General de Gaulle and his wife spent two holidays there, enjoying the food and the privacy. Sitting before a peat fire in my room, toasting my toes and leafing through a selection of glossy magazines and dinner menus seemed as good a way as any to finish another day in Connemara.

13

Getting to Galway

And this I dare avow, there are more lakes, brooks, strands, quagmires, bogs and marshes in this country than in all Christendom besides. For travelling there all my daily solace was sink-down comfort in boggy plunging deeps . . .

William Lithgow,
Rare Adventures and Painful Peregrinations, 1632

When I got to Cashel I had come about halfway on my journey through Ireland. It may have been a little more or less, but that was about right. Hence the need for a small celebration and some time for a little assessment.

I had been on the road now for nearly four weeks. This was much longer than I had intended and longer than I would usually have devoted to such a distance. If I put my foot down, I can normally cover between 500–600 miles in four weeks, and Ireland is only just over 300 miles from end to end. This allows for the curious fact that Irish miles are, or at least were, much longer than English miles. The 'Irish mile' is 2,240 yards, the English mile is 1,760 yards. Nowadays they have converted to kilometres in the Republic, but many signposts give the distance in miles as well. Are these English or Irish miles I ask myself, and end up, as ever, confused. Confusion arose because I seemed to be doing an awful lot of walking and making very little progress.

The reason is that Ireland is not the place to rush about in. Getting anywhere seems to involve going round a mountain or round a lake, or up the road to the bridge over the river, and my original calculations had been based on the idea that I could nip across the tops and through the valleys like a leprechaun. Given my normal rate of progress, this should have got me across Ireland in four or five weeks. As it was, I had a good two or three weeks to go unless the terrain became a good deal more helpful than it had been up to now.

Since I was frequently confused in Ireland this extra dilemma should not have been surprising. When I arrived at Cashel I thought I was still in Connemara, but when I woke up next day I found myself in Galway. This is because Connemara is the name given to the western part of Galway, to the country which lies roughly between the Atlantic and the Lough Corrib. A large part of this area, certainly in the south of Connemara and western Galway, is part of the 'Gaeltacht', so Irish names began to appear exclusively on the signposts. I was getting right into the heart of western Ireland now, well away from any form of tourist route, and if I had really come over halfway on my journey there was some reason for celebration. I therefore ate and drank to excess that night at Cashel Bay and felt very poorly in the morning.

I set off from the hotel at around ten o'clock next morning, smart in my clean socks and dry boots, but within half an hour I was lost. This is not hard to do in Ireland. On foot you are lost most of the time, for the maps are very little help. Indeed, one of the sights at every Irish crossroads is a driver brandishing a map and shouting at his wife. Perhaps it was the sight of one of these incidents that distracted me from paying closer attention to the route, for instead of cutting across the throat of the Ardmore Peninsula and quickly hacking off the 5 miles to Gort, I found myself 5 miles south in quite the wrong direction. I was down near Carna on the coast before it registered that I had gone wrong.

Well, no matter. The Connemara countryside was just as lovely here, perhaps even more beautiful than on the days before, and I was in no particular hurry. Ireland had got into me when crossing Connemara and I suspect it will be there for a long while yet. As my hangover faded I became almost gleeful, not least because nobody knew where I was to within 100 miles. That brought a great sense of freedom; whatever they wanted they couldn't get at me now. I strolled along in the sun, swinging my stick and shouting 'Mint Sauce!' just for the hell of it and to worry the sheep.

Then I came down to Carna and Ardmore, where I got fed up with roads and decided to cup up into the hills for some soft ground and a decent walk. A great long ride runs north from Ardmore, back up to Derrymore and Gort, the sort of sharp-edged ridge that appeals to people like me, who love ridge walking. Besides, in spite of the bogs lurking up there, I had done enough on roads and I wanted to get onto paths or tracks as often as possible during the second half of my journey. This hill above Ardmore was a fine dramatic ridge, soaring up like a wall to about 1,000 ft above the sea, and while I knew it would be boggy, I thought it would go. Go it did, and I nearly went with it.

The other purpose of climbing to this ridge was to get a good view south, over Galway Bay and out to the Aran Islands. This whole coastline is a spectacular region, constantly indented with bays and inlets, very wild and desolate, decorated offshore with a great litter of small islands. The Aran Islands, which straddle the entrance to Galway Bay, act as a buffer to the full fetch of the Atlantic, and I hoped to get a view of them from the top to see if I could spot ferries hurrying from one island to another. If so, that meant that island-hopping down Galway Bay was at least a possibility and I could save the time I must otherwise spend flogging round the shores of Galway Bay.

Getting up onto the ridge was easy enough for a rough track runs up the east face of the hill from the village of Kilkieran. Once on the top of the hill it got difficult. Ireland manages to have blanket bogs even on the tops of the mountains and the top of this ridge was very squishy indeed. Nor was it even; the ridge rolled. That long, sharp knife-edge I had seen from the road far below turned out to be a long series of dips and hollows, and these hollows fell away sharply to the edge of the ridge in a most alarming fashion.

I decided to keep well away from the edge and sploshed my way north, harried along the way by strong gusts of wind and rain. On the whole it was exhilarating. I saw a hare and several large hawks hovered off the ridge, riding the wind like children's kites. Black crows were blown past, flying down the wind like scraps of crumpled paper. It was a roaring day and I loved it.

There was even some evidence that other walkers had been up here. Stone cairns dotted the various small peaks and I went from one to another as I tacked my way north against the wind. When the rain clouds came roaring in I simply huddled under a convenient rock, hood pulled down, snug and dry in my raingear, and waited until the storm passed. After days of trudging along roads, just to be up on a hill on soft going was exciting. Then it got rather too exciting.

I have walked nearly 1,200 miles in my current pair of boots, but never before on a really steep wet hillside, so maybe that was the problem. On the other hand, maybe I was too busy enjoying myself or just not paying attention to the footing. Whatever the reason I was walking down a steep slope close to the edge of the ridge when my boots shot from under me. Suddenly I was skiing. One leg shot off on its own, pushing the other leg into a knee-wrenching 'telemark' position, and I took a heavy fall. When I stopped rolling down the slope I was only a few feet from the edge of the cliff. I got up, somewhat shaken . . . well, all right, very shaken, took another step forward and did it again. But for my stick and the rucksack I would have toppled right over the edge. A great gap appeared at my side and scared the hell out of me. I rolled over and decided to crawl back to level ground. It seemed the safest way to get there.

The problem appeared to be the sloping, cut-away heels on my boots. Many modern walking boots have this feature; the idea is that the cut-away heel offers more protection from road-shock than the sharp-edged-heel variety. This may well be true, and every little helps when walking on roads, but nothing is worse than walking on a steep hillside, unsure of your footing. It makes a chap nervous. Nor was this an isolated incident. I fell three or four more times when coming down the north face of this hill.

I eventually got to the bottom by edging across the hill and down to the flatter parts, sticking where possible to the rocks. Any attempt to plunge down even a gradual grassy incline had me flat on my back within yards. This was a real worry. I had more mountains ahead, not least in the MacGillycuddy Reeks of Kerry, and I resolved to change my present well-worn and much-loved boots for a newer pair with a sharp-cut heel before I ventured again into these wet, steep-sided, Irish mountains.

I got off the hill eventually and sat in the lee of a wall somewhere near Derryrush to rest my throbbing knee. The sun came out, the wind dropped and my spirits revived. I don't stay down for long. I had made fair time and took an hour for another trawl through Irish history from the ever-growing library of books I had assembled in my rucksack. I must be the only walker whose rucksack gets heavier as he goes along, but to make sense of the history I had to find something apposite, something suitable for wherever I was.

Leaving this journey through Ireland for a moment and reverting to my journey through history, where was I? I had begun to get the hang of Irish history by now, that 800-year-long struggle to get rid of the bloody English. What I still did not understand is *why* the Irish had not long since given up the struggle. After all, the Scots – and I am a Scot – gave up biffing the Sassanach in 1601, by getting their own King on the English Throne. They then took over most British institutions and ran large parts of the British Empire. Visit Canada or Australia or most of the rest of the world if you don't believe me. In the days of Empire it was said that all you had to do to make a friend in the colonies was to go into a bar and ask, 'Is Mac in?' There was bound to be one about somewhere. I once met a camel driver by the Great Pyramid at Giza, draped in Arab robes and as black as the ace of spades and he told me his name was MacGregor. Some sergeant in the Black Watch has a lot to answer for in Cairo.

The Irish, on the other hand, don't want to manage anyone but themselves. They are not even very good at that. That's what Sinn Fein means – Ourselves Alone – and this seems to sum up the nature of the Irish people. Because they are cheerful and friendly and easy-going, there is a tendency to think that the Irish are just like the other nations in that collection of countries we call the British Isles, but I don't think that is so. The Irish have avoided or eluded most of the formative inferences that passed through Britain. The English were shaped by the Romans and the Saxons, the Danes and the Normans. The Irish either never knew these people or fought them to the death. The Irish absorbed the English, not the other way round.

The Irish are a distinct people – almost a tribe. They may look and sound like other European people but their attitudes are different; not better or worse, just different, and they like it that way. Good luck to them, say I, and after the heavy price they have paid for simply being what they are, they deserve to be left alone, if that is what they want. It is no good trying to understand Ireland. It will simply give you a headache. Just accept it the way it is and it will all come right. I once asked a friend of mine, Seamus Redmond, if it would have made any difference if the English had treated the Irish with more kindness over the centuries, but he shook his head. 'It would have made no difference what they did; we just wanted to be left alone.' Being left alone was the mission of the Fenians.

In the middle of the 19th century, which after all is only three generations ago, the population of Ireland had been shrunk by the Famine and migration to about six million people, a drop of about 25 per cent in ten years. Of these, roughly a million had emigrated to America where, nursing their numerous wrongs, some of them set up an organization called the Fenian Brotherhood. I heard some militant Protestant in the North muttering darkly about the 'Fenians', but it transpires that the Brotherhood – named after the 'Fianna', the legendary Irish warriors of pre-history, had not been formed in Ireland at all, or not exactly. The idea was Irish–American, and funds to establish the original Fenians in Ireland were sent to the 'Auld Sod' in 1858. The Fenians were an undercover organization, sworn to evict the British from Ireland and establish a Republic.

This aim soon made the Fenians vastly unpopular with the Catholic Church. The priests linked Republicanism with anti-clericalism, and urged the people not to support them.

The Fenians staged an abortive rising in 1867, but when that failed they became involved in a much more popular movement, the Land League. The Land League was founded in 1879 with the sensible aim of recovering Irish land from the 'consolidating' and 'absentee' landlords, usually by purchase and handing it back to the tenant farmers of Ireland. The Land League enjoyed considerable success, partly because it was generally non-violent, not least because it had as its leader a charismatic speaker and a most shrewd Parliamentarian, one of the great Irish statesmen, Charles Stewart Parnell, the Member for Meath.

By the terms of the Act of Union, the Irish constituencies now sent 100 Members to the Westminster Parliament, enough to sway the voting in critical issues, and Parnell handled the Irish Party like a set of weights, putting their votes now with the Liberals and now with the Tories, not just ruthlessly or cynically, for he was a bigger man than that, but the votes usually went to whichever Party would help Ireland, for Parnell was the master of the political deal. He compelled the Westminster Parliament to buy the land of Ireland back for the Irish people; I suspect the irony amused the Irish people greatly. Where money failed to tilt the balance and achieved the sale, Parnell did not hesitate to compel.

One of the most successful tactics used to squeeze out the consolidating landlords was the 'Boycott'. This was first used to evict a certain Captain Boycott from lands he held in County Mayo and his name stuck to the process. In simple terms 'boycotting' meant sending the person involved to social and commercial isolation. No one would deal with him, speak to him, sell to him or buy from him. Even workmen were forbidden to work for him and, strictly enforced, the 'Boycott' proved a powerful weapon in Parnell's hands. The Land Acts provided the money to buy out the landlords and if they refused, a boycott would make them change their minds. Taken together, this was a situation few landlords could endure.

Parnell stated his case very clearly in a speech to tenants at Westport in 1879. 'A fair rent is the rent a tenant can reasonably afford to pay according to the times, but he cannot be expected to pay as much in bad times as in good times. What must we do to get the landlords to see that? You must show them that you intend to keep a firm grip on your land, that you will not be dispossessed as your fathers were. You must help yourself and the world will stand by you in the struggle to preserve your homesteads.' It was to help the farmers in their struggle that Parnell founded the Land League in the October of that year.

The Land Acts brought Parnell into sharp conflict with the Fenians, who wanted to nationalize Irish land, not simply replace English landlords with small Irish farmers. But the Land Acts have had one enduring effect on the Irish landscape, which still supports a great number of small and only marginally economic farms. On the other hand, it has kept the land sweet and free from the clutches of agro-business, besides creating a race of stubborn, decent, country people.

Having won a great victory for the tenants, Parnell then rode on the crest of this success towards his next aim – Home Rule. By now I was getting very used to this demand in the history of the Republic. Every time I picked up a book on Irish history, every period I studied for the journey, somewhere behind the conflict discussed comes this need for Home Rule, for Independence. I am not going to say why I think this should be; Sir Roger Casement states the case for Irish Independence far better than I ever could and we shall come to him presently. The fact is that while the Welsh and Scots have accepted the Union, periodic glitches apart, though often with difficulty and sometimes with resentment, they have never resisted it with the centuries of fervour that the Irish have.

The Irish have this need to be themselves. That need seems to come from somewhere within them, some place where no foreigner, however harsh or well-meaning, can ever manage to reach or hope to understand. I don't think the Irish really understand themselves, but it is worth stressing that while not wishing to be divided, the Irish don't want to dominate either. Ireland has never had a colony, never oppressed anyone, never stuck a long interfering nose into other nations' affairs.

In his march towards Home Rule, Parnell once again deployed the Irish Members in the Westminster Parliament, to support either the Liberals or the Tories, whichever side leaned towards Home Rule. The Home Rule issue had exhausted the English and with the French now allies and the Spanish ruined, the strategic need to retain Ireland no longer existed.

Parnell also got on well with Prime Minister Gladstone, and Gladstone steadily came to see that Home Rule would have to be conceded. In 1886 Parnell's Home Rule Bill was introduced at Westminster, where it was opposed by all the Conservatives and a large number of Liberals. The great opposition, however, came from the Protestants of Ulster, whose threats of violence enabled Lord Randolph Churchill to 'play the Orange Card' by threatening civil war if the Bill went through. In fact, since the House of Lords then held a veto on all Bills and was implacably opposed to Home Rule, there was no chance of the Bill going through, but it gave Gladstone the opportunity to say something that future Prime Ministers might have remembered: 'I cannot allow it to be said that a Protestant minority in Ulster or elsewhere shall rule on the question at large for Ireland. I am aware of no constitutional doctrine where such a conclusion could be justified.'

Parnell almost did it. Then he made the fatal mistake of falling in love with a married woman, Kitty O'Shea, whose husband cited him in a divorce case, a great scandal for any public figure in Victorian times. He fell from political grace, was excreated by the Irish Church, his enemies rejoiced and the British Parliament turned against him when the Irish Members rejected him as Leader in 1890, but he refused to resign. Worn out with the struggle, Parnell died suddenly in 1891, and then, too late, his countrymen rushed to honour him.

He now has a fine statue in his memory at the end of O'Connell Street in Dublin where the inscription states the aims of his Home Rule policy quite clearly: *'No man has the right to fix the boundary to the march of a nation'.* Under Parnell, the Irish nation had marched much nearer to their goal of Independence. Had he lived longer and been supported, a great deal of the subsequent bloodshed might have been averted, for Parnell was both a Protestant and a landowner, a human bridge between the factions.

From my lodging by the crossroads at Derryrush to the harbour at Rossaveal is a reasonable day's walk. I took my time over it, making a diversion near Derryrush to visit Patrick Pearse's cottage at Rosmac, partly because this is one of the few genuine examples left of West Coast cottage architecture, and partly because Patrick Pearse is another Irish hero. Patrick Pearse and his brother William were founder members of the Irish Volunteers, and both were shot for their part in the Easter Rising of 1916. Patrick Pearse was 'Commander-in-Chief of the Forces of the Irish Republic', and held the General Post Office against the British Army for five days before surrendering, but his struggle against the English had started long before 1916.

Patrick spent his boyhood holidays over here in the 'Gaeltacht', where he strove to learn Irish. Pearse believed that if the Irish language were to die out the people would die with it or at best lose their identity, and in this he may well have been right. He joined the Irish Volunteers in 1913 and at Easter 1916 he led 2,000 Irish Volunteers into Dublin and began the rebellion.

Patrick Pearse's cottage is a small, snug, whitewashed building, quite unlike the modern bungalows which now litter the West Coast of Ireland and do nothing to enhance the charm of the scenery. According to Fergus, my young friend from Croagh Patrick, this 'Bungalow blitz' as he called it, arose because some 'eejit' produced a book offering six basic designs for country bungalows which all the local builders adopted. Some of the embellishments may comfort the occupiers but the total effect is not pleasing. A bungalow with Doric columns at the door is a bungalow still, and only buildings like Patrick Pearse's cottage look really right in this wild Connemara landscape.

I had come out of the hills now and was on the open breezy plain on the north side of Galway Bay, crossing a country-side which was seamed with streams and rivers and dotted with ponds and lakes, each stretch of water a mirror reflecting the sky and clouds. It was all quite beautiful and I could have gone on like that for ever, and even better, this fine countryside, so close to Galway city, was still practically deserted. I was passed by the occasional car, or saw the lone fisherman here and there, but for the most part I was quite on my own, walking south towards the glimmer of the open sea.

After Pearse's cottage I marched on past the village of Costelloe where a large radio station broadcasts in the Irish language to the people of the *Gaeltacht*. My wrenched knee was still playing up as I limped on down to Rossaveal, from where a fast ferry leaves for Inishmore, the nearest and largest of the Aran Islands. Fortunately the service is irregular and I say fortunately, because the ferry was away and I was damp and soon became cold with hanging about.

I therefore gave up for the day and found a B & B where I changed my wet clothes for dry ones. Then I took a bus into Galway, heading like an arrow for Kenny's Bookshop.

Since the Irish are a literate people and I am a scribbling gent, I had heard a lot about Kenny's Bookshop which was put to me as a place no bookworm should miss. I never actually need much encouragement to visit a bookshop – I have spent half my life in them – but Kenny's Bookshop, which is still run by the Kenny family, is a booklover's mecca. It extends over several floors and has new books, secondhand books and, at the back, an art gallery. Even better, the people behind the counter actually know about books and make a point of getting to know authors. Those walls not covered with bookshelves are plastered with the signed photographs of grateful writers whose books have flowed across the Kenny counters.

Words are the basis of Irish culture. Indeed, the Irish language – Gaelic – contains the earliest surviving collection of written European literature after Greek and Latin and dates back to the 6th century. Compared with Gaelic, the Anglo–Saxon tongue is an also-ran, but when the Irish use English they still seem inspired. When I was interviewing people with my BBC tape recorder, it was striking how the Irish were fluent and the English hesitant. I think this must go back to the bardic tradition, when Ireland was a land of poets and harpists. The Irish language went into decline when its use was suppressed under the Tudors, but had been under attack long before that. 'Hang all the harpers, wherever found,' was one of Elizabeth I's most savage instructions, but it was probably a wise one, for the harpers sang the soldiers into battle as easily as any Highlander's pibroch.

Well, if Irish was suppressed, the Irish people have made good use of English. Think only of Wilde, Yeats, George

Bernard Shaw, Joyce, Beckett, Jonathan Swift and Synge, to name just a few who have used and transformed the English tongue. Dublin is the only city which has produced three winners of the Nobel Prize for Literature, and is the only city I can think of which devotes a day every year to the celebration of a literary character. This is Joyce's Leopold Bloom, and 'Bloomsday', held on 16 June every year, sees crowds of people crossing Dublin in period dress celebrating Bloom's progress that day with copious draughts of red wine. This part of Ireland around Galway and the Aran Islands is the place for J.M. Synge, who set two of his works, *Riders of the Sea* and *The Playboy of the Western World* in the West of Ireland.

Galway is a big city by Irish standards, with a population of some 37,000. I had not been in a big city for weeks and I found the traffic a problem. The traffic usually is a problem in Ireland, for be the streets never so wide, the people like to park their cars in the middle of the road or stop there for a chat. Cars can come at you from several directions in an Irish town, so it pays to be wary and light on your feet. I explored the city unburdened, dodging about the lanes and byways, poking into the small shops. After the spaces of Connemara it made a change. Galway is the County town of Galway and the principal city of the old province of Connaught, and lies at the foot of the salmon-rich Corrib river. Galway city is a later addition to the list of Irish towns, for it was founded in the 12th century by the Anglo–Norman de Burghs, or Burkes.

Galway later became the foremost port on the West Coast of Ireland, and there are still fair-sized ships moored along the quays, but the city has never really recovered from the two savagings it received in the 17th century, first from Cromwell and then from the army of William of Orange, which sailed down the West Coast to besiege the city in 1691.

Even the de Burghs were anxious that their English followers should not mix or mingle with the native Irish and were the first to support the laws against such things, introduced in the Middle Ages. These began to be passed quite early on, soon after Henry II came to Ireland at the end of the 12th century and exerted his claim to be suzerain over Strongbow and the Anglo–Irish lords.

Since Henry had no lands to spare for his son John, hence John Lack-Land, he made John Lord of Ireland, but the move was not a success. John came to Ireland with reluctance, jeered at the Irish lords, sneered at the Anglo–Irish nobles and upset everyone before he went home again. Laws were then passed prohibiting the Anglo–Irish from adopting Irish dress or hairstyles, and mixing in Irish society, until by the end of the 13th century Ireland had already divided into the resident English and the despised native Irish, and these divisions persisted for centuries. In 1518, here in Galway, an Order was posted stating: 'Neither O' nor "Mac" shall swagger thro' the streets of this city.'

Thomas Carlisle, who came through Galway in 1849, wrote of its '. . . steep, straight streets, a remarkable old city. How in such a stony country it exists, with port wine and Spanish articles coming in and Irish cattle and corn outwards. There is no other port for miles around, nothing but this stony country.' The same thought occurred to me in Connemara, to the west of Lough Corrib, but to the east of it lies the great limestone plain of Galway and Clare, running all the way south to the Shannon.

Galway has been a great trading city since the 16th century, when there were strong trade links with Spain, and it is experiencing a revival today, partly from tourism and partly because this is the capital of the *Gaeltacht*. In and around Galway I often heard Gaelic spoken in the shops and streets and found Irish used on its own on shop fronts and signposts. In other parts of Ireland, the Gaelic shares space with English, or gives way to the foreign tongue entirely, and by now I had begun to get the hang of the Irish language, or at least some of the words. 'Kil' or 'cil' means a church, as in Cill Chiaran or, in English, Kilkieran. 'Ross' means a peninsula, hence my next destination, the port at Rossaveal, which stands on a headland. 'Cashel' means a castle, 'slieve' a mountain. Some words, like 'clun' for a meadow, have similarities with Welsh, while others like 'dubh' (black) as in Dublin, are much the same as the Gaelic used by the Scots.

The *Gaeltacht* has a place in Irish history and deserves to be preserved if not expanded. I am not at all persuaded by the arguments of the various national language movements which now exist around the world and seem to take out their spleen by defacing roadsigns and inflicting a minority tongue on the majority population. Countries such as Spain and Canada are being prised apart by people like that. On the other hand, I fail to see why a country cannot contain two cultures and speak several languages. Languages are not inherently divisive. I speak three and my wife speaks five; I know people who speak seven or eight. There can be no doubt that while people can converse in one of the common international languages like English, Spanish or French, if you really want to understand what people mean as opposed to what they merely say, you will have to speak and understand the local language.

Irish was the majority tongue in Ireland until the early years of the 17th century and widely spoken in the country-side within living memory. Today it exists here only in the West and South-West, around Galway, Cork and Connemara. The Galway *Gaeltacht* consists of the Aran Islands, the small villages of Connemara and Southern Mayo and parts of the land along the North Shore of Galway Bay. These areas are served by that Gaelic-speaking radio station I had passed by on the road near Carna and by Gaelic summer schools which teach the tongue to people from all over Ireland. The Irish tongue is a nice, gentle, lilting tongue and I hope that it never dies out.

So, what with one thing and another, I had a good afternoon in Galway, lunching in McDonagh's Fish Restaurant in Quay Street, where the McDonaghs have been buying and selling fish for four generations, ambling round the shops, sitting in Eyre Square for a quiet read or sheltering from the rain in the 14th-century Church of St Nicolas which contains the tomb and memorials to the Lynch family who gave their name to 'lynching'. The story goes that in 1493 the leader of the Lynch clan, Judge James Lynch, sentenced his only son, Walter, to death for murder. When no one could be found to carry out the sentence, Judge Lynch hanged his son himself.

I prefer the wide naves of St Nicolas to the more modern Roman Catholic Cathedral of Galway, which was only dedicated in 1957. Most of the old town of Galway lies between St Nicolas and the docks around the Spanish Arch which was once the sea gateway through the town walls. Down here lots of narrow streets and alleyways are lined with little shops and cafés and bars to create a colourful part of the city where the sound of street music is heard everywhere, played by local musicians on a great variety of instruments from flutes to drums. A very enjoyable city, the good city of Galway, and I must get back there again some day.

14

Crossing the Aran Islands

The Irishman is an imaginative being. He lives on
an island in a damp climate, close to the melan-
choly Ocean.

Benjamin Disraeli, 1868

When Geoff and I sat at that map-littered table many
months before, planning this trip, one of the things that
went on the 'had-to-do' list was to travel across Galway Bay,
by ferry-hopping down the Aran Islands, from Rossaveal to
Doolin on the south shore of the bay. The three main Aran
Islands, Inishmore, Inishmaan and Inisheer, lie like a barrier
across the entrance to Galway Bay, presenting steep cliffs to
the Atlantic and are said to contain the last intact remnants
of Gaelic culture. From photographs I could see that they
were the most curious places, a great litter of stones
supporting one of those tight-knit local communities that
seem quite common on the West of Ireland and, all in all,
this was somewhere I could not miss.

Another such a Galway community, now dispersed, is the
Claddagh, a community of fishermen who once lived on the
beach – the Claddagh – close to Galway city near the present
port. As recently as the middle of the last century the
fisherfolk of the Claddagh controlled all the fishing in

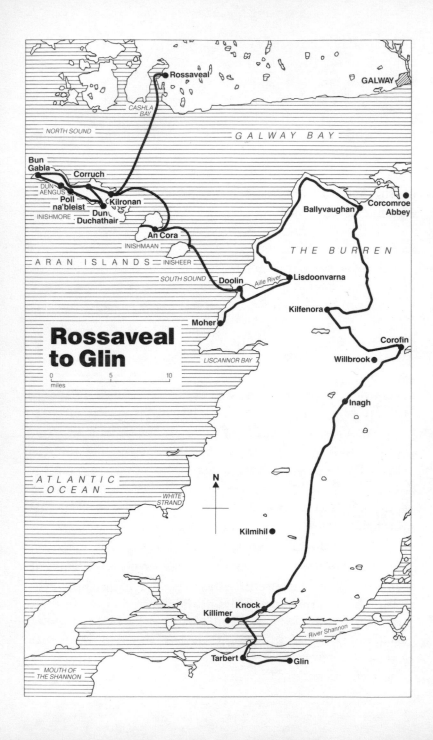

Rossaveal to Glin

Rossaveal

GALWAY

CASHLA BAY

NORTH SOUND

GALWAY BAY

Bun Gabla

Corruch

DUN AENGUS

Poll na'bleist

Kilronan

Dun Duchathair

INISHMORE

Ballyvaughan

Corcomroe Abbey

THE BURREN

An Cora

INISHMAAN

ARAN ISLANDS

INISHEER

SOUTH SOUND

Doolin

Aille River

Lisdoonvarna

Kilfenora

Moher

Corofin

LISCANNOR BAY

Willbrook

0   5   10
miles

Inagh

ATLANTIC OCEAN

WHITE STRAND

N

Kilmihil

Knock

Killimer

River Shannon

Tarbert

Glin

MOUTH OF THE SHANNON

Galway Bay and attacked any other fishermen who attempted to sail there. They had their own dialect and elected their own mayor, whose orders were obeyed without question. Strangers were driven away from the Claddagh and the natives lived in glorious if sullen isolation until quite recent times. One relic of the Claddagh folk is the Claddagh ring, a thick gold band which was handed down from mother to daughter, and examples of these can still be found in the Galway shops. The Claddagh folk are another example of how self-contained the Irish people could be, and if the Claddagh folk have gone, those on the Aran Islands still preserve their identity. Or so I had heard.

The ferry trip out to Inishmore from Rossaveal took just twenty-five minutes and the voyage got fairly lively once we were out in the North Sound, beyond the shelter of Cashla Bay. The boat put on speed and the wake grew, but so did the waves. Since we were running across the Atlantic swell the boat was soon plunging and twisting and thudding about, performing antics that had several passengers retching over the rail. Large waves sent their tops surging over the open decks, so after clinging to a stanchion for a while, until I was nicely wet, I went from handhold to handhold and made my way inside.

Everyone there seemed to be adding another tint to Ireland's famous forty shades of green. Everyone, that is, except four ladies of a certain age who were playing gin-rummy at a table by the bar. The boat rolled, reared, shook, pitched and plunged and did everything but damned well sink, and still the ladies played on, unperturbed, a glass at each elbow, their cigarettes glued to their lower lips, eyes glinting behind their spectacles as they peered down at their cards. They were still hard at their game when we came into Kilronan Harbour on Inishmore and the rest of us staggered ashore.

* * *

It would be easy for any serious traveller to get quite sniffy about the Aran Islands. I felt a bit sniffy myself. I had been told tales of gnarled fisherfolk in thick-knit sweaters and seaboots, hauling in nets full of basking sharks and singing sea-shanties. I had heard of local costumes and strange customs, and it all sounded most intriguing. The facts were somewhat different. The Aran Islands today are not at all the turn-of-the-century backwater that legend has them to be. As the passengers tottered off the ferry, a horde of touts descended on us, offering bicycles for hire or minibus trips round the island or excursions about the town in a horse-drawn cart.

Writing up my notes that evening, my nostrils were still full of the scent of horse manure, which hangs over Kilronan like a miasma. The quay leads round to the town centre, which is an alternating mixture of cafés, tourist shops and B & Bs, set along streets spattered with horse droppings. It is hardly romantic at all.

I spurned all offers of alternative transport and headed on foot for the Tourist Office, to find out if I could do as I wanted and actually island-hop down to Doolin and the Burren. The maps I had been able to buy illustrated the ferry crossings with different coloured dotted lines. Some of these went from mainland ports to the islands, and some went from island to island, and some went from the islands back to the mainland, but none seemed to confirm that I could go from island to island to island, and then south to Doolin. Neither could I get any satisfaction on this point from the people I had met so far. Constant badgering of the local people over the last few days had not enlightened me at all. Their best reply was a definite maybe.

I had now seen Galway city and had no need to go back there, and if I could get south across the sea to Doolin it would save me a good two or three days' trudging from Galway city round the southern shore of Galway Bay. My map seemed a bit equivocal on this point. It showed ferries to Galway from Inishmore and ferries from Inishmore to Inishmaan and Inisheer, but no ferries from Inisheer to Doolin, although there were, I gathered, ferries from Doolin to Inisheer. The Irish do this to confuse you.

The girl in the Tourist Office at Kilronan was equally vague, so I decided to follow the well-worn traveller's precept; when in doubt, wing it. By now I was a very well-worn traveller, so I decided to island-hop down to Inisheer anyway and take my chances on getting across from there to Doolin. That decided, I found a bed in a B & B, dumped the pack and set off to explore the island. This did not take long.

The Aran Islands are buckling under the weight of visitors but they must be doing well because the local guidebook by Pacella and Dara O'Conaola has sold over 50,000 copies and reprints every year. It is written half in Irish and half in English and gives a lot of information. From it I learned that Inisheer is two miles square, Inishmaan five miles square, and Inishmore about eighteen miles square. The total population of the islands is about 1,500 people. They work at the fishing or the ferrying and some do still dress in the traditional Aran garb of a tweed waistcoat called a 'vest', a knitted cap and rawhide shoes called 'pampooties'. I have to add that I saw no one dressed like that or any woman in a red flannel skirt and a crochet shawl, but I might just have been unlucky. I would certainly like to have seen some pampooties.

What is available and made more interesting when you know more about them, are the famous thick-knit Aran sweaters. The designs of these sweaters are of considerable antiquity. It is said that in one of the illustrations of the Book of Kells, David is seen wearing an Aran sweater and Aran socks. In former times, which means until the 1950s, the women spun the wool and the men did the knitting, using goose quill needles. Whoever does the knitting these days, they still retain the traditional stitches. There is the Link Stitch which binds the knitter with the islands, the Zig-Zag Stitch which depicts the cliffs and stone walls of the island, and which combines with the Trellis Stitch to depict the small fields, the Cable Stitch and the Basket Stitch for the fishermen, and a whole lot more.

The Aran Islands are actually part of that great limestone plateau, the Burren, that rises to the south of Galway Bay. I had not been ashore long on Inishmore when I discovered that the Aran Islands are one great fissured limestone plate. Over the centuries the islanders have tried to improve and extend the soil with a mixture of sand and seaweed, but then the wind comes and blows it all away. As a result the surface of the Aran Islands looks like the remains of a volcanic eruption. Great rocks are piled everywhere, the limestone 'karst' lies over the soil like a helmet, and green grass is in very limited supply. The eastern side, by the port of Kilronan, is fairly flat, but on the seaward side there are high cliffs, all steep and fissured, and cut with ledges where the seabirds nest. I would go mad if I had to stay there for long, but for a day or two of rest and roaming, the Aran Islands are ideal. Well, not ideal perhaps, but different.

Fortunately there is a walk, the 'Inis-Mor Way', which runs for 31 miles around this island. This can be cut into short sections by simply nipping across the narrow bits, and since Inishmore is about 8 miles long but only 2 miles wide at its widest point, I simply ticked off the places I wanted to see, beat off the touts with the pony and traps and set off on foot.

The first thing you have to do on Aran is see that famous 1930s film *Man of Aran*, which leads most visitors astray by showing life on Aran in the 1930s. The cottage where the director, Robert Flaherty, lived while making *Man of Aran* still stands and I learned that the film was processed in the fish-curing sheds. There were several curraghs on the beach at Bun Gabla, but no fishermen about to launch them or pose in their pampooties for a picture. I then took a narrow track – called a 'roidin' on Aran – back around the prehistoric fort at Dun Aengus and out to the cliff edge at Poll na'bleist, the Wormhole, one of those eerie places where the sea seems to draw you over the edge of the cliff; I don't care for such places.

I then went over to the cliffs by Dun Duchathair, another prehistoric stone fort from where I could see, across the ocean, the high cliffs of Moher on the Burren, my next landfall. Then it was over to the church at Corruch which has a healing spring, and then back to Kilronan, quite worn out and with a lot of rubber sole and leather upper scuffed off my boots. The sharp limestone slabs of the Aran Islands plays havoc with footwear and I had two more islands to go.

Most of the visitors leave Inishmore on the early evening ferry, but there were enough left to fill all the pubs to the doors. By Irish standards Kilronan is a bit short of pubs, having only three – Ti-Jo Mac's, and Ti-Joe Watty's sound authentic enough, but the 'American Bar' seems somewhat out of place. I went to Ti-Jo Mac's and tried to get some stories from the locals. This was difficult as all the customers were visitors.

The main industries of the islands are said to be farming and fishing, and some of the fishermen still use the traditional curraghs, though I would guess that tourism is what really keeps the place alive. There are few fishing boats in the harbour but everyone is first directed to the local cinema which is dark and tiny and shows only one film – Robert Flaherty's *Man of Aran*. This was made in black and white in 1934 and needs re-shooting. It shows the islanders mending nets and catching whale sharks and climbing cliffs to gather eggs and starving and drowning and generally having a terrible time.

I had already seen *Man of Aran*, which must take part of the blame for my original understanding that the Aran Islands were set in a traditional time warp. I revived my shaky humour with a pot of tea and a few drinks and went to see the church and did a bit more clambering over the sharp limestone terraces. I also went to the shop that sold Aran sweaters and decided that it would take a second mortgage to buy one for each of the family. I then talked for a while to a man gutting fish. This seemed to exhaust the immediate possibilities for entertainment, so I gave up trying and took the guided minibus tour to the prehistoric fort at Dun Aengus.

Dun Aengus is one of the finest and most intact prehistoric fortifications in Europe. I should explain that prehistory is the period before history was, or could be, written down. Britain, for example, entered history in 52 BC, when the Romans invaded and Caesar wrote about his adventures.

Dun Aengus starts right on the cliff edge, about 200 ft above the sea. It consists of three defensive walls surrounding an inner keep, with a great *cheveaux-de-frise* of up-ended stones covering the open ground in front. This fort, and three or four others on the islands, are said to date back to the Fir-bolg people. These may never have existed, so it is more probable that they go back to early Celtic times, say 2,500 years ago. I had a look around, which did not take long, and then sat on the cliffs to watch the sea for a while, but 'rock-fever' was already setting in. I am no good at small islands and here I was trapped on this one overnight. I took the mini-bus back to Kilronan and got mildly drunk.

The ferry came in more or less on time next morning, which is to say about half an hour late, and a gaggle of hopeful escapees filed on board, most of us hefting rucksacks or wheeling bicycles. It did not take long to discover that everyone else on board was either Swedish, German or French. I had noticed the night before that Englishmen were rarer than hens' teeth hereabouts. Rather more surprising was the fact that most of these people had been here two or three times before. Heaven only knows what Sweden must be like if it drives people to a holiday on Aran.

I had heard that to get ashore on the smaller islands you had to trans-ship to a curragh. This sounded exciting to a middle-aged gent with a heavy rucksack, but the skipper told me that while that happened sometimes if it was rough or the tides were very low, there was now an all-tidal pier in both places and I was not to worry. I always worry when people tell me not to worry.

Life on the next island, Inishmaan, such as it is, seems to lie in a belt across the middle of the island which is about three miles wide. As on Inishmore, there is a walk, the Inishmaan Way, which can easily be done in a full morning since it only runs for five miles and is well waymarked. I got rid of the pack in a café and set off at a smart clip, past another stone fort and the cottage of Ti-Synge, where J.M. Synge spent every summer from 1881 to 1902. He must have been mad.

The most interesting thing hereabouts was a cattle trough with a sloping sill designed to catch rainwater, for apart from only a few springs the island has no water. I took a photograph of that but it didn't come out. Beyond this the little yellow-men waymarks took me to the Cathaour Synge – Synge's Seat, where the playwright used to sit and watch the waves sweep in from America. They were sweeping in again today, sending great spurts of spray up the rocks and through the 'blowing holes' worn by the waves in the limestone. When a big wave got in a good blow at the rocks the ground actually shook. I then hurried past the knitwear factory where the sweaters come from, and the generating station, which gets a good plug in the brochure, and back to the port at An Cora just in time to leap on the mid-day ferry to Inisheer.

Inisheer has two names. The locals call it Inis Oirr, and that is the name used on the locally produced Inis Oirr map. This island has the Inis Oirr Way, which runs about the north part of the island where, it said in the guide's introduction, the island largely consists of 'clints' and 'grikes'. My dictionary proved unhelpful about 'clints' and 'grikes' and I spent most of the afternoon worrying that I was missing something crucial.

Inisheer is an outcrop of the Burren, that limestone plateau that was now in plain sight just to the south. It is another bare, white, limestone slab, cast on the surface of the sea, but unlike Inishmaan it has water. There is even a well dedicated to St Enda, which never runs dry and is said to have healing powers. Be that as it may, the well-water is cold enough to hurt your teeth.

In the spring, it says here in the guide, this island becomes a carpet of flowers. Primroses and sea pinks cloak the cliffs and rare plants like the pyramid orchid are quite common. Now, in the middle of summer, the island was just a glinting white rock, broken up with miles of interlinked drystone walls. Its gaunt appearance apart, the island was bustling. Fat cattle chomped away at hay in the tiny fields, and the tourists were everywhere. There is even an airstrip and the curragh fleet catches profitable lobsters for shipment to London. I suspect that in their own quiet, monosyllabic way, the local people are doing very well.

Inisheer is even smaller than Inishmaan, which is to say it is very small indeed. There are two or three churches and a scattering of houses on the north shore, and a small harbour where I hung about that evening, pining for a ship to the mainland. I calmed my nerves in the afternoon with an unladened sprint round the Innis Oirr Way, a 6-mile footpath waymarked with the usual symbol of a jaunty gentleman picked out in yellow paint. This walk took two hours and was most enjoyable. I saw the wreck of the steamer 'Plassey', which was tossed ashore here in 1960 and is quietly rusting away, and drank at the well of St Enda, the patron saint of Inishmaan. His church has to be excavated from the wind-blown sand from time to time. The only other notable features on the island were more troughs for collecting rainwater and stone pillars used for drying seaweed. There was hardly anyone about, except visitors, so I sat on the wall by the quay and worried about getting across the sea to Doolin.

I met a man who told me there would be no more ferries that day. Then I met another who said that there never were any ferries to Doolin and I should go back to Inishmore and try from there. At that moment, no less than two ferries came into the harbour from Doolin and the crews virtually fought each other for my custom. I went on board feeling very smug, and an hour later I was sitting in Gus O'Connor's pub in Doolin, cradling a pint of Smithwicks and grinning from ear to ear.

15

County Clare and the Burren

The Irish people are thus inclined: religious, frank, amorous, ireful, sufferable of infinite pains, vainglorious, many sorcerers, excellent horsemen, delighting in wars, passing in hospitality. Greedy of praise they be and fearful of dishonour.

Holinshed Chronicles, 1587

Doolin is a straggling little place. The village is set about a mile inland from the harbour and runs for 100 yards or so along the banks of the Aille river. The harbour was surrounded by those great limestone plaques I had got to know out on the islands, but otherwise this was pleasant farming country, where green fields were marked with small ponds and a quantity of cattle. Doolin itself is a small village with a big reputation, and at first sight I couldn't see why. The secret, it appears, is the pub.

Gus O'Connor's pub was narrow on the outside and huge on the inside and crammed with the usual crowd of locals and visitors settling down for an evening on the Guinness. The fiddlers were tuning up in the corner and the 'crack' was going full blast. Since the total population of Doolin cannot exceed a hundred souls I don't know where all these people came from, but as I soon discovered, most of them were divided into two factions.

I discovered this when someone asked how I got there and by which ferry, John-Jo's or Kevin's? When I replied, half the bar nodded and the other half scowled. There is a nice little feud going on here between the ferrymen to Aran which is dividing Doolin down the middle. I finished my pint and went off to find a B & B before the argument intensified into a fist-fight.

By reaching Doolin I had moved from County Galway into County Clare, the Banner Country, the place which has always been in the forefront of the fight for Independence and, incidentally, made another significant step on my journey. Once across Clare, I would only have one more county to go. Quite suddenly, I was getting somewhere.

Clare is a fairly flat county, bounded on the east by the Shannon and Lough Derg and to the west by the sea. There is a central limestone plain but mountains rise round the edges, most notably here on the Burren, which is a great plateau of silver limestone rearing up for 700 ft from the southern shore of Galway Bay. This is 'Karst' country, bare limestone underpinned with caverns and underground rivers, covering a region of about 100 square miles, and running out on the sea coast at the escarpment above Ballyvaughan, or at the Cliffs of Moher, which lie just to the south of Doolin.

I had anticipated crossing the Burren on the Burren Way footpath, the first long-distance trail I had encountered on this journey that was actually going my way. In my mind I could already savour it. Soft ground, soaring views, stiles ... delightful! I was quite put out to discover that most of the Burren Way is yet another tarmac'd road, bearable for walkers but far more suitable for cycle tourists, who were cruising round it in great numbers.

Ireland is not the ideal country for the long-distance

walker. On the other hand, it was becoming increasingly clear to me that Ireland is absolutely wonderful for the well-equipped cycle tourist, and cycle tourists in Ireland are very well equipped indeed. I have never seen such smart clothes, such well-geared bikes or such well-filled panniers, and I have done a fair bit of cycle touring in my time. That doyen of travel writers, Eric Newby, had gone round Ireland on a bicycle some years before I set out on foot, but he went in the winter and had a terrible time with the weather, and I hardly felt inspired to repeat his experience. In this I was wrong.

Ireland really is a cyclist's mecca. There were cycle tourists in large groups led by a guide or in couples or families, even on their own. I rather wished I had brought my bike but had I done so I would have ended up talking to other cyclists about gear-ratios and sprocket-fangling and other arcane matters so dear to the cyclist's heart. On balance I would stick to my boots and press on regardless.

Next morning promised another beautiful day. I stepped out into bright sunshine under a sky full of white, puffy clouds and an air which smelt of the sea. Sniffing happily, I opened my lungs and strode off briskly up the Burren Way towards the Cliffs of Moher, a mile or two south of Doolin and one of the major attractions on the West Coast. They are also, alas, a honeypot for tourists.

When I came in across the car park, tourists were emerging in droves from the Information Centre and running the gauntlet of the traders on their way to the cliff edge. The car park was full of coaches spilling out their passengers to wander up the cliff path in tight shoes or pulling on plastic shower-hats to preserve their hair-do's from the tugging of the wind. On the way up to the viewpoint of O'Brien's Tower there was a man with a dog and a donkey offering a photo opportunity, a man telling fortunes, a lot of people selling postcards, and three girls singing to the music of a harp. Being Irish they sang rather well.

Above this activity hung the overwhelming smell of fried onions from the Shamrock Hamburger Stall. All this was being photographed avidly by the tourists on cameras and videos. Someone even took a photograph of me. 'Look at that guy ... how 'ya doin' fella.' I was doing all right. I dodged through the blue smoke billowing from the hamburger stall and plodded up to the Cliffs.

The Cliffs of Moher are something to see. They drop away sheer into the sea, a vertigo inducing 700 ft drop, and they run for 5 miles, the steeper parts white with seabirds, puffins, guillimots, razorbills, even some choughs and ravens. How the birds survive the tourists beats me, for the flatter bits of the cliffs were like eroded terraces, full of people taking photographs from quite hazardous locations. Places like the Cliffs of Moher were put there for the profit of Eastman Kodak.

The wind on the top was sweeping in directly from America, strong enough to make me stagger or even stop the breath if I turned fully into it, and how some of the tourists were not blown off the clifftop can only be wondered at. With the wind came the rain. I turned away from the sea and was blown down-wind like a leaf, along the Burren Way to Lisdoonvarna.

Lisdoonvarna is Ireland's only spa. The description of the waters might put anyone off: '... sulphurous and chalybeale (iron) with elements of iodine and possessing radioactive properties.' Wonderful – you come for the cure and go home glowing in the dark! Several hotels advertise the cure but I have never cared for taking the waters and I arrived in the town centre after lunch gasping for a cup of tea. I found this in a café just across the way from the Ritz Hotel, which advertised among its various attractions, 'The best crack in

Town'. This statement was causing a certain amount of concern to a group of American visitors at a nearby table.

Lisdoonvarna is a holiday centre, one of those places which only comes alive when the tourists are in town, and if it isn't very, very careful, it will end up without any life of its own. Fortunately, even in mid-summer, the bar at the Ritz Hotel was full of local lads with their noses stuck in the Guinness. There seemed to be plenty of young men about, which was a good thing because the traditional attraction of Lisdoonvarna is the Match-Making.

Once a year Lisdoonvarna is the centre for the Match-Making, or Bachelor Festival, when young men and women come from all over Ireland to find themselves a mate. Such an event must drive a modern feminist crazy. I asked the young man waiting on tables in the teashop to tell me all about it and he told me that the Match-Making Festival was really a great rave. Some women come all the way from America, '... from Boston even,' to see what they could catch. Hangovers mostly, if they were lucky.

The town still supports two active 'Match-Makers' who will act for the families when a marriage needs making, arrange the wedding ceremony and even negotiate the dowry, not forgetting to take a commission for themselves before passing it on to the bridegroom's father. It all sounds very civilized, but I came here to cross the Burren.

The word 'Burren' means 'The Great Rock', and that just about describes it. Think of a great plate of stark white limestone covered with jumbled stone walls and you will have a picture of the Burren. It took the rest of the evening to get across the northern strip of the Burren and down to Ballyvaughan, where I had a rendezvous with an old friend of mine from London, Clovis Keath, who had given it all up to come to Ireland and write. This seemed a most sensible decision and I wanted to see how she was getting on.

My road to Ballyvaughan from Lisdoonvarna lay to the

west of the main Burren escarpment. This rose up like a wall to the right as I came down the hill to the sea, the limestone plates glittering red and silver in the evening light. I found my B & B by the harbour at Ballyvaughan and then had an hour or two to hang about before dinner. I tried admiring the red, blue and yellow painted houses and the Galway 'Hookers', the traditional local fishing craft moored against the harbour wall.

Then I got fed-up and went into a pub where I was set upon by an old cove in boots who engaged me at once in a quite unintelligible tongue while the lady of the house was watching television somewhere in the back and the rest of the customers sensibly refused to translate. I understood the gist of the message easily enough; he wanted me to buy him a drink.

You ordered a drink here by hammering on the counter with a tin ashtray until the landlady came cursing from the back. However, the landlady was unwilling to let me buy a drink for my new friend, who was horribly, horribly drunk. When that failed he staggered to the middle of the room and entertained the clientele with a bit of impromptu tap-dancing, the studs on his boots striking sparks from the flagstone floor. The scene was surreal. I put up with that for as long as my nerves could stand it. Then I fled, but there was no escape from lunatics that evening.

A coachload of French tourists were photographing the central roadsign of Ballyvaughan, the one that had about thirty different sets of directions on it. This took some time as they insisted on taking it in turns to pose beside it and it was practically dark before they finally left. Then I took my own photograph and fell into Claire's Restaurant to meet Clovis.

It was a lively evening; what I remember of it. We were joined by the local physician, Dr John – is every doctor in Ireland called John? – and by Claire herself, who is one of

those fine-boned Irish beauties, and by the people at the next
table, and then by a dog called Wolfgang, who appeared to
be a friend of Dr John. It all got very animated. Dr John was
a man who seemed to have got life sorted out. He swam in
the Bay every morning, kept four horses, hunted three times
a week in season with the Galway Blazers, and was just off
for a month in Ecuador. We did arm-wrestling and he won,
a lot of wine was consumed and there was some singing, and
next day I felt very, very poorly.

On the way out next morning I met Dr John and
Wolfgang returning from a dip in the Bay, looking very fresh
and healthy, blast them. I managed to sweat out a gallon or
two of booze by flogging back up the hill from Ballyvaughan
to the top of the escarpment, where I found myself at last on
the road south across the main Burren plateau. The Burren
is another place that visitors to Ireland have to see, especially
in springtime when the flowers are out and I had marked it
on my map at the planning stage. Now I had finally arrived,
I could see why people rave about it. The Burren is very
beautiful in a rather stark way, and not somewhere to miss
on any walk through Ireland.

After the Aran Islands' terrain the landscape of the Burren
was fairly familiar, a spreading carapace of limestone
littered with large boulders and standing stones, divided
here and there by long drystone walls. It all looks marvel-
lously inhospitable. There is the occasional valley where
trees, fields and small farms somehow manage to survive,
but otherwise the plant life clings to crevasses in the 'karst'.

The name 'Burren' comes from the Gaelic 'bhoireann',
which means 'a stony place', the understatement of a
lifetime. The constant rain and the numerous springs which
it supplies have enabled life to exist in the Burren since Stone
Age times. The remains of prehistoric people have been
found all across the Burren, in stone forts and circles, in
dolmens and standing stones. With all Ireland to choose

from, it is hard to see why any people should make their life more difficult than it need be by attempting to scratch a living in such an inhospitable place, but presumably the great attraction was security. No one in his right mind would envy someone who lived up here.

The first recorded habitation in these parts dates back to 1189 when a group of Cistercian monks founded an abbey near Corcomroe, close to the peak of what is now called Abbey Hill. The Cistercians were always eager to avoid soft living and the temptations of the city, and usually chose remote spots for their foundations, so the Burren must have exerted a powerful appeal. They called their abbey 'Santa Maria de Petra Fertilis', St Mary of the Fertile Rock, which is a good description of the region as a whole.

The Burren covers an area of some 193 square miles and supports a wealth of wild flowers, some endemic to the region, some rare hereabouts, like the mountain aven, the spring gentian and various saxifrages. Arctic or alpine plants grow here beside plants like the flowering orchid or the maidenhair fern, most common in the Mediterranean.

Wildlife is scanty but there are rare creatures like the pine marten. Hawks circle in the sky and there were strange scurryings in the bushes as I passed along, past the Aillwee caves and the standing stones and then tramped down on a blazing day to the Burren Centre at Kilfenora.

Kilfenora lies five miles south of Lisdoonvarna and was well worth the stop. It has a few B & Bs and stands in fine open country, but the big attraction here is the ruins of a 12th-century cathedral dedicated to St Fachtna. There are three high Celtic crosses in the graveyard and some carved tomb-slabs depicting medieval bishops. The Burren Centre nearby opened in 1975, and is full of information about the Burren, its history, flora and fauna, making the point that out here on the Burren on the West Coast of Ireland, Alpine and Mediterranean, and even Arctic plants, somehow grow together. The best of the local flowers are on display in the spring, but even in mid-summer there were enough to keep me happy, the great hedges of fuchsia, the wayside clumps of orange montbretia and the hillsides bright with spreading yellow gorse. It was almost as good as Connemara, but not quite.

It took me another two days to walk right across County Clare and down to the Shannon. For most of that time I was lost, but this did not matter too much. I got lost before I reached Corofin, which I remember as quite pretty. After that I set off for Lough Doo and missed that entirely. Who cares? As long as I kept heading south I was going in the right direction and I must hit the Shannon in the end. In fact, as I got further south and began to cross the low hills, I could see ahead the twin pencil-thin towers of the power station at Killimer, from where the ferry crosses the Shannon for Tarbert, so I was more or less on track.

I could have taken the long way round the Shannon estuary, past Ennis and Limerick, but that would have taken time and I liked the idea of a ferry ride. I just wandered along, asking directions from anyone I happened to meet. I usually got incorrect information in return, but eventually I hit the Shannon by Knock and walked around Clonderalaw Bay to Killimer. Here, on the north bank of the Shannon estuary, just above the ferry port, I dived into another pub and sat at the bar for a think. Once I crossed the river I would be in County Kerry. Valentia Island was in County Kerry, so I only had about 100 miles to go.

I could not leave Clare just yet however, for Clare is a place that has played a very significant part in Irish history. Although it lies a very long way from either Dublin or Westminster it was the people of County Clare who elected Daniel O'Connell to Westminster in 1828, and Daniel O'Connell, the 'Great Liberator' is commemorated all over

Ireland. The main street in Dublin is O'Connell Street, so what of the man himself?

To talk about O'Connell we have to go back beyond Parnell and the Great Hunger to the tricky decades after the Act of Union in 1800. This may seem a strange way to do it, but a complicated history is best absorbed in bits, and how the parts are presented hardly matters. It was hoped, and even believed, at least in Ireland, that the Act of Union would bring great benefits to the Irish people. It would give the Irish the equal status with the English and the rights and privileges already enjoyed by the people of Great Britain. They would send Members to Parliament and thus get a voice in Westminster, which must surely benefit Ireland. This belief, like so many others, was doomed to disappointment.

When the Act of Union was seen to be a fraud about ten minutes after it was signed, the first result was another rebellion, led by Robert Emmett in 1803. Emmett had been one of Wolfe Tone's United Irishmen, one of that combination of Protestants and Catholics who aimed to put Ireland first and fight for her Independence. Emmett's rebellion was on a very small scale – only eighty men took part – and it ended in disaster. Some of his supporters murdered the Lord Chief Justice of Ireland in a Dublin park and Emmett was quickly caught, tried and executed. However, in his speech from the dock he told his fellow countrymen: *Let no man write my epitaph – only when my country takes her place among the nations of the Earth, then, and not till then, let my epitaph be written.*' O'Connell's aim was to bring that time about but by peaceful means.

The most significant Irish grievance of the time was the flat refusal of the Westminster Government to emancipate the Catholics. Catholics were barred from most of the professions, from holding commissions in the Army, and from all public office. Daniel O'Connell changed all that. He was born in County Kerry in 1775 and educated in France, where his uncle had done good business as a smuggler before becoming a General in the Revolutionary Army. O'Connell was in France when the Revolution broke out and he stayed there throughout the bloody excesses of the Terror, which turned him totally against violence as a means to political ends.

O'Connell returned to Ireland, where he trained as a lawyer and founded the Catholic Association. In 1828 he entered Parliament as the Member for Clare, where he immediately refused to take the required Oath acknowledging the King as Head of the Church. From this defiance, which the Government declined to challenge, came further acts, all steps towards the granting of Catholic emancipation. O'Connell then set out to gain the repeal of the Act of Union, but in this he was much less successful. Though peaceful his mass meetings, attended by crowds of a hundred thousand people or more, worried the Government and irritated those of his supporters who wanted to use more decisive and more violent ways of persuading the British Government to liberate Ireland.

Matters came to a head in 1840 when tens of thousands of people attended meetings called by O'Connell to support his views on the repeal of the Act of Union. The biggest of these was called at Clontarf near Dublin, but when the Government banned it and called in troops, O'Connell called it off for fear of violence. This well-meaning action pleased nobody. His supporters left in droves and the Government had him arrested anyway. With the aid of a 'packed' jury full of Ulster Protestants, O'Connell was sent to gaol. The House of Lords ordered his immediate release but he emerged a broken man and died in 1847 at the height of the Great Famine, when the Irish had more to think about than liberation. His fame came later.

O'Connell is recognized today among the greatest of all

those who strove for Irish independence, a man to rank with Parnell. His advocacy of non-violence put the British Government at a disadvantage and gave him the moral authority to command the support of the Catholic Church. His success with the Emancipation Acts gave Ireland – and Irish Catholics – a political voice in Parliament and elsewhere, and that gave Parnell that support in the Westminster Parliament which he was to use with such effect. More than that, simply by calling for the repeal of the Act of Union, O'Connell put Irish independence back on the political agenda. That time was not yet, but it was coming.

I was pleased to see the Shannon. This is not because the Shannon at Killimer is a pretty river – which it is not – but because the Shannon had largely dictated my route across Ireland. This great river almost cuts Ireland in two. Since its course is slow and low-lying, from time to time the winding Shannon broadens out into great lakes, of which Loughs Allen, Derg and Ree are the largest. The Shannon is rather short of crossing places, so any journey through Ireland has to take this into account. Here at Killimer the river is wide, and supports a certain amount of coastal shipping which steams up the river to Limerick. The ferry port at Killimer contains a café, a shop, and a couple of bars. Outside one of the bars is the bronze bust of the 'Colleen Bawn', who is buried in the nearby churchyard.

When I was younger and used to hang about in bars, the young men sang songs about young virgins who fell for the wiles of wicked squires who were usually called Sir Jasper. Just such a fate actually befell poor Eileen Hamley, the 'Colleen Bawn'.

Eileen was just 16 years old in 1819 when she met Squire John Scanlan. Everyone knew he was a rotter and warned her against him but, like all young girls, she would not listen and married him. Scanlan soon tired of her. He eventually told a couple of his henchmen to take her out in a boat and drown her in the Shannon. A nice man, Squire Scanlan. This they did but the body was washed ashore on the banks of the river, the sorry tale came out and Scanlan was arrested. He was defended at his trial by Daniel O'Connell but found guilty and sentenced to hang. It is said that the horses drawing his carriage at first refused to take him to the scaffold, but he was hanged at Limerick in March 1820.

Well, it's a sad tale and to be honest, the dockside at Killimer is a sad place, overlooked by power stations which never do much for the landscape, and swarming with large and malevolent crows. I have never seen such numbers of crows as they have here in Ireland. They gather in black heaps under the roof-eaves or hop about in flocks across the roads and car parks. Here at Killimer, as I sat waiting for the ferry, it was rather like a scene from Hitchcock's *The Birds*. These menacing black spectres were hopping boldly around the cars as I sat waiting on the wall, fixing me with their bright and chilling eyes.

The ferry eventually came in and we all swarmed aboard, several cars, many cycle tourists and the solitary walker. The ferry ploughed across the river to Tarbert, where I stepped ashore and turned upstream for the short walk into Glin. This led me along the banks of the Shannon into Tarbert, past the old lock-up, the Bridewell, which is very well preserved, and round the walls of the Glin estate and into the village itself.

The Knights of Glin – which is the title of a family not a Military Order – have lived here beside the Shannon since the 14th century. Their medieval castle was destroyed by the orders of Elizabeth I in 1600, though the picturesque ruins still stand on a small hill overlooking the river. The new castle, which is a pleasant country house with some rather unsuitable towers and battlements on top, was erected in the 1780s and, times being what they are, the Fitzgerald family of Glin now opens the house to the public. I rather like old country houses, so I took an hour out here to explore the house and the grounds before I went back into Glin, found a pub and settled down for the evening.

I had crossed Clare and the mighty Shannon, stepped into County Limerick at Glin and now entered my last region, County Kerry. That was something to celebrate. There was music in the bar that night and when I complimented the barman on the skill of the musician, he told me, 'Sure, an' that boy was born with a guitar in his mouth.'

Having got this far, it was time to take stock. I was obviously going to finish the walk but what was I getting out of it? Physically, not much; I must have been fitter but I was also fatter. By this stage in my walk across Spain I had lost 24 lbs and was as thin as a rake. After a month in Ireland, I hadn't lost an ounce. Mind you, Spain does not have Irish hospitality or Ulster Frys.

I had also come a little nearer to understanding Ireland, the country of my travels, which is at least part of the reason for travelling anywhere. Events and people I had only heard about were now real and alive for me, which is one of the benefits of exploring history on the ground, in the places where the events happened or the people lived. I was also having a good time. So, all things considered, I judged the effort worth it, shouldered my pack again and pressed on across Kerry.

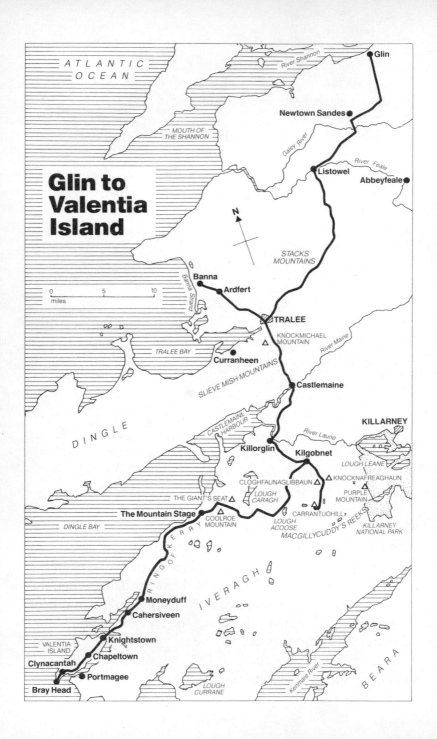

Glin to
Valentia
Island

16

County Kerry

All occlivity and declivity, without the inter-
vention of a single horizontal plane: the mountains all rocks and the men all savages.

Thomas Moore, *Journal*, 1823

Thomas Moore cannot have visited County Kerry when he
wrote that comment in his diary. I have been right across it
and Kerry is not like that at all. For all its ups and downs
Kerry has a great deal of level ground and only starts to rock
and roll in any significant fashion to the south of the city of
Tralee. Between Tralee and the Shannon the countryside is
rather gentle and, give or take the varied flowers and the
wonderful cloud formations cruising in from the Atlantic, it
is not unlike parts of Southern England.

I had become fascinated by Irish clouds. An Irish sky is
rarely simply open, or that flat grey blanket of lowering
cloud I so often endure on the mainland. Irish skies present
even grey clouds in great tumbled layers, great castles in the
air, full of threats and menace. On the other hand, when the
sun is out an Irish sky looks exactly like the ceiling in one of
those Baroque chapels, billowy and tinted with colour,
offering the distinct possibility that a cherub or two will
float from behind the cloud at any minute. I wandered on,
watching the clouds, staying off the main roads where

possible and plodding steadily towards the distant hills. I was making good time now, for the end of this journey was getting closer and like a runner in sight of the tape I was starting to sprint to the finish.

Walking flat out I can average three miles an hour, covering say 20 to 25 miles in a good day, but this does not allow for diversions off the chosen track. I usually bend the direct route at the planning stage to take in places I really want to see, but there are always more places to see and no time to see them. That was especially so here in County Kerry, which is full of attractive corners.

Kerry forms part of the old province of Munster and is best imagined like a hand laid out to the south and west. The palm is the giant limestone plain east of Tralee, the fingers the peninsulas of Dingle, Iveragh and Beara, that probe out into the rising swells of the Atlantic. Hilly or mountainous, ringed with cliffs and offshore islands, these peninsulas are the great attractions of South-West Ireland and draw the visitors by the tens of thousands. As I was to discover though, there is plenty of space down here in the South-West, and for most of the time I was still completely alone.

The main road south out of Glin leads directly over the moors to Abbeyfeale, a small town on the River Feale, but I had it in mind to visit Listowel, which lies further downstream and is famous as a place for writers. I bent my track a little once again, turning west along the Mayvane river and then over the Galey river which was foaming along, dark brown with peat, past Newtown Sandes and so back to the River Feale and into Listowel. This is a fair-sized town with a fair-sized former church in the central square which now contains an Art and Heritage Centre.

Listowel hosts an annual Writers' Week in May, when writers or would-be writers from all over the world come to mix and mingle with their colleagues and talk about their work. That might be an interesting event because I know quite a few writers and all they ever talk about is money. It is often far more interesting to get writers to talk about what they were doing for a living before they finally admitted defeat and took up writing. Look on the back of any book and you will usually see that the author has been through several incarnations – teacher, mercenary, male stripper, played the piano in a whorehouse, and so on – before turning to writing. Apart from infant prodigies and failed journalists, I suspect writing is what you do when you can't do anything else. I comfort myself with that thought, since all my attempts to become a tycoon of industry have ended in disaster.

I stopped for lunch in Listowel, sitting in another dark pub. Keane's pub in Listowel is owned by John B. Keane – always known hereabouts as 'John B.' – a successful Irish playwright and one of his plays, *The Field*, had just been made into a film, so there was great cause for celebration in the bar, where John B. Keane was drinking with the regulars. John B. Keane has also written other plays, like *Big Maggie* and *The Man from Clare*, which have done well, but like Matt Molloy back in Westport, he likes to have a pub to fall back on, a place where he can stay in touch with his roots.

After that it was south again, on over the moors on a narrow road across the Stacks Mountains into Tralee. The big event of the year here is the annual 'Rose of Tralee' competition, for which the streets were hung about with fairy lights. This festival is open to Irish girls, or girls of Irish descent from every country in the world, and they arrive by the hundreds. The town becomes colleen-infested in early August and what with the girls and their countless admirers, the event gives a real boost to the town's fragile economy.

It needs that kind of help, for like a lot of Irish towns, Tralee is not all that attractive. The parks and public buildings are quite fine but the main streets are narrow and full of pokey little shops. Memorable sights are few and far between. William Mulchinock, who wrote the song, 'The Rose of Tralee' back in the last century, has a statue in the Town Park and the town also supports the *Siamsa-Tiré*, the National Folk Theatre of Ireland, which is dedicated to keeping alive Irish art and the Irish language. Indeed, Tralee is a very Irish town, full of Irish insights, so I decided to stay on here for a couple of days before I went on across the Slieve Mish, the 'Ghost Mountains', which lie like a wall to the south of the city.

All in all it was a pleasant couple of days. Tralee used to be a stronghold of the Desmonds and after they were driven out in Elizabethan times, the lands were given to the Denny family, who ruled Tralee and most of North Kerry for the next 200 years. The Desmond story is told in an exhibition, unfortunately entitled 'The Medieval Experience', where the visitor gets transported through the past in a buggy. I preferred the ruins of the medieval castle, destroyed in the rebellion of 1641, which stand in the nearby park. I also liked the splendid working Blennerville windmill and the little trains on the Tralee Light Railway, and most of all I liked having nothing to do.

Tralee stands at the landward end of the Dingle Peninsula, at no great distance from the sea, and is linked to Dingle Bay by a ship canal. The rain stayed away on both days – as it usually did when I was in shelter – so I wandered around the sights with all the other tourists and quite enjoyed the rest. With the famous Killarney lakes and fells close at hand, Tralee was full of tourists, the streets jammed with cars and coaches, and by the second afternoon I began to think longingly of the empty hills of Connemara.

Kerry is referred to locally as 'The Kingdom' and I spent a lot of time trying to find out why. It appears to date back to the pre-Christian period when this part of Ireland was ruled by a Celtic tribe, the Goidels, whose territory extended well into Munster. Three families, the McCarthys, the O'Donaghues and the O'Sullivans – names which are still common hereabouts – tried to establish a single kingdom here in the 11th and 12th centuries, to stave off the Anglo–Normans, and though that attempt failed after the usual tribal in-fighting, this part of Ireland remained relatively free of English influence until Tudor times.

On the second day I took myself off on a trip to the village of Banna Strand, a few miles to the north. Banna Strand is really a small village set behind a great long sandy beach, and the beach has two claims to fame. It was here they filmed *Ryan's Daughter*. More relevant to my underlying theme, this is the place where Sir Roger Casement landed from that German submarine on Good Friday in 1916 with a shipment of arms for the Easter Rising.

Sir Roger Casement is an interesting man. Born into an Ulster Protestant family in 1864, he grew up deeply con-cerned with human rights, which were under severe attack at the time in many parts of the world. He became a lawyer and then a diplomat in the Colonial Service and was eventually knighted for his services as a Consular Agent. During his time as a diplomat he exposed the barbarous treatment of the natives in the then Belgian Congo and Brazil. His accusations, though true, were hardly diplo-matic, and his actions got little support from the British Government.

In spite of his Ulster Protestant background, Sir Roger was an Irish patriot. When the Great War began he followed the old rule that 'England's difficulty is Ireland's opportu-nity' and made his way to Germany. There he attempted, quite without success, to recruit Irish prisoners-of-war for the planned revolution in Ireland. He then became involved in the plans for the Easter Rising of 1916. Having arranged for a shipment of arms he went ahead to Ireland in a German submarine, which put him ashore at Banna Strand

at dawn on 21 April 1916. From that moment on, everything went wrong.

A British Army patrol appeared and captured Casement
hiding in a wood at Ardfert, which lies just behind the
beach. The arms never arrived and without the arms the
Easter Rising had little chance of success. When it collapsed
some of the other ringleaders were swiftly court-martialled
and shot, but Roger Casement suffered a more elaborate
fate. He was taken to England, imprisoned in Pentonville
and tried for High Treason.

He was found guilty. Given his actions in treating with the
enemy in time of war, there can be little doubt that he
actually was guilty. He was, however, an Irish hero – or at
least a hero to Ireland. Attempts were made to blacken his
name in the weeks before his execution by circulating
'extracts' from his diaries which apparently revealed his
homosexuality. The truth of these extracts has often been
challenged but as *The Times* wrote during his trial, such
matters, even if true, had nothing to do with the offences
with which he was charged.

I don't know or care about Casement's morals, but by the
law of the land he was a traitor to his country and his
country hanged him for it. He knew exactly what he was
doing and what would probably happen to him if it all went
wrong. The snag is that Casement served another country, a
country that had yet to come into existence – Ireland – and
by that criteria he was, and believed himself to be, no traitor
at all. It all depends on your point of view. My considerable
regard for Casement dates back to the time I read his
statement from the dock, long before I knew anything else
about him.

Casement followed the path of other Irish patriots; a
rebellion, capture and trial, a speech from the dock of
thrilling fervour, and the inevitable sentence and execution.
Irishmen are good speakers, and these speeches from the

dock must have been marvellous and tragic. Even reading them makes the nerve ends tingle. This speech of Casement's seems to sum up everything that was ever said about the state of Ireland under British rule, and since this puts the case for Ireland far better than I could ever do, I reproduce part of it here:

> We have been told, we have been asked to hope, that after this war Ireland will get Home Rule, as a reward for the life-blood shed in a cause which whoever else its success may benefit, can surely not benefit Ireland. And what will Home Rule be in return for what its vague promise has taken and still hopes to take away from Ireland? It is not necessary to climb the painful stairs of Irish history – that treadmill of a nation whose labours are as vain for her own uplifting as the convict's exertions are for his redemption – to review the long list of British promises made only to be broken – of Irish hopes raised only to be dashed to the ground.
>
> Home Rule when it comes, if come it does, will find an Ireland drained of all that is vital to its very existence – unless it be that unquenchable hope we build on the graves of the dead. We are told that if Irishmen go by the thousand to die, not for Ireland, but for Flanders, for Belgium, for a patch of sand on the deserts of Mesopotamia, or a rocky trench on the heights of Gallipoli, they are winning self-government for Ireland. But if they dare to lay down their lives on their native soil, if they dare to dream even that freedom can be won only at home by men resolved to fight for it there, then they are traitors to their country, and their dream and their deaths alike are phases of a dishonourable phantasy. But history is not so recorded in

other lands. In Ireland alone in this twentieth century is loyalty held to be a crime. If loyalty be something less than love and more than law, then we have had enough of such loyalty for Ireland or Irishmen. If we are to be indicted as criminals, to be shot as murderers, to be imprisoned as convicts because our offence is that we love Ireland more than we value our lives, then I know not what virtue resides in any offer of self-government held out to brave men on such terms.

Self-government is our right, a thing born in us at birth; a thing no more to be doled out to us or withheld from us by another people than the right to life itself – than the right to feel the sun or smell the flowers, or to love our kind. It is only from the convict these things are withheld for crime committed and proven – and Ireland that has wronged no man, that has injured no land, that has sought no dominion over others – Ireland is treated today among the nations of the world as if she was a convicted criminal. If it be treason to fight against such an unnatural fate as this, then I am proud to be a rebel, and shall cling to my 'rebellion' with the last drop of my blood. If there be no right of rebellion against a state of things that no savage tribe would endure without resistance, then I am sure that it is better for men to fight and die without right than to live in such a state of right as this.

Where all your rights become only an accumulated wrong; where men must beg with bated breath for leave to subsist in their own land, to think their own thoughts, to sing their own songs, to garner the fruits of their own labours – and even while they beg, to see things inexorably withdrawn from them – then surely it is a braver, a saner and a truer thing, to be a rebel in act and deed against such circumstances as these than tamely to accept it as the natural lot of men.

Well, they hanged him, of course. What else can you do with a man who could speak like that?

I went to Banna Strand and found Sir Roger's rather battered memorial on the sand dunes behind the beach. There was nothing else there to bring his memory back to life, just a great long beach with the waves flooding in, but I am glad I went there. It was a sort of pilgrimage. Then I went back to Tralee, repacked my travel-stained rucksack and set off again on my journey.

I had a terrible job finding the right road out of Tralee to the Slieve Mish. Since the Slieve Mish is in plain sight, that may be hard to believe, but so it was. There is a ring road to the south of the city which was not shown on my map and Irish fingerposts are not always helpful. I eventually realized that I must follow the fingerpost labelled simply 'Viewpoint', which led me through the scattered suburbs and out onto a steep, narrow lane which eventually got me to the top of the range. Those who follow in my footsteps should be grateful for this advice.

This is a sharp little mountain road up the Mish and it does indeed have a viewpoint, or to be exact, two viewpoints. The one on the north face gave marvellous views over Tralee Bay and along the north shore of the Dingle Peninsula, and from that viewpoint it is a short walk to Scotia's Glen and the stone slab of Scotia's Grave. Queen Scotia is said to be a daughter of an Egyptian Pharoah, who died in battle on the Slieve Mish in 1700 BC, after the legendary and most unlikely invasion of Ireland from Egypt, when the sons of Scotia fought and beat the native Da

Danann people. The sons won but Scotia was killed in the moment of victory, rather like Brian Boru at Clontarf. It all sounds most unlikely to me.

From there I plodded on up the road to the wind-racked crest of the hill and had my first view south to Carrantuohill and the long mountain range of the MacGillycuddy's Reeks. I spent some time up there, lurking behind the wall of the southern viewpoint, trying to spot a way up the mountain. Then I went down the hill, leaning against the wind to the shelter of the wall at the second viewpoint, and sat down in the shelter to study my map. To the right lay Castlemaine Harbour, so somewhere in the lee of this hill – Knock-michael Mountain – must lie the town of Castlemaine. After that the plains began again and took me round the shore of the bay to the foot of the Reeks. That was my route to the end of this journey and it took me over Carrantuohill.

The Slieve Mish – the Ghost Mountains or the Mountains of the Phantoms – stand like a long ridge at the landward end of the Dingle Peninsula, one of several long fingers of land that poke out from Kerry into the Atlantic. There is another of those long-distance footpaths here, the Dingle Way. This starts at Curranheen on the north of the peninsula and runs for 112 miles, right around the Dingle Peninsula and cuts off here along the Slieve Mish.

This Dingle footpath uses mountain trails and country roads, or 'borreens', and if I had not already settled firmly on a finish at Valentia Island, I would have followed the Dingle Way out to the west and enjoyed every step of it, for it is a popular and well-established route, followed by hundreds of walkers every year. However, Carrantuohill loomed ahead and I had to get over that before I could finish this walk.

As usual, going downhill played havoc with my toes. I was on the verge of another sense-of-humour failure when I met a family in a horse-drawn holiday caravan who were having a terrible time. They were hauling the horse, which was hauling the caravan, and they were not too happy about it. They stopped for a moan and put me on the road for Castlemaine, which they had been trying to get away from for the last few days.

'We want to go over the hill to Tralee but the horse won't have it,' said the wife. 'It doesn't like hills.'

'It doesn't even like slopes,' said the husband bitterly. 'Half a degree off the horizontal and we get a nasty reaction.'

'Like what?' I asked.

'Well ... to put it bluntly, it farts in our faces. Basically, we've spent a week walking around the flat bits of Kerry in the pouring rain, dragging this bloody great horse. They don't put that in the brochures.'

They were not alone in having trouble with our four-footed friends. I passed several other caravans, all of them the wooden, round-roofed gipsy kind, and everyone seemed to be walking beside their horse. Then, late in the afternoon, I turned a corner of the road and met two horses, both wearing white nosebags and trotting hard for Tralee. Further on, about a mile down the road, I found two horseless caravans drawn up off the road and two families running about blaming each other and screaming. When they stopped screaming I tried to be helpful.

'I think I've seen your horses, about a mile back ... with white nosebags – right? They were trotting along happily and quite all right.'

This news did not go down too well. Everyone started screaming at me. Apparently I should have captured the horses and brought them back. That might have been difficult and anyway it never occurred to me. The families ran off after their horses and I flogged on towards Castlemaine. Then came another unusual encounter when I was chased by a large dog. There was nothing unusual in this and I carry my stick to fight off dogs, but I had no need of it here. This dog's range of action was limited by the large slab of concrete that dangled on some shock-cord from his collar.

'He won't bite you,' said his owner, who was leaning over his garden gate. 'Well, he probably won't bite you. The old devil chases cars and I thought the stone would slow him down a bit.' The stone slab would have slowed an elephant down, but the dog seemed fairly resigned to it.

Castlemaine was another of the places I had inked in on my map before the start of the walk, for this was the home of Jack Duggan – the Wild Colonial Boy. I know that because of the old song:

> There was a wild Colonial boy,
> Jack Duggan was his name.
> He was born and raised in Ireland,
> In a place called Castlemaine.
>
> He was his mother's only son,
> His father's pride and joy,
> And dearly did his parents love
> That Wild Colonial boy ...

I've spent many an evening bawling out that song and I could hardly come all this way across Ireland without stopping in Castlemaine where, if he had his rights, there would surely be a pub named after Jack Duggan. After all in Australia they have even named a beer after Castlemaine, so fair's fair. There were several pubs in Castlemaine and although none was named after Jack Duggan, I went into one and heard a man give a curious bar order: 'A Guinness, a pint of Smithwicks, an Irish coffee, two Bush and a pint of milk.'

At Castlemaine I was down on the plains again, but clearly not for long. There were mountains all around me now, rearing up all green and dark to poke their heads into the milling clouds. After a short prowl around Castlemaine I went on to the town of Killorglin, which turned out to be jammed with people and the first place on this journey where I could not find a room for the night.

It was some time before I found shelter at a B & B some distance outside the town, near Kilgobnet, and when I got there I enlisted the entire family in my preparations for the following day. I tried to fit in all the challenges I could find on the way and one of them was to climb up Carrantuohill, the highest mountain in Ireland. It lay out there in the dark and rain, and even if Carrantuohill is not very high, mountains are not to be fooled with by anyone with even an ounce of sense. They are, as the old saying has it, perfectly safe as long as you remember they are dangerous.

This B & B would be my base camp for the assault on Carrantuohill next day, with my boots polished and as much kit as possible left out of my rucksack. I put on my trainers to rest my sore toes and went back into Killorglin in search of entertainment.

Killorglin, which lies a mile inland from the sea on the west bank of the River Laune, is unusually lively, even for an Irish town. I got there after dark when the clouds were sitting right on the rooftops and a thin, cold rain was falling, but the place was full of activity. Every bar was jammed with people, there was a band hard at it in every pub and all the restaurants were packed. It was some time, around nine o'clock, before I could find a table.

Most of the people here were young; I reflected, not for the first time on this journey, on how attractive Ireland must be for young people. There are lots of pubs, lots of chat, plenty of entertainment and, if you stick to hostels or B & Bs, plenty of cheap accommodation. Who could ask for more?

Killorglin is really not much more than a village. The population is scarcely more than 1,000 people, but it manages to support a dozen pubs as well as playing host to the annual 'Puck Fair and Pattern'. A 'pattern' is rather like the Breton 'pardon', the festival of the patron saint, traditionally held on the day of his death. The Puck Fair of Killorglin is more probably some pagan hangover, but a great excuse for a rave.

The Puck Fair at Killorglin lasts three days. On the first day – The Gathering – people come in from all over the countryside, bringing their cattle for the second day's market. This occupies all the main streets of the town and is highly successful. Now comes the unusual part. A large platform is erected at the top of the town, 10 ft off the ground. On Gathering Day, a large wild billy-goat, captured by the young men of the town in the surrounding hills is installed on this platform, his horns decorated with ribbons and a crown. This is King Puck, and there he stays, on the platform, throughout the Festival, eating the finest of vegetables, secured by straw bales, looking down on the three-day booze-up below. The livestock fair is a part of it, but there are other events too, including duck-racing, which I would like to have seen.

However, the main event of the Puck Fair at Killorglin is the drinking. For three whole days and three nights Killorglin is an open town. Nothing closes. Shops, cafés, pubs are on the go twenty-four hours a day. Why the local people don't all die of exhaustion beats me, but somehow they keep going, drinking, singing and dancing while the goat looks on. One of the nice things about an evening in an Irish pub is that there never seems to be any trouble. I am sure that there are brawls in Irish pubs, as there are in bars anywhere, but I went into a pub every night in Ireland and never sensed a whiff of trouble. In England I hardly ever go into pubs, but whenever I do there always seems to be a hint of menace from some half-drunk, crop-haired yobbo in the corner, who goes to a pub in search of trouble.

As for the origins of the Puck Fair, one tale has it that King Puck is installed on his comfortable platform as a reward for the time when stampeding goats gave warning of an approaching English army. That seems too pat an explanation for what obviously has its origins in a pagan festival, though one which has escaped the usual fate of such pagan events and been adopted by the Christian Church.

I had a good night in Killorglin. I went nipping through the rain from pub to pub and had a good supper with a plate of soda bread that could have been cut with a chain-saw. I might have stayed longer because the town was winding itself up for a good Saturday night, but there was the lurking thought that tomorrow I had to get into the Reeks and up Carrantuohill. When wisdom finally prevailed, I went back to bed at Kilgobnet and went to sleep listening to the sound of rain pelting hard against the window.

17

Climbing Carrantuohill

> Does any man do any good getting up a moun-
> tain.... The nasty, damp, slippery, boot-
> destroying, shin-breaking veritable mountain? I
> have tried many mountains in a small way and I
> protest that I will never try another.
>
> Anthony Trollope, 1859

Hill-walking in Ireland can be best imagined as climbing up
a waterfall in a thunderstorm. In other words, the experience is usually wet and always dramatic, a microcosm of
Ireland in itself. It rains a lot in Ireland and it was very wet
on the day I went up Carrantuohill. In fact, it was very, very
wet. I can see that from the map I have spread out on the
table before me as I write. Crumpled and dirty, faded from
immersion in water, it reminds me vividly of that long, hard
day on the hill.

At 3,414ft, Carrantuohill is an attractive, bulky, sharp-
summitted peak, the pride of the MacGillycuddy's Reeks, a
range that occupies the high ground at the landward end of
the Iveragh peninsula and the Ring of Kerry.

The 'Reeks' used to be called Na Cruecha Dubha – the
Black Stacks – which fails to explain where the 'Reeks' came
from, though the MacGillycuddys were a local family who
lived on the banks of the Laune river. As for Carrantuohill,

like a lot of things in Ireland the name is spelt in various ways, and it took me quite a while to realize that Carrantuohill and 'Corran Tuathail' were one and the same mountain.

Getting up, and if possible over Carrantuohill, had been another of the aims jotted down when Geoff and I had planned this walk months before. Walk the Antrim Coast, cross the Sperrins, climb Knockanrea, reach the summit of Croagh Patrick, cross the Twelve Bens of Connemara and the Burren plain, and then finish up on the top of Ireland on the peak of Carrantuohill. These were the things any walker through Ireland had to do and I had done them all but this. Once over Carrantuohill the last of my obstructions would be behind me. Now there it was, just across the valley floor, rearing up before me, cloud-capped and unfriendly.

I had got my first glimpse of the Reeks the previous day, when I came over the Slieve Mish in the teeth of the wind. They occupied the southern horizon of Kerry and they looked quite splendid in the evening light, looking far higher at a distance than they really are close-to, sharp-edged against the sky and plainly visible. That was yesterday. Today they were covered with cloud, rain was spattering against the window and the wind was up again and I felt like death.

Starting up a mountain is best done early in the day, on a day when the weather is good and the walker is rested and stone-cold sober. I awoke with what felt like a *Guinness Book of Records* hangover. This was surprising as I had drunk very little the night before. I had become a martyr to hangovers crossing Ireland but I could think of no particular reason for this one.

The idea of a wet, cold day, flogging up the mountain was awful, so I spent several hours mooching round the B & B, moaning, holding my throbbing head, crunching aspirin, having showers, drinking cups of coffee and rushing to the loo. From time to time I picked up the half-empty rucksack, which still seemed to weigh a ton, and looked out at the rain. This performance evoked words of sympathy and various home cures from my hosts.

When I finally declared that the best answer was to sweat it out on the hill, they offered me a lift to the start of the walk just a mile or two down the road, and why be a purist in these matters? At this stage in the journey I needed all the help I could get, so I accepted the offer gratefully. The entire family piled into the car and came to see me off at the foot of the mountain.

There is one rule about mountains. They always look higher and steeper at a distance. As you get closer they usually shrink in size and lean back a bit. So it was here. I must not exaggerate. In altitude at least, Carrantuohill is not much of a mountain, but it has the weather on its side and that can make a difference. I kept my head out of the window as we drove along the valley floor, partly for the fresh air and partly in case I came over poorly, but from what glances I could spare for the hills ahead, Carrantuohill was gradually becoming man-sized. It still lurked under a great, grey blanket of cloud, and the windscreen wipers were going hard, but that apart, matters were improving. The fresh air made me feel better and I was eager to be off and get it done with. Once I was out on the footpath I would probably perk up no end.

There is a waymarked trail up Carrantuohill. It begins in the yard of a small farm set in a valley between two peaks with unpronounceable names, Cloghfaunaglibbaun and Knocknafreaghaun. A plaque on the wall here remembers the crew of a US transport plane which crashed into the Reeks in 1943, and half a dozen cars were parked by the sign, indicating that I would have some company on the hill, which was a comfort.

A pair of long furry ears projected above the wall, and as I began to clamber into the hard-hitting gear, a donkey clip-clopped into the yard and poked me hard in the back with his nose, looking for sugar. I fended off the donkey and compared the wall map with my own 1:50,000 scale map. The plaque showed the route up the mountain and advised that to the top of Carrantuohill and back would take four hours. My map said something else. Humph!

I have felt better at the start of a walk. As I set off up the Hags Glen I could see the long scar on the face of the mountain a mile or so up the valley that had to be the Devil's Ladder, the main way up. The Ladder looked very steep and very long but that narrow track up the face of the cliff had been worn away by boots, so clearly it could be climbed. The Ladder is, in fact, a very steep, stony gully, 600 ft high and not a place to fall in, but if others could climb it, I could. The ascent of Carrantuohill is hardly a climb anyway. It is a lot of uphill walking and a bit of a scramble. All you have to do is do it.

The walk in to Carrantuohill is very pleasant. On a clear warm day it might even be delightful. The path is a clear track leading up an open valley and begins across a small stream. Then I was out in the open, with the Purple Mountain on my left, beyond the gap of Dunloe, Carrantuohill ahead and the River Gaddagh foaming away in a ravine to my right. As usual, once I was away from shelter the rain was coming down in vertical sheets like stair-rods. With streams foaming across the track ahead this day was going to be a wet one. Well, as we used to say in the Royal Marines, 'If you can't take a joke, you shouldn't have joined.' Someone always said that in moments of agony.

One of the things that brings the adventurous traveller down to earth is the sight of others on the mountains. I once climbed in the Cairngorms with the rest of the Commando, all of us clad in our full range of hard-hitting gear, from nailed boots to ice-axes. Halfway up the hill we met a girl skipping down the path from the White Lady in shorts and gym shoes.

All the hard men felt extremely overdressed. Walking on the top of the Pyrenees one summer, I met a young lady in a bikini, walking a poodle near Mount Canigou. I think they do it to annoy. Here, on the road to Carrantuohill, dressed for the worst and feeling ghastly, I met a group of schoolchildren coming down after two nights camping on the mountain, bright and cheerful as a flock of jays.

'What was it like up there?' I asked.

'Great,' they chorused. 'Brilliant.'

Bloody kids. Why did they have to be so cheerful? They were soaked to the skin, weren't they? How could it have been brilliant? I stood with them in the teeming rain and looked for comfort.

'Tough?' I asked, hopefully. 'Wet and cold? Bit of a challenge?'

'Easy, peasy.'

There is hope for the world yet with kids like this. Their teacher, who was bringing up the rear and draped with heavy kit, like climbing ropes, was a bit more sanguine. 'The weather is not too bad,' he said, squeezing rain from his beard. 'It was fine this morning but the visibility on the top is now about zero . . . have you got a compass?'

'I have,' I said, 'and enough kit to survive the Arctic, plus a copy of the only 1:50,000 map in Ireland.'

He grinned at me. 'You're not alone,' he said, tapping his pocket. 'But you won't find the map much use up there. The cloud is right down and visibility is non-existent. Watch your step, especially on the Ladder coming down.'

Huddled together against the rain we consulted his map and he showed me where a line of crests descended off the far side of the summit, running down to the open, flatter ground beyond. This might offer an easier way down than descending the Ladder, and it was at least something to think about, not least because it led out on my route to Kalnaa Island.

As I got closer to the hill I could see specks moving about on the side of the mountain and caught a glimpse of other walkers making their way up or down the Devil's Ladder. It was now mid-afternoon and since the climb up and down Carrantuohill is said to take four hours, I would have to press on hard if I was to be down again before dark. Having climbed Carrantuohill I might as well add that I think that four hours up and down is an optimistic estimate for anyone other than a mountain goat, but my critical faculties were not functioning too well at the time.

I crossed the River Gaddagh once or twice, picking my way across on wet boulders, sploshed across a couple of bogs and was already very wet when I reached the jumble of rocks called The Hags Teeth, and found myself at the foot of the Ladder. The path there leads between two lakes which occupy much of the land at the foot of Carrantuohill. Lough Gouragh and Lough Callee are no great size but they feed the Gaddagh river, and since they were brimful and the Gaddagh was roaring down the valley, the bog's ability to absorb and retain water must be considerable.

I could see by now that the Ladder was a steep, almost vertical rock and scree slope, with a stream running down the face. Falling water was throwing great fans of spray across the rock and I could see no obvious way up. It did not look at all inviting and I thought that while going up might be only difficult, coming down would be ghastly. I decided that, once up, I would stay up and walk off the mountain next day by following the line of peaks across the ridge and descending to join the Kerry Way by Lough Acoose in the far valley.

The Kerry Way circles Carrantuohill to the south and west, and if my map was anything to go by, there should be no great difficulty getting off the top, along a ridge and down a series of gullies, and then down to the footpath which would take me out to the Ring of Kerry and so to

Valentia. That would be a decent walk and be something worth doing ... assuming I could find the way down, that is. That decided and still feeling like death, I set off up the hill.

On a wet day the Devil's Ladder doubles as a waterfall. On a dry day – and they do have dry days in Ireland – the scramble up the Ladder might be little more than a testing bit of exercise. Today it was like swimming the Channel. My 'Sprayway' raingear was proof even against Irish rain, but jets of water were shooting over the rocks and when I took a handhold, the stream shot smartly up my sleeves and down my back. Within minutes I was soaked to the skin. As a bonus, small rocks and stones loosened by the rain or by other climbers ahead also came bouncing past, adding another worry to the fact that, climb as I would, it still seemed a hell of a long way to the top. That apart, I had no energy. I took a few paces, ran out of puff, stood hunched under the rain to get my breath back and took another few paces. This is no way to get up a hill.

Halfway up, or thereabouts, I met a French girl coming down, clad in fetching but unsuitable yellow oilskins, and we sheltered under a rock for a chat. Ireland was '*très belle*,' she said, and the people '*très sympa*,' but the rain ...? She could not think of anything good to say about the rain. She looked very tired with her hair hanging in wet skeins about her pale face. She had clearly done more than enough and I warned her to be very careful over the rest of the descent. Then I turned again to the Ladder.

I don't want to make a great to-do about this. The Devil's Ladder is not the North Face of the Eiger. It only felt like it. Since I knew enough to realize that the hill was not the problem, I finally concluded that I was ill.

The trick for getting up a steep slope is to pick the easiest route, take the shortest possible steps and keep going, however slowly. The snag is this trick doesn't always come off. There is a rough sort of route up the ladder, a path of sorts made by countless other walkers, but this route is sometimes obvious and sometimes disappears. On a day of low cloud and pelting rain any route would be hard to make out, but I just plodded on, picking handholds where I could, scraping off the mud, watching the water flow into my boots and wishing I was twenty years younger. I eventually got to the top of the Ladder, but getting there took more than twice the time I had allowed.

Even worse, everyone I passed was heading down and giving me worried looks. Over the last few yards up the Ladder the route left the rock behind and led through a narrow gully of earth and mud. On the lip of this gully a family sat in the rain eating sandwiches. One of them, a boy of about eight, wearing a cycling helmet, looked as fresh as a daisy, blast him! Anyway, I had done it, or so I thought.

'That was a tough one,' I said to the family as I flopped wearily onto the grass. 'Where is the summit?' Since I had been at it for hours I expected the summit to be in sight and the family could take my photograph to prove I had got there and the worst would be over.

They looked surprised. 'You're not there yet,' said the father. 'It's another forty minutes or so ... up there in the clouds somewhere.'

My heart sank. Those who choose to climb Carrantuohill should know that when they get to the top of the Ladder there is still a long way to go to the top and all of it uphill. This can be even more depressing when the rain is coming down at the end of a dark afternoon.

I lay there for a few minutes, chatting with the family, and the father took my photograph since it would be cloudy at the top. Then I had to get on. The family urged me to get a move on as the day was getting late, so I left them at a fast clip, which slowed to a stagger within yards.

The path from the Ladder to the summit of Carrantuohill runs uphill over very rough ground and is marked by large stone cairns. Had I been feeling well, had the weather been better, and had it not been so late in the day, I might have enjoyed it. On a good day the views from the path up Carrantuohill must be spectacular. On this particular day I could sometimes see for yards. I plodded painfully uphill, my head butting into the pelting rain, exchanging greetings with other, younger walkers, who came bounding down out of the mist in a shower of stones.

'Keep going,' cried one. 'It's not far now,' said another. 'Only another half hour,' added a third. I hardly had the strength left to even pretend I was enjoying myself, but I kept going.

Like a lot of mountains, Carrantuohill has false crests. Every so often, looking up from my bent-double position over my walking stick, I would see what appeared to be the top of the mountain, a curving, grey line in the mist up ahead, and think, 'I've done it, by God!' Then, as I staggered on upwards, another dim crest would appear behind that, then another and another, endlessly upwards. I began to think of abandoning the attempt, of turning back and telling lies. It was late, I felt ill, I was too old, and there was no point in it.

On the other hand, to hell with it. I had not come all this way across Ireland, braving countless hangovers and endless conversation only to turn back now. The summit was up there somewhere and I was bloody well going to find it. One of these days, and with luck quite soon, I will outgrow these childish fancies.

Quite a few years ago I entered the Engadine Ski Marathon. This is a classic 26-mile race on cross-country skis along the valley below St Moritz. The fit types train for weeks, live on health food and zip around the course in something under two hours. I trained in the bar at the Kulm

Hotel and decided that I might get to the finish in five hours, which allowed for lunch. The snag is that when you enter a race you end up being competitive. I set off with 15,000 others at far too fast a pace but I flogged on round the course until everyone else had either finished the course or given up, and I was quite worn out. Later that day I was still plodding along, hoping only to get to the finish before the race ended and everyone went home, when out of the evening gloom appeared two warmly-clad figures – Jim Rivett, the friend I had driven out with, and my wife. They urged me on with encouraging cries but fell silent when they saw the state I was in, my face haggard, my hair thick with frozen sweat.

'Come on,' said Jim. 'Look at you! Be sensible . . . I've got the car over there and we can drive down to the town and have a few drinks. Pack it in, man.'

I have to say that I thought that a most seductive suggestion. I was just about to kick off the skis and reach for Jim's hip-flask when my wife stuck her oar in.

'If you think my husband will stop now,' she declared, 'then you just don't know my husband.'

I could have killed her.

The upshot was, then as now, that I plodded on, and far too late in the day, the finish eventually came in sight. The cloudy summit of Carrantuohill is marked by a tall, green-painted metal cross, and I was very, very glad to see it. I shrugged off my rucksack and wandered about the hilltop, worried that in that dim light my pictures, taken here as proof of arrival and evidence of effort, would not come out or be fogged by rain on the lens. Then I put the camera away and turned my thoughts to the next problem. How was I going to get down? I was alone and weary in a dull, grey, dripping world, and it would soon be dark.

I didn't have to go down. I am often foolish but I am not a fool. I had my tent and my sleeping bag, some dry clothes and some chocolate. I am quite a wily old bird really. A night on the mountain by myself would be no hardship. On the other hand, I was ill. I certainly felt ill. Though soaked to the skin I was sweating like a pig and my head ached. I had already abandoned the idea of pressing on over the mountain to the Kerry Way. Wandering about an unknown mountain when you can hardly see your hand in front of your face is a sure way to commit suicide. After a short ponder I decided to start down again. If I felt ill now I would feel much worse later.

Had the weather been good and the route visible, or had it been earlier in the day, I might have tried walking out to the west, partly because I hate turning back, and partly because turning back meant going down the Devil's Ladder. I didn't fancy that at all.

Going down a mountain is usually worse than going up, particularly if you are heavily loaded and tired. All the weight of the body and the rucksack falls on tired legs and the risks of a stumble and a fall are therefore quite high. I did not fancy a 600 ft fall down the Devil's Ladder. It was now getting dark, it was still pouring with rain and all the sensible people had long since left the hill. If I came a cropper on the Devil's Ladder it would be next day at least before anyone found me, but since I didn't intend to come a cropper, this thought did not bother me unduly.

Getting down was a painful business. My wet socks were bunching up in my boots, my toes were raw and the weight of the rucksack was crushing. When I got back to the top of the Ladder I was already quite shattered. I sat down on a rock, pulled my boots off and poured out a stream of peaty brown water. Then I put on dry socks and squeezed my feet back into the boots again. That done, I picked up my stick and rucksack and started down the Ladder. It went like a dream.

Most difficulties back away when you confront them, and

in the event getting down the Ladder was not too bad. Looking down from above I could see a fairly obvious route, and although it was wet and muddy and my toes were jamming painfully into the front of my boots, I got down in one piece and without undue difficulty. It took me a fair amount of time though, and took a lot out of me, but in about an hour I was at the bottom. I am now in my late fifties, and at that age you don't bounce back like you used to; and when the ground finally flattened out into bog and the track through the Hags Glen appeared ahead across the moor, I was very glad to see it. I limped off across the plain and over the river as fast as my trembling legs would carry me.

I got back to the farm at eight o'clock. Night was now beginning to fall, but – there is a God! – there was a car in the car park. Not everyone is willing to offer a lift to a soaking-wet, muddy 'eejit' with a great big rucksack, so God Bless Ireland, where people are kind to the wet and weary. These were walkers who had returned to the car park half-an-hour before and they were drinking hot toddie from a Thermos and as tired as I was – a fact which I found comforting. They all swore they would never do it again, and we had a dram or two while we agreed on that.

Back at the B & B came the divestment. This took time and help from the family to peel off my wet, muddy clothes. Then came the ecstasy of a hot bath and dry garments. Even after that I didn't feel too good.

I sat on the sofa that evening, declining all offers of food, drinking endless cups of tea, shivering and sweating. It finally occurred to me that the 'Bug-Which-Was-Going-Around' had stopped going around and pounced on me. This BWWGA was causing people to keel over right and left and I certainly felt like death. Death actually seemed like quite a good idea as I crawled into bed. Even so, I was determined not to stop now. In another day or two at the most I could be on Valentia Island, this trip would be over, and I could go home again. Normally I hate that final moment. This time I could hardly wait.

18

Valentia

There lay the green shore of Ireland, like some
coast of plenty. We could see the towns, towers,
churches, houses; but the curse of eight hundred
years we could not discern.

Ralph Waldo Emerson, 1856

I felt all right next morning until just after breakfast. My
clothes were dry and the day was fine, and I had slept like
the dead. Then, half way through breakfast, I began to
disintegrate. Getting into the hard-hitting gear took a great
deal of time and someone else had to pick up the rucksack
and hold it while I backed into the straps like a tired old
plough-horse. This was bad enough but I began to feel really
shaky as I said goodbye to my hosts, who stood watching
anxiously in the doorway as I plodded off down the drive.
Within half an hour I was definitely ill again, but no matter.
I had a bug, not bubonic plague. A hard day would not kill
me, and I only had about 20 – maybe 30 – miles to go.

I never seem to have a good day for the finish of my
journeys. When I walked across France I reached the
Mediterranean on May Day, when every car in France was
on the road and trying to kill me. When I reached Tarifa
after walking across the parched desert of Central Spain, the

rain was washing boulders off the hillsides of Andalucia. When we came to the Jordan after riding right through Arabia, the Israelis would not let us in. Now the pattern was repeating itself. This Iveragh peninsula on the western edge of Kerry is one of the most beautiful places on Earth, but not today. Today it was wet, cloud-covered and dreary.

I have brooded at length on the weather of Western Ireland. It should be said that while it rains a lot in Ireland, the rain hardly matters. Up to now it had arrived in the form of rainstorms, sharp and dramatic, quite exciting and no problem at all if you are dressed for it ... and I was dressed for it. On this last day, when I could have used a little sunshine or some exciting storms to take my mind off things, I met the archetypal British Isles downpour, with lowering skies and visibility of a hundred yards at best. Everything dripped.

Given half a chance and another lifetime, I could spend an entire trip just sauntering round the Ring of Kerry. The Ring of Kerry is a road which runs right round the Iveragh Peninsula through all the beauty spots, a route that will take the traveller right round the coast and back to Killarney through the Killarney National Park. There is also a footpath, the Kerry Way, the Republic's longest waymarked trail, that runs right round the Iveragh Peninsula, right out to the far west point and back to Killarney, a total distance of some 135 miles.

This path follows tracks and green roads with some tarmac'd sections here and there and a number of drove roads or 'butter' routes which once took sheep or produce to market. The Kerry Way flanked the Ring of Kerry road but lies inland, keeping to higher and hopefully drier ground, and I hoped to pick it up as soon as possible. There was also the remains of the old railway line that once ran out to Valentia, and although the track has gone, the bridges and embankments remain, so what with one thing and another I had the possibility of dry-going for the last part of my journey ... but now it had to rain.

I was in no state to hang about or make diversions. My B & B near Shannera was close to the road running round the Reeks to Lough Acoose, and I marched there as fast as I could to pick up the Kerry Way and then cut north, sometimes on roads, sometimes back on the Way itself, across the col between Coolroe and the Giant's Seat, two small hills which overlook Dingle Bay, to stumble down to the Ring of Kerry at the café at the Mountain Stage.

From here, I could follow the Way or the railway, or the road west. There was no need to wait and not much to see, for the cloud base was just above the tops of the telegraph poles and the visibility restricted by great drifts of rain. My temperature was now over the 100° mark but with coffees in the occasional wayside café and a few hot toddies in every open pub, I got along well enough. This was no day for pin-point map-reading and there was no need for it either. I veered right up the coast road, driven on by a gusting wind.

This brought me along the main Ring of Kerry road to a point near Daniel O'Connell's country house at Moneyduff and here I swung left for Cahersiveen, a straggling sort of village, surrounded by rain-drenched fuchsia bushes. I was striding along, concentrating only on putting one foot in front of the other as fast as I could, making good time, my head lowered against the gusts. Then the offshore mist lifted for a moment as the wind shredded it away, and there, across the rooftops and the green wave-tipped Sound, lay the green hump of Valentia Island.

I had thought with a name like that, Valentia must be called after some Armada galleon which had come to grief here in 1588, but not so. Scores of galleons wrecked themselves down this coast, from Antrim and Malin Head to the Blaskets, but the Spaniards who survived never had the time to give their names to anything. Those Spaniards who got ashore had a hard welcome from the local people, and most of them were murdered on the beach. Even if they had wished to be hospitable the English prevented it.

The Lord of Connaught even declared that anyone sheltering a Spaniard would be declared a traitor. Some 10,000 Spaniards were therefore slaughtered on the beaches or pushed back into the sea to drown, and those stories which trace the dark-haired Irish people of the West back to some Spanish survivor are simply fancies, nothing more.

Valentia Island takes its name from 'Beal Innse', the name for the channel that is now Valentia Harbour. This lies at the landward end of the island, which is most easily reached over a new bridge further west at Portmagee. I had no intention of walking one step further than necessary and there was a short cut, at least for wise people who came here on foot. I veered off the Ring of Kerry and down a minor road to Reenard Point, following the signs marked 'Ferry'.

The first person I met at Reenard Point was Mickey Dore, the ferryman, who looked like a canary, wrapped in his bright-yellow fishermen's oilskins and was clearly looking for trade. He came skipping across the puddles to help me with my rucksack, and told me that he could whip me over to Valentia Island in no time, as long as the tide was right. The tide would be right for an hour or two yet, and as it was about two in the afternoon it was time for a nip of something on a soft day like this. Having had several nips of something already that morning, I agreed with this and we went on together to the pub.

By the time I emerged from Bridie O'Neill's pub by the ferry slip at Cahersiveen I was walking on air. The Point Bar by the slipway at Reenard Point is a very friendly pub and run by Bridie O'Neill, who is a fine-looking woman for someone who had eight children by the time she was thirty-one. There were children everywhere in the Point Bar, running among the tables, ducking under the counter, all chattering like jays. The regulars included visiting French fishermen trying to hire a boat, and a French resident from Bordeaux who spoke English with an Irish accent.

I sat at the bar talking to Bridie and to Mickey while they poured various remedies down my throat, all suggested by their grandmothers. Most of these contained lavish amounts of whiskey. I translated for the Frenchmen who wanted to go shark fishing off the Skelligs, and picked feebly at a grilled trout, until Mickey said that the tide was falling and we would have to be off. One boat ride and five miles after that and my walk would be over.

The wind and rain were still hard at it, chilling me instantly as we emerged from the pub. Mickey took my elbow down the seaweed-slimy slipway and helped me onto his open launch, and I must be getting old or feeling sick to need help like that. Then we were off across the Sound, the launch digging its nose into the waves, the spray coming back in capfuls over the bow and dashing into my face.

This ferry crossing lies at the narrow landward end of the Portmagee Channel and runs across to Knightstown on the island. Knightstown, the island capital, was the former home of the Knights of Kerry, another local lord like the Knight of Glin, and the town once supported a large monastery. John Paul Jones, the Welsh privateer who preyed on English shipping during the American War of Independence often came into Valentia to rest his crew ashore before another foray up the English Channel, but those dramatic days are long gone. Knightstown today is a quiet little fishing port, dreaming away in the West.

Getting ashore at Valentia was not all that easy. The falling tide kept Mickey's launch well off the pier as we circled around for a look, and we finally got ashore by climbing up and over a series of unsteady trawlers. Mickey came along to give me a hand and heaved me over the rail, but I arrived on the quay feeling very poorly. After that the state of my health meant we had to go to the pub. The pub was naturally crowded on this wet day, my condition was explained and various cures were suggested. These were then consumed, I bought a round or two myself, and there was some singing.

It was mid-afternoon and still raining hard before I could set off on the last short walk to Bray Head. A number of kindhearted people had offered me a lift but this last bit I had to do by myself. It was a quiet afternoon in Knights-town with no one about, and only the sound of the rain pattering on my raingear to break the silence.

I left the carousing behind me and plodded on up the western road, trying to think philosophical thoughts, but none occurred to me. The westerly wind was flaying towards me between hedgerows thick with fuchsia and on I went, ever more slowly, through Chapeltown to the Bray Headland. Low cloud hung all along the coast and nothing moved on sea or land except the small ferry which was ploughing back up the Portmagee Channel after an excursion to the Skelligs. I was quite alone at the end of my walk and I liked it that way.

Past Chapeltown the country became more bumpy but the road led on and eventually brought me to the little village of Clynacantah, where the road swung back and a track pointed west to the end of my journey, a mile further on across the wind-tugged grass.

I would like to say that my walk led me to some definite conclusion about this fascinating, friendly and frustrating island, but no thoughts came to me at the time. I was too tired and poorly for introspection. Besides, my journey had been a happy time. Ireland has its problems, God knows, but this is a cheerful, lighthearted country. You would have to be a great pessimist or a terrible poseur to walk among these cheerful, philosophical people and end up gloomy. I might feel as sick as the proverbial parrot at the moment, but I had no regrets.

Even so, I felt I should come to some conclusion. I had, after all, come a very long way and learned a lot, and it should have taught me something, and as I walked along I tried to puzzle it out, to come up with some phrase, some epigram that, if it could not manage to encapsulate Ireland might at least find a place in a book of quotations. In both aims, I failed.

Only later did it occur to me that Ireland is not a place of the head but a place of the heart. It is a waste of time trying to understand Ireland. You have to feel it and let your feelings take over. When people ask me what I feel about Ireland and why I enjoy it, words won't do. I usually end up saying that they will have to go and see it for themselves and make up their own minds. There was also the worry that, honest as it was, this was only Ireland as I saw it, as it appeared to me as I wandered along. Had I gone too deeply into Irish history, written too much about the Northern Troubles, spent too much time in pubs, or ranting about the rain? Well, if I have, what matter? This is Ireland as I saw it, and everyone must find it for themselves.

So I went on through the sad, grey day on the wet road above the heaving ocean and on to the end of my journey, and I kept going until I could go no further. I could have wished for better weather; there are great tall cliffs around Bray Head, and from my path I could see the coast to the South, the seas breaking on the shores of Puffin Island, and along the cliffs that shelter Portmagee, but the other things I might have seen, the Blasket Islands to the North, the Skelligs to the South, all that wonderful seascape of the West, was completely hidden in the cloud and rain.

Out there, beyond the tip of Bray Head, across that grey sea, lay America, 3,000 miles away. At my back lay Ireland, a country I hardly knew at all six weeks before, but where I now felt quite at home. I felt ghastly but that was just the illness, and I felt contented enough to shrug that off for a few moments as I flopped down on the wet grass and looked out at the ocean. This was probably my last long walk. Crossing three countries on foot is enough for any lifetime. Mind you, I said that on the beach at Tarifa and then look what happened. I already have a couple of thoughts on things I might do next.

Although there is an exhilaration in coming to the end of any journey, there is also a sense of relief that you have done it, a sadness at the end combined with the thought that you have got away with it once more, that nothing disastrous actually happened. That can lift you over any temporary touch of gloom and, with this task completed, there is time to think about the future. So there I sat, in the wet grass on the Western tip of Ireland, wondering where to go now.

The world is a very big place and although most of it has been discovered and explored, there is still space and distance for the individual traveller. What seems to count today is not where you travel but how. No one has yet come down the Amazon on roller-skates, but such gimmicks are not for me. Walking has the advantage of simplicity, and that is hard to find these days, but if you just keep walking you will get where you want to go in the end.

Right now I wanted to go to bed, so I turned my back on the Atlantic and let the wind and rain blow me gently down the hill and back into the pub. When I finally got into bed I didn't get out of it again for two weeks.

Kit List

The golden rule is to take everything you need and leave out anything you can do without. My kit list was as follows:

CLOTHING:
6 pairs loop-stitched socks
1 pair Daisy Roots 'Vetta' boots
1 pair trainers
2 pairs Rohan trousers (1 on, 1 off)
2 shirts (1 on, 1 off)
3 pairs underpants (1 on, 1 off, 1 in the wash)
3 handkerchiefs
1 hat
1 neckerchief
1 set 'Sprayway' raingear
1 tracksuit top
1 set washing gear

All the above in one Karrimor Jaguar rucksack, with:

EQUIPMENT:
1 tent
1 sleeping bag
2 Silva compasses

1 notebook
1 Nikon FM2 camera
6 rolls ASA 400 black and white TMX film
6 rolls ASA 64 Kodak colour film
1 Buck knife
Maps and guidebooks (various)
Water bottles 1 × 1 litre
1 mug, 1 plate, 1 plastic food-box
First-Aid kit
Lip salve
Money
Credit cards
Sunglasses

Bibliography

Beckett, J.C., *The Making of Modern Ireland 1603–1923* (Faber, 1985).

Belfrage, Sally, *The Crack* (Grafton, 1987).

Brown, Terence, *Ireland (A Social & Cultural History 1922–85)* (Fontana, 1985).

Chadwick, Nora, *The Celts* (Penguin, 1981).

Coogan, Tim Pat, *The IRA* (Prager Publishers, 1970).

Doran, Sean *et al*, *Ireland* (Rough Guides, 1992).

Duff, Charles, *Ireland and the Irish* (Boardman, 1960).

Duff, Charles, *Six Days to Shake an Empire* (J.M. Dent, 1966).

Ellis P.B., *Hell or Connaught* (Hamish Hamilton, 1975).

Evans, Rosemary, *The Visitor's Guide to Northern Ireland* (Moorland, 1981).

Farrell, Michael, *Northern Ireland (The Orange State)* (Pluto, 1980).

Hennessy, Maurice, *The Wild Geese* (Sidgwick & Jackson, 1973).

Inglis, Brian, *The Story of Ireland* (Faber, 1956).

Jeffares, A. Norman (ed.), *W. B. Yeats Selected Poetry* (Pan, 1990).

Jenner, Michael, *Ireland Through the Ages* (Michael Joseph, 1992).

Kee, Robert, *Ireland – A History* (Weidenfeld & Nicolson, 1980).

Lyons, F.S., *Ireland Since the Famine* (Fontana, 1980).

Macrory, Patrick, *The Siege of Derry* (Hodder & Stoughton, 1980).

Morton, H.V., *In Search of Ireland* (Methuen, 1930).

O'Eiskin, Breandan, *A Pocket History of Ireland* (O'Brian Press, Dublin, 1989).

Porter, Peter (intro.), *W.B. Yeats – The Last Romantic* (Aurum Press, 1990).

Robinson, Tim, *The Stones of Aran* (Viking, 1989).

Rogers, R., *Irish Walks Guides* (Gill & Macmillan, 1980).

Toibin, Colin, *Walking Along the Border* (Macdonald, 1987).

Warner, Alan, *On Foot in Ulster – The Ulster Way* (Appletree, 1983).

Woodham-Smith, Cecil, *The Great Hunger (Ireland 1845–1849)* (Hamish Hamilton, 1962).

Woodham-Smith, Cecil, *The Reason Why* (Constable, 1953).

Yeats, W.B., *Collected Poems* (Papermac, 1982).

An Ireland Guide (Bord Failté – The Irish Tourist Board, 1982).

The Gill History of Ireland (11 vols.) (Gill & Macmillan, 1975).

Ireland (Michelin Green Guides, 1992).

Further Information

THE NORTHERN IRISH TOURIST BOARD
River House
High Street
Belfast B41 2DS
Tel: (0232) 2311221

In London:
11 Berkeley St.
London W1X 5AD
Tel: (071) 493 0601

In USA:
276 6th Ave.
Suite 500,
New York, NY 10001
Tel: (212) 686 6250

BORD FAILTÉ (IRISH TOURIST BOARD)
Baggot St. Bridge,
Dublin 2
Tel: (01) 765871

In London:
150 New Bond St
London W1Y 0AQ
Tel: (071) 493 3201

In USA:
757 3rd Ave
New York, NY 10017
Tel: (212) 418 0800

Walking Information from:

The National Sports Council (COSPOIR)
Hawkes House,
Dublin 2
Tel: (01) 714311

Sports Council for Northern Ireland
House of Sport
2A Upper Malone Road
Belfast BT9 5LA
Tel: (0232) 661222

Maps & Guides:

Stanfords Map Shop
12–14 Long Acre
London WC2E 9LP
Tel: (071) 836 1321

The Travel Bookshop
13 Blenheim Crescent
London W11 2EE
Tel: (071) 229 5260

Index

Note: The names of all loughs appear under the heading 'Loughs' and those of all rivers appear under the heading 'Rivers'.